Tourism and Community Development

Asian Practices

Tourism and Community Development – Asian Practices
ISBN: 978-92-844-1305-8

Published and printed by the World Tourism Organization, Madrid, Spain
First printing 2008
Second reviewed edition 2009
All rights reserved

The designations employed and the presentation of material in this publication do not imply the expression of any opinions whatsoever on the part of the Secretariat of the World Tourism Organization concerning the legal status of any country, territory, city or area, or of its authorities or concerning the delimitation of its frontiers or boundaries.

World Tourism Organization
Calle Capitán Haya, 42
28020 Madrid, Spain
Tel.: (+34) 915 678 100
Fax: (+34) 915 713 733
Website: www.unwto.org
Email: omt@unwto.org

Table of Contents ———————————————————

Foreword

As a continent with the largest population in the world, Asia has a variety of tourism markets with different characteristics. Meanwhile, it is also a new and booming international tourist destination. Many Asian countries, especially the developing ones, are witnessing a fast growth of their tourism industry. Tourism has become a new economic growth point for their national economy.

While most tourist activities are carried out at the level of local communities of various destinations, tourism has played an important role in the development of national economy, and has brought about substantial social and cultural changes. In order to guide local communities to develop tourism under the principal of sustainability, UNWTO has conducted community-based tourism projects throughout Asia mainly in the form of formulating tourism development plans, guidelines as well as institutional strengthening and capacity building. The projects themselves revealed the enormous influence tourism imposes on the local communities and the incapability of existing theories in accommodating the rapidly growing tourism in this region.

UNWTO has, therefore, commissioned this study on Tourism and Community Development: Asian Practices with the technical assistance of Sun Yat-sen University. With a view to identify the in-depth linkage between tourism and the community development so as to evolve strategic guidelines and a common approach for the region, a selected number of Asian cases are reviewed and evaluated. It is hoped that the study of the Asian cases can serve as a reference not only for tourism professionals in Asia, but also elsewhere in the world.

I thank the Regional Representation for Asia and the Pacific of UNWTO for producing this study in a timely manner.

Francesco Frangialli
Secretary-General
World Tourism Organization

Acknowledgements ————————————————————————————

This book is the result of a joint project between the World Tourism Organization (UNWTO) and Sun Yat-sen University of China.

Thanks go to the Regional Representation for Asia and the Pacific of UNWTO led by Mr. XU Jing, for its overall supervision in publishing the book. Mr. Francesco Frangialli, Secretary-General of World Tourism Organization (WTO) supported the co-operative effort between World Tourism Organization (WTO) and Sun Yat-sen University, China.

Thanks also go to Walter Jamieson, professor and dean of the School of Travel Industry Management in the University of Hawaii, who provided in-depth suggestions in editing the book.

James L. Secor, doctor and faculty of the School of Foreign Language, Sun Yat-sen University, undertook the proof-reading for the book. HU Wei, doctor and faculty of the School of Tourism Management in Sun Yat-sen University, translated chapter two: Community Participation in Tourism in China: the Case Studies across Regions from Chinese into English. ZHANG Xiaoming, doctor and faculty of the School of Tourism Management, Sun Yat-sen University, did a great amount of work in formatting the book. Thanks are due to their efforts and supports.

The editors thank all the contributors for their persistence and efforts on accomplishing the book. In particular, we would like to thank the following authors:

XU Honggang, Trevor Sofield and BAO Jigang (Chapter 1);
SUN Jiuxia and BAO Jigang (Chapter 2);
Trevor Sofield (Chapter 3);
Walter Jamieson and Pawinee Sunalai (Chapter 4);
Jan Burrows (Chapter 5);
Douglas Hainsworth (Chapter 6);
Timothy Jeonglyeol Lee (Chapter 7);
Jan Wigsten and D. Gantemur (Chapter 8);
Emiko Kakiuchi (Chapter 9);
Sanjay Nadkarni and Osama Manzar (Chapter 10);
Zahed Ghaderi (Chapter 11);
Kamal Hapuwatte (Chapter 12);
Indra P. Tiwari (Chapter 13).

Chief Editor's Word ————————————————————

Today in Asia, the issues on tourism and community development, in particular community's sustainable development, have drawn wide attention of various stakeholders, including policy makers, professionals, NGOs and others who are interested in sustainable community tourism. There are limited numbers of successful sustainable community tourism models. Debate on the good community tourism models and practices is ongoing. Yet, a shared vision has been reached that theories and approaches developed in the developed world cannot be simply transferred to Asia. Long term efforts are needed to accumulate our learning and understanding of community tourism.

The idea of initiating a publication on the issue was formed at the "International Conference on Cultural Tourism and Local Communities" which was held in Yogyakarta, Indonesia, from Feb. 8 to Feb. 10, 2006 during which Mr. XU Jing of UNWTO discussed with me about the rapid development of tourism in Asia and the need for more extensive and intensive studies on the development of destination communities.

Accordingly, this book, Tourism and community development—Asian practices, concentrating on the case studies of a selected number of countries in Asia, aims to share some experiences among Asian countries as well as the similar countries and regions elsewhere in the world. There are many issues to be studied or addressed on the community tourism. This study does not propose a standard model and is not an attempt to develop a rigid framework or guideline for the emergence of participatory tourism development strategy in developing countries and peripheral areas of the developed world, but attempts to provide examples, through a variety of case studies, of how community tourism is developed in the region and how tourism can contribute to the development of local communities. It aims to improve the understanding of the contextual factors and the complexity of the situational elements which need to be taken into account for better policy guidance.

The preparation of the book started in July, 2006 and lasted for more than one year. In the book we have included cases and practices from 12 countries, Cambodia, China, India, Iran, Japan, Korea, Lao PDR, Mongolia, Nepal, Sri Lanka, Thailand and Vietnam. Most of the contributors are natives from the country and have different backgrounds, such as academicians, government officials and international consultants. The perspectives and examples therefore cover a wide range.

I am pleased to present the publication to all interested parties, especially those policy makers and professionals working in community tourism. The book can also serve as a reference for academicians, university students and those who are interested in sustainable community tourism.

BAO Jigang
Professor and Dean
School of Tourism Management and School of Geography and Planning
Sun Yat-sen University, China
October 2007

Chapter 1

Community Tourism in Asia:
An Introduction

1.1 The Growth of Tourism in Asia

Tourism has been growing very rapidly in Asia (1998). Tourism will not only play an important role in the economic development but also bring enormous social and cultural effects. Many Asian countries positioned tourism as a leading industry and as a change agent and a tool for development. However, experiences showed that unplanned growth and mismanagement of tourism can damage the natural and social-cultural environments of many tourism destinations (Hall & Lew, 1998). The problem of sustainability is emerging with tourism development and community tourism is believed to be an effective approach. Voices for promoting community tourism and involving community in tourism development are widely heard. However, until now, most of the research only focuses on what should be done to develop community tourism but not enough cases have been accumulated to support proposed community tourism development models and proposed policies.

This book attempts to contribute to the understanding of community tourism practice in Asian countries and to examine the factors which influence the dynamics of community tourism. It can be seen that community tourism is developing in all these Asian countries although experiences varies from country to country. These cases also show that community tourism develops within the particular social, political and cultural context of each country and as such there is not necessarily a 'one-model-fits-all' application, or universal consensus on definitions or processes. These cases will provide knowledge for practitioners, policy makers and researchers in sustainable community tourism development in Asia.

1.2 Community, Tourism and Sustainable Development

Tourism, communities and sustainable development are closely linked in traditional research in tourism though they are all problematic concepts because of lack of clarity and common agreement. There are hundreds of definitions of communities, tourism, and sustainable development. However, the key concept here is the sustainable development which links these issues together.

Sustainable development has been used both in the tourism industry and community development. Sustainable community development is a subset of sustainable development and is based on a consideration of the relationship between economic factors and other community elements such as standards of housing, education, the natural environment, health and accessibility. It has emerged as a promising alternative to conventional approaches to development, a participatory, holistic and inclusive process that can lead to positive, concrete changes in communities by creating employment, reducing poverty, restoring the health of natural environment, stabilizing local economies, and increasing community control.

Sustainable tourism development is also a subset of sustainable development. According to the World Tourism Organization (2001), sustainability principles in tourism refer to the environmental, economic and socio-cultural aspects of tourism development, and a suitable balance must be established between these three dimensions to guarantee its long-term sustainability. Thus, Sustainable Tourism should:

- Make optimal use of environmental resources that constitute a key element in tourism development, maintaining essential ecological processes and helping to conserve natural resources and biodiversity.

- Respect the socio-cultural authenticity of host communities, conserve their built and living cultural heritage and traditional values, and contribute to inter-cultural understanding and tolerance.

- Ensure viable, long-term economic operations, providing socio-economic benefits to all stakeholders that are fairly distributed, including stable employment and income-earning opportunities and social services to host communities, and contributing to poverty alleviation.

Community tourism development is proposed in the context of sustainable development. Two researchers have systematically analyzed the community tourism development. After the examination of the relationship between communities and tourism, Jafari (1990) positioned these studies into four platforms which generalized major movements in the study of tourism. The first platform is the Advocacy Platform which gathered strength in the 1960s when the economic effects of tourism were perceived in an optimistic light. In the 1970s the overly positive views of the Advocacy Platform were challenged because the unperceived problems associated with tourism development especially in socio-cultural terms accumulated and became readily apparent. These studies were centered around the negative impacts of tourism on communities, and therefore termed as 'the Cautionary Platform'. The Adaptancy Platform followed the first two platforms and was an attempt to avoid the extremes of the first two platforms with their contradictory arguments by positing 'alternative tourism' development models. Both ecotourism and community based tourism grew out of the Adaptancy Platform. Another thread is from the tradition of sustainable development which was studied from two approaches (Saarinen, 2006). Natural based sustainability is grounded on the idea of a non-touristic change which can be compared and evaluated based on the concept of the spatial unit as an original resource for tourism. However, this approach indicates a sacrifice of the local communities. Activity based sustainability is industry oriented. It refers to a tourism-centric approach similar to Butler's tourism destination model which emphasizes the sustainability of the industry where it is necessary to reduce negative impacts on communities, the environment and societies due to lack of proper management. Since the relationship between the resource based and activity based sustainability appears to be impossible, efforts have been made to overcome the dual nature of sustainability by invoking different negotiation process and participation process which often broadly refers to community participation. Jafari's fourth platform emerged in parallel with the other platforms and is called the 'Knowledge Base Platform': its central thesis advocates the need for rigorous research into all aspects of tourism, including community tourism, in order to reduce polemic and increase objective analysis and understanding.

Overall, community tourism is closely linked with sustainable tourism. It is a regarded as a solution to resolve conflicts between environmental protection and local need for development. Therefore it has multiple roles which aim to improve the residents' quality of life by optimizing local economic benefits, by protecting the natural and built environment and provide a high quality experience for visitors (Choi, 2006; Hall and Lew, 1998; Murphy, 1985; Stevens, 1999). From this perspective, the community tourism is dynamic in nature and a systems approach should be adopted to understand the interactions among the factors.

1.3   The Scope of Community tourism

There is a wide scope of community tourism. With the rapid development of tourism, more and more communities become stakeholders of tourism, either because they are affected by tourism development passively, or because they are using tourism as a tool for their development. As a matter of fact, most communities can use tourism as a development tool to some extent. Also all the community may be influenced by the tourism directly or indirectly.

A spectrum of community tourism can be recognized based on the importance of the tourism to the host and the importance of the host to the tourism product. The two may not overlap. Some of the tourism activities rely on host communities, such as village tourism, while others can survive without communities' support even though these activities have impacts on the communities. For example, some enclave resorts attract foreign investment and foreign tourists who want little contact with the local communities. There is limited opportunity for local communities to participate and many such developments will tend to be exploitable and not necessarily sustainable.

However, as the so-called 'triple bottom line' which combines social and environmental responsibility with economic efficiency becomes more widely accepted, examples are occurring where all inclusive enclave resorts can have a major impact on poverty levels in surrounding communities. Research by the German aid agency, GTZ, into the poverty alleviation impacts of the Jamaican-owned chain of four and five star "Sandals" resorts (22 properties throughout the Caribbean) demonstrate that because of their pro-poor policies they can make a significant contribution to poverty alleviation (Lengefeld and Stewart, 2004). The "Sandals" company targets local community members for up skilling and training, pays wages that are often two to three times the average, sponsors backwards linkages into local agricultural and market garden production (e.g. through Small Farmers Cooperatives, and paying for an agricultural extension officer in the Jamaican Ministry of Agriculture to work specifically with local community primary producers and the hotels on quality control standards and crop diversification), and the sponsorship by each resort of a local poor community facility (a school, a clinic, an orphanage, etc.) A report by Karammel & Lengefeld (2006) recorded that two resorts owned by Sandals in Negril, Jamaica, showed the most positive practices, including the fact that 99 percent of permanent employees were local (approximately 780 people); they enjoyed secure incomes (half of the interviewees had worked for Sandals for between 3 to 12 years); sound career structures and options were in place (foreign language courses abroad were the career advantage most often cited by interviewees); and in terms of staff development: each Sandals employee received extensive training, including HIV prevention, customer service and environmental awareness. Because of high take-home rates of pay, the tourism dollar multiplier was reaching into almost every corner of surrounding communities where levels of poverty had been substantially ameliorated.

Most community based tourism indicates a close relationship between tourism and community. Communities use tourism as a development tool and tourism activities rely very much on communities.

Community based tourism product often refers to village tourism, rural tourism, ecotourism and etc. Most of the cases provided in this book belong to this category.

However, it needs to be understood that community based tourism so defined is a niche market and only covers a limited segment of community tourism. To fully use tourism development opportunities to achieve sustainable development, a broader and wider scope of community tourism should be considered.

In this context, a review of CBT literature indicates that two quite different types of activities encompass most community involvement. However they are often used interchangeably without the differences being delineated and to avoid confusion it is therefore suggested that clear definitions for the purpose of this chapter be established at the outset.

CBT most commonly refers to communities which engage in 'front line operations' that incorporate direct interface with tourists, such as home-stays and lodges; small eco-tours; guide and porter services for local tours/treks; cultural performances for fee paying visitors; teahouses, refreshment kiosks and restaurants; and souvenir/curio/handicraft outlets. These will generally be co-located within the residential boundaries of a community, or in close proximity adjacent to the community. Many of these activities will be initiated in advance of visitation to the area and will be based on the development of local resources as attractions or as direct services to tourists. By definition, they will tend to be small — SMEs owned either by the community on a cooperative basis, or by families and/or individuals within the community.

A second set of activities relate to the value chains of tourism operations and the capacity to harness community resources and labor to provide goods and services for existing tourism businesses. In such instances, with the exception of the provision of labor for tourism businesses not operated by the community, the community will not interact directly with tourists and may be physically distant from tourist operations. For example, hill tribe communities in Thailand that grow orchids under contract to Thai Airways for the airline to present to their passengers may never see a tourist and since the orchids are handed out on arrival at the destination they may be thousands of miles from the point of origin. The income from such activities will be dependent in whole or in part upon the tourism industry at large, but the interaction with tourists is indirect, mediated by those who occupy the front line sector. In such indirect cases it would be more accurate to use the term 'Communities Benefiting through Tourism' or CBT.

The provision of goods and services through the supply chains for front line operations extends the potential to involve communities in literally hundreds of different business activities from what has been termed: "the Secondary or Support Sector of the Tourism System" (Sofield, De Lacy, Bauer, Moore and Daugherty, 2002). Tools such as tourism value chain analysis assist in identifying such entrepreneurial opportunities. This is in contrast to the more conventional approach to CBT which focuses on trying to identify and help communities develop businesses in the front line sector that operate and interact directly with tourists.

While CBT will invariably refer to small operations, CBT offers possibilities of tapping into mass tourism with economies of scale that have the potential to make very significant contributions to poverty alleviation on a magnitude that will tend to be much greater than more traditional CBT activities. The International Trade Centre initiative with the Export-led Poverty Reduction Program/Berimbau Project in Brazil is a case in point (International Trade Centre, 2006).

Box 1.1   Berimbau Project, Brazil

In Bahia, a Brazilian state not only well known for its beautiful natural environment but also for low human development levels, the International Trade Centre's EPRP (Export-led Poverty Reduction Program) launched a CBT pilot project in 2003 to integrate eight communities into the value chains of the nearby mass tourism resort Costa do Sauípe.

Seven productive chains were analyzed and developed in close cooperation with the poor communities: organic waste recycling, fruits and vegetables, soaps and shampoos, clothing, fishing, artisan products, and cultural activities.

Building on this, project activities included the construction of a waste recycling plant and a warehouse for agricultural products. Run by a community-based cooperative, the plant is now processing all organic residues of the resort. The warehouse, managed by a cooperative composed of 190 farmers, is marketing honey and other organic produce of the region.

Agreements were signed with the hotels encouraging increased local sourcing of products and services. The project also facilitated the creation of a cooperative that produces uniforms for the hotels' staff, organized the construction of an artisan shop in the resort and created five associations of local artisans. In addition, two "Capoeira" and "Samba de Roda" performance groups were founded which not only give presentations/concerts in the resort but also support the communities in preserving their cultural heritage.

In the 8 communities, the project contributed to the improvement of the livelihoods of 7,000 people through the creation of new employment and substantial increases in income. For example, monthly incomes of the 390 local female artisans rose from US $ 40 to US$ 400. A replica project in the neighboring resort, "Reserva Imbassai", involved 2,700 more people in tourism related activities. (International Trade Centre, 2006).

This case demonstrates that the two approaches are not mutually exclusive. On the one hand, the establishment of two cultural troupes is examples of CBT through direct ownership and community based provision of an attraction for tourists. The handicraft (artisan) shop inside the resort is also a traditional CBT SME. On the other hand, the backward linkages into agricultural produce – fruit, vegetables, honey – to supply the resort, and the recycling of waste generated by tourists for organic mulch as a spin-off business are two examples of the second CBT approach.

Upscaling of community involvement in tourism can therefore take a broad holistic approach and look beyond SMEs to engagement with mass tourism and the provision of goods and services for operations that are owned outside the community. Empowerment through tourism will then be derived not only from community owned and operated tourism businesses, but from a wide range of other businesses, some of which may not even be recognized as tourism. Recycling for example is not normally regarded as a tourism business! Education and training for secondary or support sector ventures will also provide empowerment even if it does not lead to direct ownership of a CBT or CBT business because it will provide choice of a future beyond the restricted confines of an uneducated or unskilled community member.

1.4   The Different Patterns of Participation in Community Tourism

Yang and Wall (2005) point out that public participation in decision making is advocated so that people can have some control over resources, initiatives and decisions which affect them (2005). Although there are many dimensions of sustainable tourism, community participation has obtained special attention since it linkage between the resource, development activities and the benefits sharing from development. It is argued that participation has the following virtues:

- "Top down" approaches have failed in the past to resolve the intractable problems

- Community will build up the capacity to tackle any future problems

- Community tourism allows host to break away from the control by tour operators and other powerful groups

- Community is about grassroots empowerment as it seeks to develop tourism in harmony with the basic needs of the community (Fitton, 1996)

Policies and support for community tourism are increasing. The empirical studies presented in this book show that the positive results are found out in the rural development (the case of Iran), increase of awareness of cultural resource (Vietnam) and the protection of natural resources (Yuban Village, China; the conservation of the Mekong River Dolphin, Cambodia).

Despite these positive results, there is also no clear policy frame on how to intervene for community participation, which may be a result of a mélange of place specific conditions much influenced by the social, cultural, and political contexts. There is lack of shared vision on the participation model which can lead to the sustainable development at the local level and contribute to the global sustainability. The origin of current community participation is based on three main historical antecedents: western ideologies and political theories; the Third World community development movement of the 1950s and 1960s; and finally Western social work and community radicalism (Medley, 1986). According to Western paradigms, little resident and private-sector involvement appear to occur in decision making for tourism in developing countries (Timothy 1999). Therefore there are arguments which danger of deny any public participation in the developing countries.

Different forms of participation are identified in the developing countries. For instance, Tosun (1999) classified three types of community participation: spontaneous community participation, coercive participation and induced community participation. Spontaneous community participation means that community has a high level of citizen power and can control the whole process of tourism development. It represents an ideal model of community participation. Coercive participation is manipulated and contrived. The real objective does not enable people to participate in the tourism process but to enable power. Induced community participation is the most common mode to be found in the developing countries where the local communities are consulted but the decisions have been made by others.

France (1998) pointed out seven types of participation, (i) plantation, a kind of exploitative development; (ii) manipulative and passive participation; (iii) consultation in which the residents are consulted but the development problems are defined by externals; (iv)material incentives including the employment opportunities in tourism; (v) functional participation often used by outsiders as a way to achieve their goal; (vi) interactive participation, in which locals take control of local decisions; and (vii) independent initiatives, meaning that the local people have accumulated capital from tourism.

A simple model proposed by Yang and Wall (2005) uses two dimensions to categorize the patterns of participation, the benefits of tourism development to the communities and the role of community in the decision making. Four basic patterns can be recognized: (i) participation in decision making and benefits; (ii) participation in decisions with no benefits; (iii) acquisition of benefits without participation in decision making; and (iv) no decision-making power or benefits.

- The communities control the decision making process in tourism development and obtain benefits. Yubeng (chapter 2 in this book) is such a case where tourism started to develop 3-4 years ago. Although the villagers have not fully understood the potential impacts of the tourism and reached agreement on limiting tourist numbers within the carrying capacity, they have agreed on and designed a management structure on how the benefits should be distributed and how each household should participate in the tourism business.

- The communities participate in the decision making process but they cannot obtain benefits. It happens in many top-down planning exercises. The communities are consulted in the planning process. Later on, some of communities consulted may not have been selected in the development and lose the chance to participate in tourism development exercises.

- The communities do not participate in the decision making process nor choose the way that tourism is to develop, but they share some benefits. They can get some compensation because their right to the cultural landscape is acknowledged but they have limited power in the bargaining process. Or they are employed or operate their own business in tourism. In the chapter on Sri Lanka in this book, the Jetwing Youth Development Project run by the large Sri Lanka hotel management company Jetwing, trains rural youth to be employed by Jetwing Hotels.

- The rights of cultural landscape and the tourism resources of the community are not recognized and the communities are completely excluded from the tourism development. Sometimes, they are not allowed to participate in the tourism industry. Sometimes they are re-allocated to other far away places with little compensation. There are also cases that the tourism product is so designed that they simply only bear the costs of tourism development with no benefits. For instance, Tiwari (2006) argues that in Nepal many of the group trekking tourists do not spend any money along the trekking route and their contribution in those areas is virtually nothing as they stay in open camps, use tents and prepare their meals carried along with them by porters. But they bring negative environmental externalities to the locals by littering empty cans, plastics, water bottles and so on.

1.5   Factors Influencing the Participation Pattern of Community Tourism in Asia

Overall, community participation in most of the Asian countries is at a low level although diverse patterns also exist, as illustrated by the various cases included in this book. Factors which contribute to community tourism participation level are from the macro-political-cultural context, the tourism industry and the micro community-level.

1.5.1   The Macro Environment

1.5.1.1   Political Cultural System

The social and political system sets the power structure between communities and other stakeholders and therefore the participation patterns. Timothy (1999) pointed out that in societies with centralized political structures, members of the community may feel that it is the government's duty to plan economic development opportunities for development. He found out that most Javanese communities are not interested in being involved in tourism planning. The social-cultural tradition accepted that central government and the head of the villages have the power and right to control communities. Most Asian counties, China, Korea and others are all centralized structures historically; as a result, local communities and individuals do not have high motivation to participate in the decision process at the community level.

Property rights determine the legal role of community in tourism management. The unclear property right of tourism resources is the most challenging barrier for the communities to obtain legal right to participate in the development process, share benefits and participate in the decision making process, especially when tourism development is associated with national parks and protected area where lands belong to the State although the local communities have been traditionally living there for centuries.

Considering the global-local linkages, the governments in developing countries are facing pressures to promote economic growth and modernity and reduce the gap with the developed countries in the shortest possible time. Mass tourism industrial development seems to be an effective and quick tool to achieve the goal while the community issue which usually involves long time commitments and also political risks seem not easily to be accepted and promoted by governments at various level.

1.5.1.2 Economic System

In many developing countries, the economic structure is determined by its duality which brings constraints to community tourism development. Most of the public economic infrastructure, such as financial institutions, transportation systems, information networks and other are usually designed for big enterprises and mass production. The majority of community businesses which are in small and middle size enterprises, even family businesses, face difficulties to start up, to maintain and grow due to lack of accessibility to formal financial institutions, to market information and know-how and the business network. Therefore, often communities are forced to give up their right of development to the outsiders.

1.5.2 The Structure of the Tourism Industry

The tourism industry is also characterized by a dual structure. There coexist a few multinational corporations (MNCs) which control and dominate the international markets and a large volume of small enterprises in a vulnerable position. For example, in a 1996 study of global tourism, the 35 largest outbound nature tour operators had 90% of the market and the five largest operators alone held 40% of the total market (Higgins, 1996). In many cases, the communities have to rely on the mercies of MNCs to be able to get access to the market. Participation of local communities in mass tourism therefore seems difficult (Tosun, 2005).

The stage of tourism development also influences the participation process. Overall, the tourism industry is a relative new business. Communities have difficulty perceiving the opportunities, challenges and risks in tourism development. And there is a lack of local expertise in community tourism planning and management and communities who can help them. As a result, the local communities are in a weak position facing outsider investors. In the initial stage of tourism development, when tourism benefits are not perceived, the motivation and the enthusiasm of the locals to participate are often low. When tourism begins to develop, it will attract outside large investments. The arrival of MNCs normally forces the small enterprises out of the market, although, in many cases, the decision to exit tourism development opportunities can be made voluntarily by local communities. For instance, in many heritage sites, the local people prefer to rent out or sell their houses to outsiders at high price and the funds enable them to move to other places and invest in other business.

1.5.3   The Development Stage of Communities

The development stage of a community influences its capacity to manage itself (Holden 2003). Tosun (2005) pointed out that a higher level of development of economic, social and political life ushers in a better condition for the emergencies of participatory tourism development. For instance, those communities which are accessible to a city are often in a relative developed stage and the capacity and the motivation for the locals to manage themselves are high. The suburban communities can often initiate farm tourism product and can manage its development.

1.6   Challenges of Sustainable Community Tourism in Asia

Sustainable community tourism is a complex system. There are many dimensions of sustainable community tourism covering ecological, social, economic, institutional, political, national, regional and local levels. These dimensions are interdependent and mutually reinforcing (Mowforth & Munt, 1998). This complexity raises the question about what is appropriate community participation that will lead to the sustainable development in the long term, whether a high level of community participation is a pre-requisite and sufficient condition for sustainable development and whether there is a correct path for community tourism to follow to attain sustainable development. The answers are not so obvious. There are many challenges facing communities, researchers and policy makers.

1.6.1   The Question of the Participation 'Ladder'

Based on the World Bank's participatory model in the development process, Wang and Wall (2005) proposed a participation ladder model which goes through impactee, beneficiary, client and owner. Other ladder models are also available. Yet, as Tosun (2005) pointed out none of these models is grounded on empirical cases. Very few practices in the real world have been found to have taken places beyond the community consultation or manipulative participation. Even in the developed countries, few cases have followed the path which is suggested by these authors. Therefore, the model can provide little guidance to practical issues. It is still unclear that intervention on participation alone can lead to long term sustainability of community development and to contribute to global sustainability.

An ideal community-based tourism model is often described as a form of tourism where the local community has substantial control over, and involvement in, its development and management, and a major proportion of the benefits remain within the community. Yet, it also does not address whether the state is in dynamic stable condition leading toward sustainability. The ideal state may be in a disequilibrium condition that is moving toward collapse. For instance, although the case of Yubeng Village seems quite ideal, it is uncertain whether the community can really handle the huge impacts of mass tourists when demand is high and when natural resources are also national property. Higher participation levels are not necessarily 'better'. A high level of participation can not guarantee a more sustainable path towards development.

1.6.2   The Limits of Local Solutions to Global Issues

Community tourism is usually considered a local solution to the sustainable development conundrum. Yet, there are many national and global social, political and environmental backgrounds which have to be considered that are beyond the capacity for local communities to manage. These challenges exist not only within the tourism sector but in fact within a broader social and economic context.

1.6.2.1   The Low Awareness of Sustainability Issues

Although sustainable development has been promoted worldwide since the Rio Earth Summit of 1992 and as a concept it has spread out all over the world, most of the developing countries in Asia are still under the pressure to achieve economic growth where sustainability is regarded to some extent as a brake on that growth. The awareness of sustainable development has not really turned into actions among the public.

For instance, from the demand side, a substantial number of tourists are not particularly interested in community tourism. Bierman (2006) argues that most tourists who visit Jamaica are beach tourists who do not really care about the local culture for these places, and rejecting these tourists in favor of more 'sensitive' or more 'socially responsible' tourists may lead to a loss of development opportunities. Only a small part of the tourism business in Asian destinations has shown interest in obtaining accreditation for being environmental friendly. Most tourists seem to display a lack of awareness of sustainability issues and their consumption behavior puts additional pressures and stress on resources. Also, few tourism companies have really implemented eco-strategies. Price competition, networking and cost reduction seem more popular.

1.6.2.2   The Lack of Institutional Commitment to Sustainability

Tourism is a new industry in Asia, and in spite of much cautious advice about the perceived vagaries of tourism, all countries in Asia (with the exception of North Korea) have perceived the economic opportunities of tourism development. In this context they have also perceived the possibilities to use tourism as a development tool for poverty alleviation and for reducing the gap between rural and urban, the gap between the core and the peripheral regions. Policies which attempt to guide long term sustainability are under studied and supported.

Yet, the concepts of sustainable development have not fully been transformed into policies and regulations and integrated with government institutions. The policy framework is still formulated to achieve economic growth, usually narrowly defined in tourism terms as increased visitation numbers regardless of yield, and without reference to carrying capacity issues and sustainability. Sustainability sometimes is only a token rather than the action.

1.6.2.3   The Resource Stress and Competing Use of Resources

In most of the Asian counties, the consumption rate of natural and cultural resources is high because the resources are needed not only to meet the basic needs of their large populations but also to provide the foundation for economic development. Many of the environmentally friendly and resource efficient technologies are not available and affordable. Exploitation for short term profit rather than sustainable utilization for a more enduring contribution to national needs are the norm. Therefore, the natural resource stress is high and the environmental problem is serious.

Although community participation was proposed to set up a negotiation process for the use of resources in a sustainable way, risks of overusing natural resources are high. The stakeholders can choose to increase the consumption rate of natural resources and lower the goal of resource protection in order to enlighten the present social pressures due to the increasing and conflicting use of resources. The target of maintaining a balanced stock of resources can be eroded in the long run.

Community tourism is a resource based development (Murphy 1985). The additional consumption of the resources by tourists would exaggerate this stress, especially when a large volume of domestic Asian tourists, without high environmental awareness, become reality. That the community can effectively resist the temptation of turning their resources into economic benefits within the short run is a big assumption.

One of the traditional management tools assumed to ensure local communities adopt the sustainability principle is to demonstrate the risks of losing tourists due to improper management of tourism resources. Sofield's case of Dolphin provided such an example. Persuading the local communities to understand the danger of losing the tourists once the dolphin is gone is a major focus of village awareness workshops, hence the project aims to have all the communities work together to protect and conserve the few remaining dolphins and to protect their riverine habitat form pollution. However, in most places in Asia, an understanding of the risk of losing tourists is low when the demand is high and when income generation is correspondingly high, and so the scarcity of the resource and dangers to it are conveniently overlooked in the pursuit of short term monetary gains.   Many tourists are simply not so sensitive to environmental quality and do not want to be 'burdened' with an understanding of the complex interrelationship between their activities and adverse impacts on the environment which could cast a shadow over their pursuit of pleasure. As a result, due to market pressures the motivation for communities to preserve resources is often not strong. Therefore, the effectiveness of the policy tool is thus reduced.

1.6.3   The Heterogeneous Community

Another factor seldom discussed is the social and cultural structure within the community and among the communities. There is no strong evidence to show that local communities have automatic privilege or higher moral value over other groups from the sustainability perspective and they did not automatically choose the sustainable way of development. Often the low level of traditional technology simply meant that such communities had limited capacity to cause major environmental degradation. There is thus an appearance of sound environmental practice but in some cases there is no scientific understanding of sustainability. They may also not necessarily have the knowledge to understand the impacts and scale of their impacts on the environment.

Community tourism and community participation do not guarantee equal opportunities and equal benefits to the internal members within the community. In some societies, women and youth are not permitted to participate in business let alone in the decision making process. Local elites may prevent the spread of benefits and the participation of marginalized people in the decision making process. Tosun's research (2005) pointed out that the internal structure of client-patron relationship prevents a wide sharing of benefits from tourism development. Nyaupanea, et al. (2006) found that tourism development in Annapurna exacerbated the socio-economic inequities previously existent in the host community.

Community tourism participation also cannot guarantee a bigger multiplier effects and an equal share of benefits among communities. Those who happen to get access to roads or tourism resources obtain more benefits while leaving other communities in poverty. For instance, in China the World Heritage listed ancient village of Xidi in Huangshan has obtained advantage by being the first in the market and has therefore developed far ahead of the surrounding villages which have similar heritage (The Center of Tourism Research and Huangshan Tourism Bureau, 2006). However it has been reluctant to share its good fortune with its neighboring communities which it views as competitors. In the tourism development process, the tension among communities to get access and control the tourism resources may increase. Communities may compete viciously among each other and lock in a low efficient situation. The tragedy of the commons in the making is often observed among these communities.

The unbalanced human-resource-economic development pattern in these communities indicates that the traditional way to manage resources in a sustainable way is not always working. Without proper support, communities will often experience difficulties to manage the additional demands that tourists place on their resources. Nyaupanea, et al. (2006) compared a community based system and externally controlled tourism development and they found out that government controlled development can prevent the destruction of tourism on the environment where communities could not.

The interaction between communities and tourism is complex. The degree to which host societies embrace tourism development depends on a number of critical socio-political, economic and environmental factors (Briassoulis & Van der Straaten, 1992; Chee-Beng, 2001). If community tourism models are to be of assistance in developing countries, they must at the outset be based on a valid theory of where tourism fits into the particular socio-economic structure. Without understanding the linkages, policies may create counter-intuitive behavior.

1.7   A Systems Intervention for Sustainable Community Tourism

1.7.1   A Systems-oriented Dynamic View of Community Tourism

The importance is to use a systems approach to understand the long term dynamic behaviors between tourism, community and sustainable development. There is a need to adopt a systemic approach to address the underlying causes in an integrated way, focusing on the entire systems that are affected rather than only problem symptoms. The evaluation of community tourism should be viewed from a long term point of view and the policies should be based on pattern change rather on short time issue. The attraction of a simple solution to complex intractable problems is obvious but the likelihood of finding a 'magic bullet' is low (Botterill and Fisher, 2002).

Two systems should be examined for understanding community tourism: the global tourism system and the local political-cultural, social, economic and environmental systems in which community tourism is embedded. The community tourism interacts with the systems and there are feedback relationships among them.

1.7.2   Stakeholder Cooperation

All the chapters inside this volume express the importance of obtaining a shared vision and commitment among stakeholders. A holistic and long term commitment to community tourism from various stakeholders is needed. The stakeholders include business sectors, the tourists, government agencies, the communities who are directly and indirectly impacted, the NGOs and others. Experiences also show that when agreement is reached by the stakeholders, it must regenerate accountability among these parties with regards to further investment, practices and policies and be reflected in institutional action. Therefore, government support and institutionalization of these agreements are crucial.

1.7.3   Government Supports to Sustainable Development

Government supported policies can cover a wide range of initiatives. Community development is one important solution for sustainable development yet there are no quick solutions for it. Long term commitment is a pre-condition.

Importantly, governments in Asia should support the participatory process. According to Tosun(2005)'s three stage participatory tourism development model, at present, external pressures from the internal and external factors on central governments to accept and support the participatory development approach have emerged and therefore governments began to support and initiate community development. Some Asian governments have moved into the second stage which is the emergence of political will at the central government level. For instance, in Sri-Lanka, the national government formulated policies which require that "any new tourism development project/program should contain a community development component incorporated, in addition to providing employment opportunities for the community, purchasing goods and obtaining services from them" (Chapter 12). At the third stage, the government should legislate for participatory processes at the operational level.

1.7.4   Empowerment

Empowerment is the starting point for the community to participate in decision making processes and to bargain for their benefits. Empowerment has to be provided economically, socially and politically. Empowerment usually requires the provision of financial and public infrastructure help communities to develop tourism. Socially, empowerment means an equal access to education, and the know-how to enable community members to have the capacity to develop. Politically, the rights to tourism development opportunities and the right to their own places and the right to choose their development should be guaranteed and protected by law. Wigsten and Gantemur (Chapter 8) points out that empowerment is also needed by other stakeholders in order to avoid the tragedy of commons.

1.7.5   The Role of Information and Communication Technology (ICT)

The diffusion of ICT technology may also be effective in enhancing the capacity of communities to manage tourism by them. Village based ventures generally lack the capacity to market them effectively. As a result, most communities have to rely on outside companies to attract tourism. Development and implementation of ICT tools will help communities tap the international market by strengthening and including local institutional and human capacities and promoting local involvement and ownership.

1.7.6   Protection of Ecological Environment

Community tourism by itself is not enough to ensure the integrity of local ecosystems. There is a need to understand that depletion of natural resources is not a local issue and it is not purely caused by the mismanagement of the natural resources locally. Institutional instruments should be built to maintain a sustainable level of resource stock and help communities by reducing the demand and consumption of their resources, rather than shifting all these management pressures to the local communities. Under the current situation, if the demand for natural and cultural resources is increasing, and the standards for the natural resource protections can be negotiated and adjusted in the decision making process at the local level to accommodate that increased demand, then there is high potential to end up with the resources being sacrificed instead of protected.

1.8   The Structure of This Book

There are many issues with the community tourism. This study does not intend to propose a standard step and is not an attempt to develop a rigid framework or guideline for sustainable community tourism development strategy in either developing countries or in the developed world in Asia. We feel it is too early to generate a generic model for sustainable community tourism development. As Jafari (1990) claims that much of former work on the community and tourism is subjective, there is need to move into a Knowledge Base platform which should be based on research not opinions and emotions. We are still in the process of examining different patterns of community tourism and different paths to sustainable community tourism. This book therefore attempts to assist understanding of the contextual factors and complexity of the situational elements which need to be taken into account in considering the role and intervention of community tourism.

We have included cases and practices from 11 countries, Cambodia, China, India, Iran, Japan, Laos, Mongolia, Nepal, Sri-Lanka, Thailand, and Vietnam. These countries are at different development stages. Japan is a developed country. China, Iran and Thailand are developing countries; Sri Lanka is positioned below them but above the least developed countries of Nepal, Laos, Cambodia, and Mongolia. The importance of tourism to the different countries and to their local communities is also quite diverse although all the countries have perceived the economic potential of tourism. The tourism industry plays very important economic role and contributes significantly to the export sector in Sri Lanka, Nepal, Laos, Cambodia and Mongolia. Thailand and Indonesia have been traditionally international tourism destinations and have accumulated substantial experience in tourism industrial development and community tourism development. China, India and Iran have become important players in the international tourism market and the impacts from the domestic tourism are substantial and wider than for international tourism.

Most of the contributors are nationals or have worked in this region as consultants for a long period of time. They come from different background, academicians, government officials, international consultants, and some with tourism industry backgrounds and experience. Some are more theoretical in their approach to tourism development, others are practitioners, and all are interested in the application of the principles of sustainable development to community tourism. The cases included in the book cover a wide range of community tourism developments and initiatives, and the guiding objective for including these contributions inside the covers of this book are to widen the availability of case studies for the enquiring mind.

Overall, the importance of community tourism has become recognized and community tourism has developed in all these countries although some have only recently commenced. It has been well accepted that community tourism can play an important role in poverty alleviation, rural development and the protection of cultural and nature resources. However, it is also demonstrated that there is a wide spectrum of community participation patterns and few cases have been found to have followed the path defined by Wang and Wall (2005).

The cases also demonstrate that there are multiple sources which lead to the emergence and growth of community tourism, including government initiated poverty alleviation programs (Masuleh, Iran; Chapter 11), non-governmental organization and international donor agency sponsored programs (dolphin case, Cambodia, Chapter 3), national park initiated development (Kanas, China, Chapter 2; Gorhi-Terelj National Park, Mongolia,, Chapter 8), the village itself (Yubeng, China, Chapter 2), even community tourism development programs initiated by outside business (Dai Folk Village China, Chapter 2) and multiple forces (Klong Khwang, Thailand, Chapter 4).

These case studies cover the macro-level (international aid), the meso-level (the formulation of the tourism development plans for community development) and micro-level (village level). The papers are therefore organized into three sections.

The first section covers different patterns of community tourism in practice. These cases show that community models are often situational and influenced by political and cultural factors. SUN and BAO (Chapter 2) present three cases in China. The participation levels in three cases are different yet all of them are groping their own ways towards sustainability with little external support. International donor agencies are a major driving force for community tourism development. Therefore two cases have been selected to provide experiences and lessons from their practice. Hainsworth (Chapter 6) introduces an 18- month project on community cultural tourism development in Vietnam that presented positive results. Burrows (Chapter 5) describes the process of community tourism development of a Buddhist cave in Laos from the perspective of an international consultant. He also discusses the role of international consultants in community tourism development. The lessons learned from the case are that "tourism advisors should perhaps focus on existing tourist attractions rather than develop complex CBT models that often fail once the advisory assistance has gone, particularly those that did not involve private sector from the outset".

Methodologies and techniques for community tourism are discussed in the second part. There are two cases on how the participatory community planning process is implemented, one is in Kanas provided by SUN and BAO (Chapter 2), the other is by Jamieson and Sunalai (Chapter 4). In the case of Kanas, mass tourism had already developed and problems were highly evident when the consultants began the planning exercise. Therefore the goal of tourism planning was to control the negative impacts. Consultation was conducted to improve the feasibility to implement the plan. In the case of Klong Khwang Thailand where tourism had just started, an integrated simulated tourism experience was introduced during the planning stage to increase the community's understanding of t tourism impacts, in addition to public consultation techniques and focus groups. Proactive policies were thus formulated.

Stakeholder analysis is widely applied methodology. Sofield (Chapter 3) presents a project on the conservation of dolphins in Mekong River through the development of community based ecotourism. The key element of the project and the challenge is to network the 104 communities that inhabit the 200 km stretch of the Mekong where the few remaining dolphins live and persuade the communities to work together. His case study provides a good example of how to construct cooperation among the communities through the analysis of differing objectives held by the varied stakeholders. Wigsten and

Gantemur (Chapter 8) developed a framework to identify stakeholders for community tourism development in Gorhi-Terelj National Park, Mongolia.

Kakiuchi (Chapter 9) suggests the application of willingness to pay methodology to design a pricing structure for collecting fees from tourists to finance the restoration and maintenance of the Hamlets of Gokayama, which are World Heritage Listed Sites. Nadkarn and Manzar design a practical approach on utilizing ICT for community tourism in India.

The third section of the book includes country experiences in addressing community tourism issues. They are meso level studies. Some countries, like Sri Lanka and Nepal have initiated national programs for community tourism and the significance of community tourism is recognized. Sri Lanka is a pioneer in developing a tourism plan that incorporates community consultation (WTO 1994).

The cases have shown that each type of community participation has its own strength and weakness. Some cases reflect the fact that local sustainability does not guarantee global sustainability. Overall tourism development, especially community tourism development is a new phenomenon in much of Asia. Most cases need to be monitored for a longer time to be able to determine whether they are on a stable path to development. As yet not enough cases with a long record have been accumulated. Therefore, theories which support a generic model for application in every country often lack empirical support. This study leaves us with more questions and few definitive answers but it does provide rich insight for the understanding of the problems and possible approaches to address these issues. More studies are needed to develop models to better understand what sustainable community tourism means and how it can be achieved.

References:

Bierman, D. (2006), 'Commentary on 'Connecting with Culture': the Challenges of Sustainable Community Tourism', *Cornell Hotel and Restaurant Administration Quarterly*, 47, pp 382.

Botterill, L.C. and Fisher, M. (2002), *Magical Thinking: The Rise of the Community Participation Model*, Paper presented at the Jubilee conference of the Australian Political studies Association, Australian National University, Canberra.

Briassoulis, H. and Van der Straaten, J. (eds.) (1992), *Tourism and the Environment: Regional, Economic and Policy issues*, Kluwer Academic Publishers, Dordretch.

Chee-Beng, T., Cheung, S.C.H. and Hui, Y. (eds.) (2001), 'Tourism and the anthropology in China', in *Tourism, anthropology and China*, White Lotus Press, Bangkok, pp. 1–26.

Choi, H.S. and Sirakaya, E. (2006), 'Sustainability Indicators for Managing Community Tourism', *Tourism Management*, 27, pp.1274-1289.

Fitton, M. (1996), *Does Our Community Want Tourism, Examples from South*.

France, L. (1998), 'Local Participation in Tourism in the West Indian Island' in Laws,E. , Faulkner, B. and Moscardo, G. (eds.): *Embracing and Manaing Change in Tourism: International Case Studies*, London: Routledge. Quoted in Tomothy, D., 'Tourism and Community Development', in Sharpley. R and Telfer. D. (2004), *Tourism and Development: Concepts and Issues*, Channel View Publication.

Hall, C.M and Lew, A. (eds.) (1998), *Sustainable Tourism Development: A Geographical Perspective*, Addison Wesley Longman, New York.

Higgins, B. R. (1996), 'The Global Structure of the Nature Tourism Industry: Ecotourists, Tour Operators, and Local Businesses', *Journal of Travel Research*, 34 (2), pp.11-18.

Holden, A. (2003), 'In Need of New Environmental Ethics for Tourism?', *Annals of Tourism Research*, 30(1), pp. 94.

International Trade Centre (2006), *The Export-led Poverty Reduction Programme/Berimbau Project*, ITC Bahia, Brazil. Geneva..

Jafari, J. (1990), 'Research and Scholarship: The Basis of Tourism Education', *Journal of Tourism Studies*, 1(1), pp. 33-41.

Karammel, S. and Lengefeld, K. (2006), *Can All-Inclusive Resorts be Pro-Poor?* Department for International Development and hosted by the Institute of Development Studies, at the University of Sussex, UK, (Online), available: http://www.id21.org/insights/insights62/art05.html (30-5-2007).

Lengefeld, K. and Stewart, R. (2004), *All Inclusive Resorts and Local Development: "Sandals" Resorts as Best Practice in the Caribbean*, Presentation at World Travel Market, London, November 2004.

Midgley, J. (1986), 'Introduction: Social Development, the State and Participation', in *Community Participation, Social Development and the State*. J. Midgley (ed.), Methuen, London.

Mowforth and Munt (1998), *Tourism and Sustainability: New Tourism in the Third World*, Routledge, New York.

Murphy, P.E. (1985), *Tourism: A Community Approach*, Routledge, London.

Nyaupanea G.P., Morais, D.B. and Dowler, L. (2006), 'The Role of Community Involvement and Number/Type of Visitors on Tourism Impacts: A Controlled Comparison of Annapurna, Nepal and Northwest Yunnan, China'. *Tourism Management*, 27, pp.1373–1385.

Sarrinen, J. (2006), 'Traditions of Sustainability in Tourism Studies', *Annual of Tourism Research*, 33(4), pp.1121-1146.

Scheyvens, R. (1999). 'Ecotourism and the Empowerment of Local Communities'. *Tourism Management*, 20, pp. 245-249.

Sofield, T. (2003), *Empowerment for Sustainable Tourism Development*, Elsevier Science Ltd, Oxford.

Sofield, T.H.B., et al. (2002), *Pro Poor Tourism: A Scoping Study*, Brisbane: CRC. Tourism.

The Center of Tourism Research, Huangshan Tourism Bureau (2007), *The Master Tourism Development Plan*, Chinese Tourism Press, Beijing.

Timothy, D. (1999), 'Participatory Planning: A View of Tourism in Indonesia', *Annals of Tourism Research*, 26 (2), pp. 371–391.

Tiwari, I. P. (2006), *Regional and Poverty Orientation of the Tourism Development in Nepal*, Proceedings of the International Conference on Tourism and New Asia: Implication for Research, Policy and Practice, Beijing, China, 9-12 August 2006, pp.571-583.

Tosun, C. (2005), 'Stages in the Emergence of a Participatory Tourism Development Approach in the Developing World', *Geoforum*, 36, pp. 333–52.

Tosun, C. (2000), 'Limits to Community Participation in the Tourism Development Process in Developing Countries', *Tourism Management*, 21(6), pp. 613–633.

Tosun, C. (1999), 'Towards a Typology of Community Participation in the Tourism Development Process Anatolia', *An International Journal of Tourism and Hospitality Research*, 10(2), pp. 113-134.

Wang, Y. and Wall, G. (2005), 'Sharing the Benefits of Tourism: A Case Study in Hainan, China', *Environments*, 33 (1), pp. 41-59.

World Tourism Organization (2001), *The Concept of Sustainable Tourism*, UNWTO, Retrieved March 2003, (Online), available: http://www.worldtourism.org/sustaianble/concepts.htm (30-5-2007).

World Tourism Organization(2001), *Tourism 2020 Vision*, UNWTO, Madrid

World Tourism Organization(1998), *Tourism: 2020 Vision*.

The Implementation of
Community-based Tourism

Chapter 2

Community Participation in Tourism in China: The Case Studies across Regions

2.1 Introduction

China's tourism has developed rapidly since the 1990s and has become one of the major tourist destinations in the World. The nation is rich in community resources and various tourism activities are mainly developed based on these communities. As the tourism industry largely affects community life, raising awareness of the locals towards the values of tourism resources leads to an increasing involvement in tourism industry and the hope that they will benefit from this participation.

Community participation in tourism development (CPTD) implies that during the process of decision-making, development and planning, management and inspection, the community views and their needs are fully considered: the community is regarded as a vital entity in tourism development, so with their participation a sustainable community tourism is ensured (Sun & Bao, 2006). Community tourism development has achieved great success with community participation in tourism activities presenting a multi-faceted situation.

As the development pace of tourism is faster than that of tourism studies, researches on communal participation in tourism development are notably inadequate. The Chinese version of "Regarding the 21st centurial agenda on tourism development" by Zhang (1998) remarked that the Chinese researchers realized that the tourism growth cannot be maintained at the cost of resource and environment. Since the 1990s, in searching through models of tourism sustainability, Chinese researchers began to study the dynamic linkages between tourism destination and the community. Communities can be functional not only in all phases of tourism sustainability, but also they are tangible bodies of management, searching for an appropriate sustainable development model for their community in the most feasible way, considering their community-specific problems (Tang, 1998). Moreover, community participation in tourism development is an indispensable mechanism of sustainable tourism systems (Liu, 2000). In reality, CPTD in China has a long way to go and presents a low degree of community participation. To some extent, CPTD has experienced little activity and there is a lack of an incentive mechanism to guide an involvement in tourism resource protection (Zhuge et al., 2000). On the other hand, the social systems of China and the West vary in many ways in from the, tourism development stage on; and, therefore, the CPTD model cannot be fully transplanted into China (Bao & Sun, 2006). As such, some scholars initiated special CPTD models for China (Sun & Bao, 2006).

However, under the driving force of pro-development and economic gain, community- involved tourism in China has developed faster than many other countries. This, coupled with the immense problems associated with the beneficiaries involved in community tourism, contributes to a series of particular issues for China to deal with. As the situation stands, there is a need for tourism researchers to conduct in-depth case studies on the CPTD so that these problems can be brought to light and solved.

This project selects four study sites to carry out such research. These are: Dai nationality-based community in Xishuangbanna, Dai Autonomous Prefecture, Yunnan Province; Xidi Community in Huangshan City, Anhui Province; Yubeng Tibetan Village at Diqing Tibetan, Autonomous Prefecture, Yunnan Province; and Kanas tourist area in Buerjin County, Xinjiang Autonomous Region. Site observations, detailed interviews and questionnaire surveys were developed to obtain first hand data. Starting from 2002, the authors paid several visits to the target sites, looking at community-based tourism activities, which are also linked to the social and economic nature in the areas, and extracting relevant information from selected representatives in the community. The study was intended to demonstrate case studies in common and in difference so that a picture of CPTD can be reflected as a whole in China.

2.2   Case of Dai Village: A Multi-Faceted Participation in a Minority Nationality Area

2.2.1   Introduction of the Case

Dai Village is situated at Menghan Township, Xishuangbanna Autonomous Prefecture, Yunnan Province. It is 27 km from Jinghong City, the capital city of Xishuangbanna Autonomous Prefecture. The area covers five well-kept Dai villages alongside the Lancang River. It is a typical tourist attraction zone characteristic of Dai nationality religion, history, culture, customs, architecture, clothing and food. These five natural villages are built up on the basis of the Dai community ethnicity, under which the entire residential area (and also part of the production area) form the tourism zone. As such, community life plays a leading part in which religion, culture and architecture of the Dai nationality are fully reflected, as well as production activities and life presented. The administrative work of these five villages is under the leadership of Manting village committee of Menghan Township. In 2002, there were 314 households, making up a population of 1487, of which the Dai nationality accounted for 99.26%. With the development of tourism, the average annual income of the villagers was notably increased: in 2002, it was 2315 Yuan per head, whereas the 2005 figure was 3571 Yuan, higher than the average income of 3005 Yuan for the township.

Dai village was founded in 1998; it was jointly managed by two stakeholders, Ganlanba Frm and a Kunming architecture company. Having commenced business in August 1999, the Dai Community travel zone was soon awarded 4A grades in China. By 2006, around 2.69 million inbound and outbound tourists were received, generating a total income of approximately 63.65 million Yuan from the industry. Tourists visiting Dai Village are mainly in collective groups, given that individual tourists increase year by year. Under the management body of Dai community zone, 10 departments were put in charge of various works in the environment, such as engineering, performances, guiding, ethnic affairs. In 2005, there were 463 employees in total.

2.2.2   Participation Modes by Dai villagers

2.2.2.1   Participation in Tourism Activity

All five villages in the zone are characteristic of the Dai Nationality in Xishuangbanna, which presents the best combination of Dai nationality culture and tropical beauty, each village having its own instructive name for these places. For example, "Man" in the Dai language means Village, Man Chunman means Garden village; Man Zha means Cooks Village, and Man Ting means Grand Garden Village. The villagers and the resort are integrated in all ways and cannot be separated from one another. On the one hand, the travel activities and products promoted by the Dai Company are mainly demonstrated at the various cultural sites of the community premises; for example, it is always the case that a Dai temple is used for such activities. On the other hand, such activities require extensive participation from the villagers (Table 2.1).

Table 2.1   Main Entertaining Activities Associated within Dai Community Zone

Items	Contents
Water-Sprinkling festival	Allowing tourists to feel the fantastic atmosphere of the Water-Sprinkling festival
Dai Home Visiting	The raised-wood board architecture of Dai and allowing tourists to experience the Dai greeting ceremony.
Seasonal festivals of Dai	Organizing dragon boat racing, bamboo-made-rocket launching, chicken fighting, drum competition, lantern lighting, open-access Market、 offerings to Buddha. . .
Demonstration of folk arts and crafts	Hand-made brocade, Dai jewelry-making process, engraving on palm leaves, pottery-making, extracting sugar and other culture-specific activities.
Hinayana Culture show	Visiting the ancient temple of Man Chunman; and the White Pagoda of Manting with its surrounding trees; Participation in fastening strings, reciting scriptures, drawing lots and other Buddhism activities
Song and dance show	Demonstrating the dancing culture of the Dai

Source: Based on field survey between 2002 and 2005

These events organized by the Dai Company mainly are types of folk custom used in promoting Dai culture and satisfying tourists' needs and, also, obtaining economic benefit for the villagers involved in the events.

2.2.2.2   Economic Activities Involved

Dai Village Company has made great efforts to balance the projects in which the various villages within the community participated. Under its leadership, the natural and economic situation of each village is considered, project participation guided and conflicts or fractious encounters avoided; hence, a multifaceted economic structure was formed. As a result, the economic activities involving mainly the Dai can be classified into three types, as follows:

Home Visiting of Dai

The operation model of Home Visiting by the Dai was originally copied from Han Chinese. In the 1990s, Han Chinese from Sichuan, Jiangxi, Guangxi and other provinces started renting businesses of Dai buildings in order to sell tourist souvenirs made of fake Sand Gold or Sand Silver. They offered a high sales commission for drivers and tourist guides so that more tourists could be taken for shopping. In the beginning of 2002, such activities were banned. However, being driven by the profits as such, the native Dai copied such business models and carried on selling the fake sand gold and sand silver souvenirs. The Managing Company acknowledged the business tacitly by registering such buildings as "Site of Residential Buildings of Dai" (Photograph 1). Meanwhile, in order to avoid complaints from tourists, tourist guides are required to ensure tourists know beforehand that the purchase is not real.

Currently, such business activities are mainly operated by the villagers from Man Chunman. Under the leadership of senior members of the villages and the village committee, 108 households in the village were divided into two groups, receiving tourists every other day. Later on, each group was sub-divided into two under which business was run and profit shared. Thus, the households of each group ranged from 28-30. Within every household, one family member was held responsible for business operations; most are women under 50.

The cost of purchasing souvenirs was shared among the group members and accounts settled on a daily base. As business was only run every other day, on the following day, these members would either sell fruit or collect rubber resin. In 2003, the daily income for each member running Dai Buildings was over 100 Yuan; however, since 2005 this figure has shown a sharp decline — currently it is below 20 Yuan.

Figure 2.1   "Visiting Site of Dai Residential Building" Labelled on the Dai Home Visiting

Enjoying Dai family life

Enjoying Dai Family Life refers to a home-based service in which a Dai family provides tourists with accommodation, food and entertainment. In 2005, 20 households were licensed by Dai Village Company to run such businesses. These, coupled with other 7 households that run the similar businesses but remain unauthorized, provided about 100 jobs annually for the community. Within the periods of Golden Week, around 200 villagers were employed for the service. As a result, the business attracted 50,000 tourists. During the Golden Week of Chinese National Day, two families, Aiguang and Aiyue in Manzha village, on a daily base accommodated 100 person-times tourist and served food for 600 person-times. On average, each family earned 3000 Yuan a day. In September 2003, the Manzha village had 48 households, of which 32 families formed two cooperative groups: two women from two households form a team and run Enjoying Dai Family Life as host families (Photograph 2). To start the business, each family invested several hundred Yuan to purchase crockery and Hi-fi equipment; profit obtained from the business was shared after deducting the initial input. These host families normally earn a bit more thanks to the charge for water and electricity. The cooperative was formed on a voluntary base and, in most cases, such a group was formed by relatives.

Things have changed since 2004: one of the groups dissolved and some members tended to become financially independent. This led to the closing down of the cooperative. At the moment, there remain 12 families running the Enjoying Dai Family Life. This figure is still second to none amongst the community villages. The monthly income of each family was around 1000 Yuan, subject to seasonal variation.

Figure 2.2   Service Women of "Enjoying Dai Family Life" Washing-up at Mihaguang Host Family in Manzha Village

Stalls in markets

By the end of 2006, there were more than 200 stalls in the Dai Village, of which 80% of the slots owned by Dai Village Company were provided free of charge. Fruit, farm commodities, barbecue shops, small food stores and souvenir shops were the main features of these stalls, providing flexible job opportunities for the residents of the five villages.

2.2.2.3 Employment with the Dai Company

The Dai Village Company had 249 staff in total in October 2003, of which 83 were from the five villages which make up one third of the employees of the company. While in 2005, these two figures were up to 463 and 248 respectively, the latter were more than half the number of the total employees. As can be seen from the Table 2.2, the employees from five villages worked in different departments, amongst which they formed the greatest proportion of the environmental department, mainly undertaking labor-intensive jobs, such as porters or gardeners. Again, more than 40% worked with the

Department of Performances. This is because the Department has attracted most folk artists from the locals, given that not many actors were from villages. Moreover, one third of these villagers worked within the Resort Management Department. This is because they were originally from the local villages and there was a need for them to be coordinated with the locals. Nevertheless, only one of them worked in the office of the administration; at the management level of the Company, there is not a single one of these people.

Table 2.2   Village-Origin Staff in Each Department of the Company

Departments	Number	Of which village–origin staff	Percent of village-origin Staff
Office	34	1	2.9
Travel Zone Management	56	17	30.4
Environment	48	27	56.3
Tour-guide Dept	43	10	23.3
Performance Dept	68	28	41.2
In total	249	83	33.3

Source: Cited and calculated from "Staff name list of Dai Village Company in October, 2003".

The monthly wages of these employees of village-origin ranged from 400-600 Yuan, of which tour-guides earned the most, about 1000 Yuan during peak season. As regards those folk artists involved in the demonstration of folk customs, the Company only pays 150 Yuan a month as they earn money from their performances. They were recruited initially because their land was to be rented by the Company. As a result, the company is obliged to arrange a job for one family member.

2.2.3   Positive Effects of Community Participation in Tourism

Over the years of development process by the Dai community, tourism has brought about more positive effects, despite some negative elements. Tourism, as an externally driven force, has led the Dai Community to a far-reaching change effect. First, it accelerated the transformation of the population structure, creating more off-farming jobs within the communities. Second, it facilitated the diversification of the economic structure, transforming traditional agriculture into a more commercial and modern mode. Third, it enabled a diversification of agriculture to occur along with development of industry and tourism. As a result, family-run and kinship-associated businesses turned into the main style of production organizing. Fourth, it promoted urbanization and changes in life style. Frequent interaction between hosts and guests impacts the life style of the community and hence speeds up the transition process from rural to urban. Yet, the positive effects of the Dai community participation in tourism activities need to be considered further.

2.2.3.1   Traditional Culture Rediscovered and Preserved

The rediscovery of the traditional culture heritage by Dai Village has greatly stimulated community residents to inherit and study their music and dances. Experts and famous dancers in Xishuangbanna are invited to act as supervisors and directors for the folk dancing shows in the community tourism quarter. Combined with folk singing and dancing, these women, who run the "Enjoying Dai Family Life" program, have re-created performances of their own minority nationality enabling many lost pieces of music and song to circulate again. Although their participation via art performance aims to make more money, it has to a great extent played a significant role in restoring and preserving their traditional culture as a whole.

Through the tourism development process, Dai community residents are largely involved in the making of handicrafts and demonstrating their folk customs. The former covers hand-made sweets, bamboo-made souvenirs and grinding rice. Other customs can be identified such as elephant feet drum dancing, dancing with knife, Water-Sprinkling show (Photography 3), bamboo-rocket-launching, chicken fighting, as well as wedding and love-matching rituals. Folk customs and arts of Dai community used to be regarded as their especial way of life, but now also are recognized by the market and outsiders. Thus, the community residents benefit from their traditional customs. Thus, the re-discovery process as such is promoting the survival of traditional customs of the Dai community.

Figure 2.3   Tourists and Local Women of the Dai Community Enjoy Water-Sprinkling

2.2.3.2   Ethnic Identity Raised in Community Participation in Tourism

Community participation in tourism provides more opportunities to make contact with "the other". In comparison with "the other", the Dai community has perceived their cultural values and identified themselves with a strong sense of self. This in turn enhances the coherence and harmony of the community.

On October 5, 2003, Manzha villagers were *offering* "Salashuai" (Photograph 4). "Offering" here originated from east and south China where the minority nationalities atoned for their sin with gifts. "Offering Buddha" means to offer gifts to Buddha. On that day, 50 families in the village prepared plentiful tributes and started to deliver them to the temple. The entire temple became full of the various tributes. At 10 am, 60 monks from 5 temples nearby presented themselves and addressed their scriptures and delivered their best wishes to the villagers offering Buddha. The atmosphere of the ceremony was grand and the sight magnificent. The event continued till 5 pm, leaving tourists' eyes satiated. The Dai community residents, having placed themselves as the support of tourism, keep the most in-depth cultural elements of their own alive: the Water-Sprinkling festival, dragon-boat racing, the offering to the well, the offering to the pagoda, and "Salashuai" are notable examples of the splendid customs they are brought up with. The values of these customs are reflected in the tourists' eyes. With such appreciation by tourists, the Dai community feels cool and composed.

Figure 2.4   Dai Villagers Offering Tributes in Temple

2.2.3.3   Awareness for Protecting Culture and Natural Resources

Protecting the cultural heritage and natural resources with tourism development presents challenging tasks. In practice, policy, regulations and law too often play a limited role and the achievement does not meet the goal set. Therefore, such tasks cannot be completed without community participation. It has ever been the case that many projects fail because of a lack of local community participation.

In the area of the Dai minority nationality, residents involved in community tourism raised awareness of their culture. For example, the landscape used to be regarded as nothing special in their eyes, whereas now they cherish it because of the tourist perspective and increasingly realize that the landscape protection is crucial to future development. Again, as far as traditional Dai architecture is concerned, the developers of the Dai Village Company enacted decrees entitled "Measures and methods of protecting buildings of Ganglan style" on April 23, 2002. The introduction of these decrees into the community enabled residents to understand the detailed measures for Ganlan building, through which a majority of residents became aware of the values of traditional building. As a result, amongst all the five villages, only one site of non-traditional architecture can be located in Manting village, where tourism activities are not as popular as other villages. Alongside a higher degree of community participation in tourism and the awareness of culture protection, the Dai community participation in tourism provides both motivation and supportive notions for culture protection and its promotion.

2.2.3.4   Extending Traditional Culture of Dai

Traditions and customs cannot easily vanish; they show a strong vitality. No matter what life style a human chooses or how the world changes, traditions will continue for generations to come. To cope with the various impacts brought about by tourism activities, people invent new customs and extend their culture of nationalities into a wider space. Dai community residents are capable of taking measures against impacts on their traditional customs. For example, traditional bedrooms of the Dai have no doors, just a curtain, and residents of the Dai community itself do not approach another's bedroom. However, alongside an increase in tourists who are too often ignorant of the taboo, bedroom doors have been added and, also, locked. Again, concerned about tourists' interruption of the soul of a host family, old people in the community will pray for cleansing when tourists have left. Gradually, the make-up ceremony has become a new-style custom. The formation of new customs as such is thus a direct consequence of the community participating in tourism.

2.3   Case of Xidi: Relatively Reasonable Mechanism of Benefit Distribution

2.3.1   Profile of the Case

Xidi village is located in Yi County, in the city of Huangshan in Anhui Province. It lies 8 kms from the county seat and 40 km to the southeast of Huangshan National Park. On November 30, 2000, Xidi, together with the adjacent Hong Village, was formally included in the list of the World Heritage Sites of the UN. These sites cover three ancient ancestral shrines, one monumental archway and 224 ancient residential buildings, which are amongst existing groups of ancient residential buildings built in the Ming and Qing Dynasties.

Through the efforts of Confucian officials and businessmen, Xidi was established and kept alive throughout the generations. Over the most prosperous era of Xidi village life, during the Jiaqing years of the Qing Dynasty (Photograph 5), with a population of 5000, there were more than 600 houses, 99 alleys, over 90 wells, 34 ancestral shrines and 13 monumental archways. At present, Xidi on the whole preserves the pattern of village and streets of this prosperous period and constitutes a unique cultural landscape feature, demonstrating sophisticated architectural art and scenic panorama designed to be in harmony with nature. With notable features of the regional culture, it is highly regarded as an ancient village of great comprehensive and overall value amongst the traditional villages of Wannan (south Anhui) (Table 2.3). Xidi village reflects outstanding talents and achievements in creating a living environment characteristic of traditional villages of Wannan. It provides priceless information for an in-depth research on unique architecture, village and regional history, culture, art and economy, in addition to the feudal patriarchal clan system. All this makes the Xidi village a precious cultural heritage.

Figure 2.5   The Ancient Xidi Residential Buildings during Its Prosperous Period

Table 2.3   Basic Architecture and Technology Indicators of Xidi Village

Protecting category	Preserved buildings	Preserved buildings	Preserved buildings	Total
Period of construction	Jiaqing years to the end of the Ming Dynasty	Jiaqing to Xuantong years of the Qing Dynasty	P.R.C	
Modes of buildings	Typical characteristic of traditional buildings	Characteristic of traditional buildings	Characteristic of traditional buildings	
Historical, artistic and scientific value	Very high	Relatively high	medium	
Intact degree	Very good	Relatively good	good	
Number of preservation (Blocks)	29	95	47	171
Area (M^2)	6380	21,080	9,870	37,330
Remarks	Including three ancestral shrines, zouma building and monumental archway			

Source: http://www.yixian.gov.cn/yxdy/xd-7.htm (25-4-2005)

At the beginning of the reform and opening up of China in 1980, the architectural and cultural value of Xidi village was known to the world, according to experts' research at home and abroad. In 1986, the County Party Committee of Yi County set up a "Leadership Committee of Development and Utilization of Tourism Resources in Yi County". The Committee included 11 heads from relevant departments, in charge of the county office, office of publicity, culture affairs, transportation, construction, finance. The Party Secretary and the County Magistrate acted as head and deputy head of the committee, respectively. On October 15, 1986, the "Xidi Tourism Site" was formally opened. Nominally, the Xidi spot was headed by the county office, but in fact, it was chiefly operated by villagers under the inspiration of the village cadres. In 1994, the Xidi Tourism Site was reorganized as Xidi Tourism Service Company and the Xidi Tourism Holdings Ltd was set up in 2005 (abbreviated as Xilu Company). Presently, the villagers of Xidi mainly engage in agriculture and the tourism industry, besides their other business activities (Photograph 6). For the more than 300 households of Xidi village, what interests them most is the bonus from ticket revenue.

Figure 2.6   Xidi Residents in Handicrafts Business Using Residential Buildings

2.3.2   Earnings Distribution Mechanism of Tourism in Xidi Community

2.3.2.1   Principal Ways of Distribution

Tourism enterprises in Xidi are owned by the village committee. At the early stage of Xidi's tourism development, its main distribution method was to evenly allocate benefits to the villagers, excluding taxes and costs. With the rapid development of tourism, distribution of benefits in Xidi became more developed and more reasonable. Excluding taxation and the cultural heritage conservation fund, the profit-sharing of Xidi tourism enterprises' ticket revenue accorded the ratio of 1:1, allocated to Xidi village.

Within the half profit from tourism enterprises being distributed to Xidi village, 20% was kept as a village collective fund for communal projects; 80% was distributed to the villagers. The latter were then allocated to the individual villagers according to two standards: distribution by population of Xidi and distribution by housing construction area. "The Population Standard" and "The Housing Standard" were used to be considered at a ratio of 1:1 before 2002; afterward, in order to enhance the protection of the World Cultural Legacy, the ratio was adjusted to 4.5:5.5.

Since 1996, the villagers of Xidi have begun to enjoy a dividend income from Western Trip Company's ticket revenue. The dividend situation from 1999 to 2003 was as follows: allocation for Ancient Dwellings in 2002, 14 Yuan per square meter to each household according to the housing standard; and according to the population standard, the subsidy was 430 Yuan per capita in 2002. However in 2003, because of the "SARS" impact, ticket sales declined and the dividend was reduced to 324 Yuan per capita. At present, more than 1000 villagers in Xidi will gain about 800 Yuan per capita annually from tourism ticket dividends.

2.3.2.2   "Population Standard" Distribution Program

"Population standard" is not simply according to distribution through the criterion of population, it also implies other criteria and distributes in the name of "Environmental Protection Fees." It can be divided into three distribution ratios by a benchmark of environmental protection standards: Full employment (100%), Partial employment (40%) and Nil employment. There are detailed regulations in the "Population standard" which was formally implemented from 2000:

The conditions of full employment:

- Agricultural resident population with a local account

- Local residents who go out for study or a job

- Conscript service, demobilized soldiers in the village

- Agricultural laborers with an account in the village, live outside but still come back to engage in the paddy contract; or the elderly relying on their children

The conditions of partial employment (40%):

- Counting the number of months through the accessing and quitting months of the accounts, either for immigration, emigration, birth or death

- Children with an account in the village and who live in the village, one of the accounts of whose parents is in the village will enjoy a halved share (except for the resident household)

- Those under 14 years of age and own an only-child certificate will be granted 5 Yuan per month for boys and 6 Yuan per month for girls. If one of the couples' accounts is not in the village, the grant will be halved

- A residential account in the village

The conditions of nil employment:

- Those with an account non-registered in the village and those with off-farming accounts

- Those with an account in the village who have been settled outside for more than two years

- Temporary residents with emigrant accounts

There is a slight change in the standards for 2001 and 2002 according to that of 2000: a new regulation will join in the 4th condition of full employment in 2001 — the college students admitted to high school and up (regardless of the accounts' moving out or not) are entitled to the above standards, but this right will be lost automatically after their graduation. In the 4th condition of full employment in 2002, the changes read, "the elderly relying on their children" for "persons over 60 years old".

Because of different tourism revenues each year, the environmental protection fee is adjusted according to the population standard. Take the full employment standard for example: the fees for 2000, 2001 and 2002 were respectively 270 Yuan per person, 320 Yuan per person and 430 Yuan per person.

2.3.2.3 "The Housing Standard" Distribution Method

The Housing Standard distribution method in Xidi is provided under the terms of the Ancient Building Conservation Fee and acts as the charge of the villagers for the Ancient Dwellings' repair and maintenance. There are some distinctions between new dwellings and old ones. They are as follows:

- Differentiating old dwellings from new ones by the construction time of before or after the founding of The People's Republic of China.

- Grading the dwelling according to its condition and function when the house was mapped – in Dec. 2000.

- Newly constructed buildings are not contained in the conserved charges unless authenticated before Dec. 31, 2000.

- After UNESCO's investigation of Xidi (Feb. 2000), all the new, unfinished houses, and those which had been demolished or not restored to their original appearance and structure (whether or not holding land use permits and real estate certification) do not enjoy the protection fees.

- The Ancient Dwellings protection fee is distributed based on square meters.

The Ancient Dwellings protection fee is allocated according to the ratios as followings:

- 100% payment: including ancestral houses, kitchens, additional halls for living use, and so on – which are called "Old Houses" by the villagers in Xidi.

- 60% payment: including those main houses for living use built after the founding of the Republic, before the investigation of UNESCO (Feb. 2000) and were finished before the mapping time – they are called "New Houses" by the villagers in Xidi.

- 20% payment: including the rooms for feeding silkworms, hovels and houses for production use.

2.3.3   Evaluation of Benefits Distribution Mechanism

Rationale

The distribution method of "Population Standard" reflects the villagers' equal rights toward the ownership of the resources. What's more, it affirms the critical role played by each villager in the fabric of the whole environment.

Scientific approach

The distribution method of the "Housing Standard" differentiates the heritage value and tourism value of the residential buildings, the private estates of the villagers according to quality and grade of the houses. Although some aspects of the method still need be detailed and elaborated, they have embodied the science of the distribution system.

2.4   Case of Yubeng: Self-Actualized Sustainable Tourism

2.4.1   Introduction

Yubeng village is situated in eastern Deqin county, Yunnan province, about 60 km from the town centre. People who want to reach the village need to go along an 8 km-long mountainous road on foot or by horse. As it is difficult to access, the village is virtually isolated from outside world. This, together with its unattached nature, makes the place more alluring. So, as a desirable tourist spot, it attracts eco-tourists at home and abroad who prefer nature, a rustic village life and Tibetan culture. With an altitude of 3.2 km above sea level on average, Yubeng is ranked the highest village in the Meili snow mountain area. It is divided into two parts of natural habitations, the upper and the lower village. Holy Waterfall, Mountain-climbing Base (Base Camp) and Ice Lake are the main tourist attractions. Heading off about 7 km from lower Yubeng to Holy Waterfall (at the foot of Miancimu peak), you will see an important religious place with bathing for Tibetan pilgrims. There is a mountain-climbing camp to the southeast of Kawa Karpo. Two attempts have been made to conquer Mt. Kawa Karpo by a Sino-Japan joint climbing team in 1991 and 1998 and both teams chose this site as base camp. As the southwest of Base Camp lies at Ice Lake (Naiqinlacuo), even in summer, ice blocks avalanched from snow-mountains can be seen floating on the water.

Yubeng village is characteristic of a small Tibetan community and consists of 34 households with a population of 163. Yubeng means "where classics are founded" in Tibetan. It is seated at the foot of Mt. Meili and surrounded by snow-mountains, virgin forests, marshy grassland, valleys and farmland. Such scenery greatly satisfies tourists' needs of returning to nature. Its villagers dwell in Tibetan houses and believe in Tibetan Buddhism. Most earn their living by doing farm-work, though some operate home-stays as a sideline. The village is preserved like "a heaven of peace and happiness" with an unadorned folk way and beautiful scenery（Figure 2.7）.

Figure 2.7   Beautiful Yubeng

2.4.2   Community Participation in Tourism at Yubeng

With exploration conducted by such pioneers as climbers, adventure tourists, hikers and photographers, Yubeng is gradually becoming known by the outside world. Especially, in recent years, reported via the Internet, TV and other media, it has become a worldwide popular tourist attraction. What's more, it has been highly praised by those tourists who very much prefer nature, ecotourism, folk customs and religious culture.

From the mid-to-late 1990s, villagers began to run home-stays and horse-riding businesses, providing tourists with accommodation, transportation and other basic services. There were 10 family hotels and 350 beds as of 2003, all providing food and baths.

In terms of the information provided by the local government, the annual combined household gross revenue from the tourism industry at Yubeng rose from ￥ 139300 to   ￥ 628100 between 2001 and 2005. In 2005, its household earnings was￥ 18500 and per capita income was ￥ 3853 per year, which exceeded the average level for Yunnan province.

2.4.3   Interest-Sharing System of Community Tourism

2.4.3.1   The Development of Interest-Sharing System

With an increasing number of tourists coming to Yubeng, more villagers started to run family hotels after 2000 increasing their potential for competition. This, to some extent has led to factions and even conflicts amongst the villagers.

As a teacher of primary school (Photograph 8), A-Rong worked in another village prior to 2004. Whilst visiting Yubeng in 2002, he noticed the phenomenon of mass competition. Concerned that this might threaten tourism development and damage harmonious relationships among the villagers, he initiated a scheme and appealed to villagers to host tourists by turns. In the beginning, his proposal was opposed by the leaders of Xidang village committee (as a natural village, Yubeng belongs to the

Xidang administrative village) who said it was the era of market economy, so there was no room for egalitarianism. But A-Rong insisted that they had not yet reached the stage of free market economy because of their economic and cultural condition. "If they do, some of them will earn no money and be much poorer." Finally, his realistic scheme was approved by the villager committee. In their view, a few dwellers would earn more money with the influx of travelers but when all villagers identified the interest and then rushed to pursue it, competition could not be avoided. So, if there were no effective mechanism for coordinating competitive activities or for reconciling conflicts, the simple relationship between villagers would be threatened and the unadorned folk way would cease to exist. Thus, the humanistic environment which attracts tourists and promotes Yubeng's tourism development would be degraded. Undoubtedly, this could precipitate a fatal attack on Yubeng arising from tourism development.

Figure 2.8   Simple and Intelligent A-Rong

At the beginning of 2002, under the leadership of elite villagers headed by A-Rong, a simple "tourism-revenue equal distribution system" was formulated after several householder meetings. They also decided to make a billboard to announce their findings at the village entrance, reminding travelers of the arrangement. Villagers put the tourism-income sharing system (including income from home-stays and horse-riding) into practice after voting in Villagers' Congress in 2003. Then the actual disposable household income rose, meanwhile reducing the income inequality attributed to the difference of activities in the tourism industry.

2.4.3.2   Basic content of interest-sharing system

Leading horses carrying passengers and running home-stays are the main ways that Yubeng's villagers participate in the tourism industry. This original closed-door village adopted an original but fair way to distribute opportunities and interests, just as a primitive communist society. They established a distribution system to share the income from running family hotels, delivering food and beverages as well as horse-leading. In the meantime, dwellers regulated the obligations of cleaning when they acquired interests.

Accommodation-income's equal opportunity and distribution system

Thirty-four families of Yubeng were selected randomly. Workers (generally two people) were requested by the village committee to record tourist groups at the village entrance. Visitors would be rostered into families in turn according to the tourists' entry sequence and Yubeng family numbers. This regulation aimed at bringing every family an accommodation income. At first, tourists were forced to reside with the families in turn but they tended to want to select by themselves, so changes occurred for the sake of the visitors. Visitors can now select families to live with based on their needs. If the family on duty is chosen, it gains all the income; if not, the selected off-duty family should give half of their profit to the family on duty.

Guests to the home-stays were assigned in terms of group arrival times, regardless of the number of tourists. This meant that the number of tourists accommodated by the families in turn was not the same. This is a matter of chance but the way of distributing profit conforms to the villagers' thoughts of equality.

This system directly considers the interest of the families which could not run home-stays for one reason or another and it took the active families in the accommodation business into account. A simple community interest-sharing opinion was reflected. Considering the intention of system design, the system avoids not only further gap-widening between the rich and the poor, but also the cut-throat competition among family hotels, thus maintaining community harmony.

Catering income's distribution-according-to-work principle

Tibetan food is the main staple of these Tibetan people: Zanba, beef, mutton, yak butter tea and so on. Most Tibetans are not used to the food of other nationalities, like the Han. They are not good at cooking these dishes either. But to satisfy the tourists' demand, some competent families started to provide a more diverse diet. In the Tibetans' subconscious mind they believe in "more pay for more work". Naturally, all of the catering income belongs to the operators, which means these families gain all the profit from catering, if they supply meals. This principle considers the work efficiency of home-stays and what it reflects is people who get paid according to their work.

Public-participation system on horse business

Yubeng's transportation and communication to the outside world are difficult because of its distinctive location and the harsh road conditions. This is also why its eco-system is well-preserved and its sustainable use of tourism attractions is ensured. The fact that tourists and their baggage are carried only by horse is emphasized. Consequently, villagers can earn a lot by leading horses, which has proved to be a significant income-resource. Specific management measures for horses are as follows:

Unified administration

Each household is required to provide two horses for the horse-riding business and they serve by turns according to their numbers. The elected head of the horse squad takes charge of designating which horses are to be used and supervises the earnings. Assignment of passengers is resolved by drawing ballots. When travelers need horses, the head hands each of them a number randomly, then calls the horse matching that number. In the business of horse-riding, equality is represented by drawing ballots. Although those drawing women or light weight tourists are delighted, those drawing heavier weighted men are a little unhappy. It depends on luck. Everyone would accept the result. As it turns out, they all have the chance to carry lighter passengers. Some of the horse handlers (Photograph 9) are members of Yubeng households, others are hired from neighboring villages; wage rates average between ￥ 300 and ￥ 400 a month.

Figure 2.9   Pretty Horse-Leading Girl and Tourist

Unified price

In the management process, horse-riding was priced uniformly according to the distance and difficulty of the routes (for data, see Table 2.4), of which tourists' insurance is included. The price allows a visitor plus baggage under 5 kg, the overweight would be charged extra. Again, a horse specializing in carrying luggage costs as much as a horse carrying a person.

Table 2.4   Estimated Distance, Time and Prices of Yubeng's Tourist Routes

Tourist routes	Distance （km）	Time (hours)			Price (RMB yuan)	
		Experienced hikers	Ordinary hikers	Horseback riders	Up	Down
Xidang hot spring － Lower Yubeng	18	4.5	6.5	5	165	
Xidang hot spring － Upper Yubeng	17	3.5	5	3.5	145	
Xidang hot spring － NanZong Mountain Col	12	2.5	3.5	2.5	105	
Lower Yubeng － Holy Waterfall	7	2	2.5	2	75	30
Lower Yubeng － Xidang hot spring	18	4	6	4	145	
Lower Yubeng － Nanzong Mountain Col	6	1.5	2.5	1.5	75	
Upper Yubeng － Nanzong Mountain Col	5	1	1.5	1.5	75	
Upper Yubeng － Base camp、Ice lake	12	3	4	3.5	85	50

2.4.3.3   Integration of Responsibilities, Rights and Benefits: Responsibility System of Environment and Sanitation

The sustainability of Yubeng's community tourism lies in the fact that they strengthened environmental protection when they were trying to acquire economic benefits. Under the supervision of foreign NGOs, they put a subsection sanitation care contract system in place. Every household is responsible for waste disposal in their area. In the mid-1990s, an investigation of Yubeng's biodiversity was conducted by The Nature Conversancy (TNC, American). Investigators also assisted villagers in establishing an elementary contract system of subsection-sanitation care. They also raised money and reinforced the drinking water pipeline project for both humans and livestock.

The responsibility system for managing the environment and sanitation impacts of tourism can be regarded as an "exogenous" system design in comparison with features of the tourism-industry-revenue equal distribution system, which are "endogenous", since the former was put into practice with the support and assistance of TNC. The basic requirements of the system are as follows:

- Effective spatial scope of the responsibility system of environment and sanitation: This starts at Nanzong Mountain Col in the east and ends at Holy Waterfall in the west. It extends from the southwest foot of North-South Zhengla Mountain to the north and the entrance to the Ninong village of North-South Zhengla Mountain's section to the south.

- Dividing responsible areas: Villagers divided the spatial scope above into several parts for households of Yubeng. Each family is responsible for cleaning an area, including roads, forest, marshy grassland, temporary constructions, etc.

- Tag to confirm: To confirm who was responsible and to facilitate supervision, villagers marked each householder's name on a board both in Tibetan and Chinese, and then hung the board in his responsible area (Photograph 10).

Figure 2.10   The Wood Sign Which Identifies Persons Responsible for Environmental Management in Tibetan and Chinese

With its implementation, it seems that the simple and feasible system above was carried out well. The subsections were divided and assigned along the main tourist lines. And they were publicized in the form of tagging. So far, good sanitation has been preserved in most regions where travelers may arrive.

2.4.3.4   Assessment on These Systems and Measures

Accommodation revenue and horse leading income bring villagers significant economic benefit. When conflicts concerning interests appear, villagers work out a reasonable balance system so that conflicts are effectively resolved inside Yubeng. They develop tourism, gain and share the profits without the operation, management, advertising and promotion conducted by external investors and developers. Further, tourist income was earned prior to the large-scale investment of local government. Villagers even put an interest allocation system in place, lacking the organization and administration of local government. Villagers themselves are exactly the system designers and operators, illustrating that villagers can bring local wisdom into full play with the direction of elites and the support of the native equal provincialism. In consequence, the majority of villagers obey the system and community tourism is naturally accomplished.

Similarly, although public sanitation is treated as a public good by government or charity organizations, and good public sanitation cannot be provided in Chinese private areas at present, villagers consider the eco-system and nature as their public zone even more when Yubeng as a collective stood to benefit from effective tourism development . As a result, when a foreign NGO brought in sanitation techniques, they all agreed quickly. The easily-implemented sanitation system was put in place and the responsibilities were shared by all households.

Yubeng's tourism-administration systems and measures are basically cooperatively managed and equal allocation modes result from self-creation, self-development and self-consciousness. These systems satisfy and coordinate most villagers' and their families' tourist revenue fairly and openly. Meanwhile, villagers' awareness of effects of acting as hosts was aroused to some extent. The pressure put on the environment and sanitation has eased, although the number of Yubeng's visitors has increased.

2.5   Case of Kanas: Effective Community Tourism Planning

2.5.1   Case Introduction

2.5.1.1   The General Situation of the Community Residents in Kanas Tourism Zone

"Kanas", located in the north of Buerjin county 150 km away from the county seat and centered on Lake Kanas, is a National AAAA class tourism zone. Most of the visitors are group packages, apart from some backpackers. Kanas community is an ethnic community living off pastureland with a long history of maintaining its national culture, which is a striking and unique and colorful community culture. There are fascinating Chinese Mongolian-Tuwa people and Kazakhs with a long history of culture, mainly living in Kanas village and Hemu village (Photograph 11) of the Hemu & Kanas town in Buerjin county, and also Baihaba village of the Tielieketi town in Habahe county.

Figure 2.11   Hemu Village: Photographers' and Backpackers' Attraction

The Kanas tourism zone makes up a large area, given that the community residents in the area are not many (more then 2800, see Table 2.5) but they possess considerable national and regional characteristics. A low level of economic development is a common problem in and around the Kanas tourism zone. In 2004, Per Capita income of farmers of the Kanas village, Hemu village and Baihaba village was ￥ 1,539, lower than the average of ￥ 1,718 for Xinjiang and far lower than ￥ 2,634 for all of China the same year.

Table 2.5   The Make-up of Community Residents in Kanas Tourism Zone

Villages	Households	Population	Nationalities	
			Mongolian-Tuwa	Kazakh
Kanas village	188	773	502	271
Hemu village	291	1226	797	429
Baihaba village	172	834	358	476
Total	661	2833	1657	1176

2.5.1.2   The Situation of the Community Residents Participating in Tourism Industry in Kanas Tourism Zone

At present, the community residents taking part in the tourism industry are at the stage of running their own businesses. The community tourism of Kanas tourism zone has been developing very fast these past three years, at first being started in 2000 by outsiders and then gradually gaining greater native involvement. They engage in tourism business during the peak travel season, making local delicacies, selling handcraft products, running shops, horse renting and leading, taking a single person or a family as a unit for a homestay.

All of the residents of the three communities are very enthusiastic about participating in the tourism industry and they set up new houses for operating the tourism industry. There are altogether 27 families engaged in tourism in Baihaba village, with 481 beds in all. The most common key benefit of the community residents is the rent. The highest rent of Kanas village in peak travel season can be more than ￥ 200,000, while most of the families receive ￥ 30,000 to ￥ 50,000. Some residents also sell agricultural products, rent horses, lead horses or visit families out in rural areas.

2.5.1.3 Problems in the Community Tourism

Trends of operating disorder

There is a tight combination between the community residents and the Kanas tourism zone while the government took part in the community tourism a little late. There have been so many residents coming in and out of the community (especially outsiders) that the community tourism program is in disorder. For example, the advertisement boards are in a disorderly condition around the rural and the family inns; houses are built randomly; rivers are polluted and the natural views and historic buildings are damaged. The environmental sanitation is bad in the scenic zone. A lot of economic loss was caused by the blind pursuit of cash incomes by the residents.

The commercialization of the tourism community

Chinese Mongolian-Tuwa people have lived in the mountains for such a long time, seldom in contact with outsiders, that they are not known and are considered very mysterious. At the same time, the population of Tuwa is so small that it is called "the last Tuwa people" in China. Since more and more tourists have come to Kanas in the last five years, the way of life of the Tuwa people has aroused a lot of interest. The way of culture and life which the outsiders bring in has accelerated the process of local commerce but it is aggressively overtly commercial and results in an incorrect understanding of the local nationality culture.

The outstanding contradiction of community

There have been a series of contradictions and problems arising from some of the formerly harmonious and peaceful ethnic communities in the process of profit chasing. The complex commercial relations between villages, villages and enterprises, villages and the government, and individuals result in deep collaborations, difficult to dissolve, presenting the following aspects:

- Conflicts of the resource use between scenic zones and communities, between tourism and husbandry, as well as leading to management problems.

- Conflicts between communities and the government in the development and the fairness of distribution of benefits due to the historical reasons.

- Conflicts between different communities between the communities in and out of the core zone of the scenic area.

- Conflicts among community distributions due to the difference of management capacities and location results in unequal income.

2.5.2 The Process and the Principals

In order to resolve the problems of tourism development, the project team proposed that tourism planning be based in the community to promote the participation of the communities in developing themselves. The members of the project team, composed of the Zhongshan University Center for Tourism Planning & Research, have done research into the communities of the Kanas village, the Hemu village and the Baihaba village and visited many of residents on the way, delivering altogether 200 questionnaires to acquire knowledge of the background of the residents, the sources of income, willingness to be trained, the content of training, the recognition of the impact of tourism and the willingness of participating in community-tourism. The project team has given training about community-tourism and has held conferences with the community residents, introducing the relevant situations and seeking public comments and suggestions on tourism planning (Figure 2.12 & Figure 2.13). According to the research and analysis, "The community tourism planning of Kanas" has proposed a corresponding scheme on community tourism planning based on the situations and the problems of Kanas community.

Figure 2.12   Kanas Villagers Listening to the Lecture about Community Tourism

Figure 2.13   Hemu Villagers Participating in the Seminar for Community Planning

The orientation of the tourism development plan is changing from the economic and material approach to the development of community and service. The following basic principles should be adhered to.

- *Principle of protection* – Economic growth seems to be the first priority of the local government now, so there is thought of "GDP supreme," "growth supreme" and "profit supreme," however, the principle of protecting both the natural and the humanistic resources of the community must be followed if appropriate tourism planning is to result.

- *Principle of participation* – Community residents are important forces of tourism development, so they are encouraged to participate in the process of developing, planning, managing and supervising their tourism. On the one hand, community residents will receive more benefit from the process of participation; on the other hand, it is a democratic decision-making process which provides opportunities and duties pertaining to civil rights and self-management.

- *Principle of restriction* – The number of community residents who participate in the house-reception and other programs must be restricted. The number of tourism communities to be developed, the development of tourism activities and the tourists to be allowed into the communities must also be restricted if adverse social and cultural impacts and environmental degradation are to be avoided.

2.5.3   The Main Contents of Tourism Plan

2.5.3.1   The Basic Strategies for the Tourism Plan of Kanas Community

The following strategies in community participation are proposed on the basis of the situation and the problems in tourism development of Kanas community.

- Providing the community residents with the opportunities of participating in decisions on tourism development. The government should get advice and suggestions from the residents representing their needs.

- Improving the control and the guidance of planning. The government should supervise the social and economic well-being of the residents by effective measures. The intention of the government is not only to bring benefit to the residents but also to have them maintain the arrangement, without which there will not be sustainable development.

- Making the best use of the management of the base organization in community participation, the government should take great consideration of the specialty of villagers' roles and professional attainments at the grassroots level, giving them freedom to improve the organizational and management ability in community-tourism development in promoting the healthy development of a community-tourism industry. The village community should prevent an increasing gap between rich and poor among residents and prevent a monopoly of local elites and the economically able in tourism administration.

- Traditional communities should play an important role and make the "Village Regulations and Folk Conventions" with preferential binding force. They should be entitled to new tourism participation functions and should lead the community residents to participate in tourism management in a good order. New organizations, such as a "community tourism association," could be set up in the tourist communities. This should also lead the residents to make the rules as it comes from the inner rule power of Chinese village governance.

- Residents in the communities should have priority to participate in the tourism industry and outside interests should be restricted. More employment and management opportunities should be provided to the residents of the communities. Providing numerous people with employment and investment opportunities and offering the chance of controlling and managing the relevant natural resources and participating in the benefit distribution in the process of tourism development should be left to them. They should prevent occupation by outsiders in running restaurants, hotels and shops, especially Kanas village and Hemu village where the problems are very noteworthy in this respect.

- Hold the principle of "not to participate is to participate the most" to prevent over-participation. To other residents who don't participate in tourism directly, not to participate is to participate the most, for according to the relevant scholar (Steven Schipani & Souksanh Pakasy, 2003) only a small portion of the tourists live in the village communities, so community residents should be led to conduct other business activities in order to prevent over-participating in and losing the attraction of the "heaven of earth" and "idylls" of Kanas community, especially the Kanas village in the center of Kanas community.

- Establish a mechanism of benefit distribution that prevents the tourism community becoming commercialized. Most of the tourism communities of Kanas are facing the problem of going commercial and there has been less traditional environment of ethnic communities and worse visitor experiences than before because of this. In order to maintain a balance between residents who don't participate in tourism management and those who do, tourism profits must be shared by means of compensating them through collective funds and twice-profit distribution to prevent the communities from becoming too commercial.

- Strengthen the education and training of community residents, including the training of the staff, the education of all residents and establishing learning programs of community culture and handcrafts.

- Make good use of the general consulting function of NGOs to attract the attention and technical support of all kinds of non-governmental organizations, non-profit organizations, academies, specialists and scholars.

- Provide tourism information and set up an information platform. The government or private developer should make information about tourism development known to the public regularly. The community itself should actively participate in setting up a tourism market information service system, since it is both information provider and information receiver.

- Set up a tourism coordinating committee made up of directors of the tourism department of the local government, representatives of enterprises, owners of local individual enterprises and local community representatives. Hold coordinating conferences regularly, consulting and handling problems in the development in order to coordinate the benefits for all interest groups.

2.5.3.2 Planning Programs the Status Quo of the Three Communities

Kanas Village

- Planning purpose: Prevent the community from becoming a business district run by outsiders. Restore the original lifestyle of the community.

- Problem diagnoses: Because of the over-operating of family hotels by outsiders, the total number of beds in both new and old villages is up to 1800 but the traditional custom and culture of the Tuwa are threatened, which in turn affects the cultural landscape of the core scenic area and contributes to an unpleasant experience for travelers.

- Solutions: Close down all the existing family hotels and restaurant businesses at this stage. Redesign the benefits distribution system in the community to protect residents' interests. After the growth of the residents' participation capacity in a specific period in the future, development will be controlled. Encourage e residents to display such ethnic cultural programs as folk customs and crafts.

- Community interests: Franchise fees, ticket dividends, focus on catering and souvenirs (the Authority operating area for the villagers to draw concessions), riding schools, company workers, and the reconstruction of the community environment, protection of the natural environment, improvement of the quality of the villagers, and the protection of national culture.

Hemu Village

- Purpose of Planning: To protect the harmonious cultural landscape of World Heritage significance which has been accumulated by Hemu Villagers for generations, while at the same time expanding the space of follow-up development for the Kanas Lake area.

- Diagnosis of the Problems: Driven by economic interests, a growing number of outsiders and the locals motivated by profit have flooded into the business of tourism, leading to the explosive growth of newly-built properties in the community, with over 100 new houses built. This has transformed the structure of the traditional dwelling places of the Tuwa and Kazakh people. As one of the representatives of Kanas tourism image, 'the amazing paradise village' is now under threat.

- Program of problem-solution: Stop all outsider operations of "family" hotels and other businesses; launch a training program for local people in accordance with planning of operation rules; improve local participants' abilities and raise awareness of planning. Also, remove business construction which seriously affects the landscape with the local government promulgating regulations of house construction and enforcing evaluation and approval of land for construction of a new house, and setting rules for house appearance, material, size, color and so on. The planning committee selects other sites to focus constructing business service areas. Encourage community residents to operate businesses displaying folk culture and nationality culture.

- Interests of the community: Family hotels (on average three beds per family in accordance with the right to operate, can be operated collectively or be contracted to the village residents), farmhouse beverages (concentrated distribution and operation to avoid contamination), tourism handicrafts and other operating income, riding schools, company bonus tickets, community infrastructure construction, improvement of village quality, multi-ethnic cultural heritage, typical landscape protection.

Baihaba Village

- The purpose of program: To preserve the tourism value of Baihaba Country as the No.1 country of the northwest, the No.1 sentry of the northwest and the paradise of photographers.

- The diagnosis of problem: Some aberrant architecture appeared around the villages, which affected the sight. Nonstandard phenomena existing in the management of family hotels will have a negative impact on the local image if it further develops.

- The projects of solution: Constitute rules and admission qualifications in order to standardize the operating activities of local people and prevent external people to begin business by tenancy. Encourage the residents to operate ethnically cultural projects such as the exhibition of ethnic customs, folk handicrafts, etc.

- The focus of interest of the community: family hotels (designed according to management rights that one family may have five beds on average, the family hotels can be collectively managed by several families or contracted with local inhabitants), happy farm restaurant (design concentrated layout and manage on the basis of avoiding pollution), revenue from tourism crafts, tourism public facilities and accommodations which are shared by all villagers, the countries became real tourism destinations after the building of roads, heightening of residents' comportment, preservation of ethical culture.

2.5.3.3 The Development of Community Tourism Controlled Standards

The community should be fully involved in community-based tourism, but this doesn't mean an excessive involvement, in other words, participation without limitation. For orderly, proper community participation in the development of tourism, and also in the needs of tourist village elements of the tourism product, a series of controlled standards are as followed:

- Standard of farmhouse restaurant operation

- Measures of residential hotel management

- Norms of tourist practices

- Norms of civilized host Kanas

- Implementation of the "western national park community management" system

- Presentation to tourists of a "Community Tourism Handbook"

2.6   Conclusion and Discussion

2.6.1   Basic Conclusions

Based on the analysis of the four different cases above, the following conclusions were reached:

The Case of Dai Village

Ethnicity under the development of tourism will not emphasize the authenticity of new folk but pay more attention to the economic value of culture. Driven by interests, people will begin to have some sense of the adoption of new practices. They will then accept these new folk bringing the Minority a sense of belonging and identification, a clearer ethnic identity. Cultural tourism development encourages villagers to take an active look at their own culture and amend and reconstruct their own cultural values, which may require a compromise process. With levels of community participation of Dai Park raised, the residents' awareness of the need to protect the culture will become greater. Community participation provides some instinctive motivation and sense of support for the Dai community in actively and consciously protecting and retaining their nationality culture. However, conflicts of interest exist between the enterprises and the community, between village and village, and there are internal conflicts of interests in various villages.

The case study also supports the hypothesis of Mckean: tourism may actually strengthen the protection, improvement and innovation process of tradition (Mckean, 1989:120). In fact, general awareness of the negative impact of the demonstration effect is enlarged, which supposes the destination residents will be suspected and rebel against the local tradition; local cultural mode could fall apart. Actually, the keen interest of foreign culture shown by tourists promotes awareness of the destination to explore tourism resources of cultural values. Traditional culture obtains a certain degree of protection, although associated with pseudo-folk.

The Case of Xidi

The mechanism of tourism income distribution at Xidi Village was based on the administrative villages at the rural grassroots level, so the collectively owned enterprises operated as a basic management framework. This implied a dual significance of tourism income and heritage protection and embodied economic means and administrative measures together. Xidi's implementation of population and housing standards has become an effective way to protect the village's cultural heritage. In a sense, it can serve as a model for the protection of the heritage of other cultures and can be used as an example for other tourism development. By putting the economic and administrative means together, over a period of time they will gradually become internalized as a sense of community awareness.

Currently a prominent issue exists in the distribution of interests of Xidi Village: exclusive distribution accounts for 50% of tourism income, in addition to the other 50% taken by the company (village-run enterprises). Villagers do not have the right to share, control or supervise the income allocation. This is a point on which most resident comments focus and is also one of the problems Xidi's collective enterprises must solve in the process of transformation to a modern enterprise system.

The case of Yubeng

Yubeng has implemented a balanced interest-sharing arrangement and pro-active protective methods of the environment and control of outside (foreign) investment. As a result, it has already developed a sustainable tourism community that is independent and self-fulfilling. This kind of self-control mechanism reduces the conflicts between people, also between people and nature, and thus maintains the tourism ecosystem of Yubeng. The community-tourism in Yubeng is the most representative case found in China at present. That is, the villagers really participate in each part of tourism decision-making, management and interest allocation.

The various management systems of Yubeng are plain and simple; however, they come from practical knowledge originating in the community. The institutional system is bottom-up and has positive effects on maintaining tourism management order, vindicating community inhabitants' benefits and promoting the sanitary quality of the villages. The establishment and carrying out of the present method in Yubeng depended on the lead and guidance of county elites, to a certain extent, but also depended on the equitable concept of the Tibet inhabitant inheritance. The experience of Yubeng County is valuable; nevertheless it is hard to copy in the process of developing tourism in other similar villages. Undeniably, the present participation system of Yubeng will be impacted by the in-flow of mass tourism. At the same time, the benefit allocation concept that combines responsibilities, rights and interests together doesn't extend to the field of public property; therefore, it leads to a loss of public resources. Moreover, supervision of the system itself and its exemplary mechanisms are expected to be more mature.

The case of Kanas

In the Overall Plan of Xinjiang Province Kanas Tourist Areas, which was undertaken by the Center for Tourism Planning & Research, Sun Yet-San University in 2005, community tourism planning was given an important role.

On the basis of in-depth investigation and analysis, the Tourism Plan of Kanas Community ascertained the purpose and principle of planning and studied thoroughly the present situation, management pattern, characteristics of community participation and problems of tourism development. The plan looked at the reality of community based tourism in Kanas and a series of problems was confronted. Learning from related experiences, both domestic and international, it put forward the some basic principles about community participation as follows: Firstly, strengthen the control and guidance of community participation. Secondly, fully develop the management function of skeleton organizations. Thirdly, establish a reasonable interest allocation mechanism. Fourthly, control the commercialization of tourism community. Fifthly, strengthen some basic policies in community participation to the community residents, such as education and training. To ensure community participation can process orderly and moderately, the plan set up operable controlling standards for family restaurants and hotels, also regulations for respecting hosts and tourists.

2.6.2   Discussion

In the course of studying the above cases, it was not difficult for us to find that: no matter the conservation of ethnically traditional culture, world heritage, country ecological landscape or the process constituting a community interest allocation mechanism and tourism plan, we needed a multi-faceted participation of the community. The community is the host of the local resource and culture; they are the creators of a variety of systems and, at the same time, have extraordinary collective wisdom. However, the community is not after all a rational colony. Although some communities, such as Yubeng Village, are comparatively rational management systems, this kind of rational approach takes time to develop. When the interest conflicts and developing contradictions accumulate to a certain point, the direction of community tourism must be deeply reflected and needs the comprehensive participation of more groups.

Scholars should realize that cultural variance is inevitable when confronting communities for tourism participation. The variance of a community is not led by tourism, but the common response under the background of modernization and globalization. The form and reform of culture is a phenomenon that exists everywhere (Ma, 2002:53-54). No matter the variance is active or passive, it occurs inevitably. At the same time, nearly all ethnic culture has a strong compatibility; therefore, tradition is unlikely to be defeated in contest with the modern. The real valuable achievement of scholars, perhaps, is to guide the tourism community to carry out conscious cultural changes, and also get residents to participate in-depth.

From another aspect, scholars should have exact judgment as to the relationship of stakeholders. Driven by interest, community-based-tourism in China is developing rapidly because of the active participation of various stakeholders, such as enterprises, government and community; but since they focus on different interests and there are gaps in the balance of forces, contradictions commonly arise during the process of community participation. Enterprise and government often hold a dominant role. As strong powers, they cannot conduct an equal dialogue with the peasants as the weaker and this leads to greater complaints from peasants after government and enterprise make profits. These are the problems that the four communities mentioned above are going to or will be confronting and thus this field also needs the constant focus of scholars.

Finally, the cases of community based tourism mentioned above have provided us some successful experiences. Nevertheless, we cannot emulate every system, even if they are scientific and reasonable, as a great deal depends on the cultural foundation of the society. Community-based-tourism in China has achieved breakthroughs in a relatively short time, while many communities have found their own way of interest allocation and mode of participation. Indeed, the participation and behavior of residents are more rational, and the government and enterprise should consider this in the planning and management of the community. Because of the geographical diversity and multiform ethic and culture, the researchers should be more thoughtful and cautious when facing practice and test of methods in tourism development.

References:

Bao, J. and Sun, J. (2006), 'A Contrastive Study on the Difference in Community Participation in Tourism Between China and the West', *Acta Geographica Sinica*, 61(4), pp. 401-413.

Center for Tourism Planning and Research, Sun Yat-sen University (2005-2007), *The Tourism Master Plan for Shangri-La, Tibetan, Yunnan, and Sichuan Province* (Funded by China National Tourism Administration).

Center for Tourism Planning and Research, Sun Yat-sen University (2005-2006), *The Tourism Master Plan for Kanas, Xinjiang Province* (Funded by China National Tourism Administration).

Liu, W. (2000), 'Some Theoretical Thoughts about Community-Involved Tourism Development', *Tourism Tribune*, 15(1), pp. 47-52.

Ma, G. (2002), *Enter to the Other's World*, Xueyuan Publishing Company, Beijing, pp. 53-54.

Mckean, F.P. (1989), 'Towards a Theoretical Analysis of Tourism: Economic Dualism and Cultural Involution in Bali', in Smith V. (ed.), *Hosts and guests: the anthropology of tourism* (2nd ed.), University of Pennsylvania Press, pp. 119-138.

Schipani, S. and Pakasy, S. (2003), 'An assessment of international tourists in Luang Namtha LAO PDR', (Online), available: www.ecotourismlaos.com/.../publications/anassessment_of_international _tourists_in_luang_namtha_province.pdf (31-5-2007).

Sun, J. and Bao, J. (2006), 'From Absence to Distinctness: the Research Context of Community Participation in Tourism', *Tourism Tribune*, 21(7), pp. 63-68.

Sun, J. and Bao, J. (2006), 'The Community Participation Model of Tourism: an Empirical Study of Yunnan and Guangxi', *China Tourism Research*, 2(1-2), pp. 137-145.

Tang, S. (1998), 'Commodification of Tourist Destination and Community Tourism', *Geographical Research*, (2), pp. 145-149.

Zhang, G. (1998), 'Agenda 21 for the Travel & Tourism Industry towards Environmentally Sustainable Development', *Tourism Tribune*, (2)-(5).

Zhuge, R. et al. (2000), 'An Approach to Involving Local Communities into Participatory Management of Natural Resources in Wuyishan National Nature Reserve in Fujian', *Rural Eco-Environment*, (1), pp. 47-52.

Chapter 3

The Dolphin Discovery Trail:
A Proposal for Adventure Tourism,
Conservation and Poverty Alleviation in
Cambodia

3.1 Introduction

In the past five years there has been heightened global interest in the freshwater Irrawaddy Dolphin (Orcaella brevirostris) as its numbers have declined in all known habitats across southern Asia (in Cambodia the dolphin is popularly known as the Mekong River dolphin). The Irrawaddy dolphin is now listed by CITES (Convention on International Trade in Endangered Species of Wild Fauna and Flora) as an Appendix I (critically endangered) species (IUCN 2006). In Cambodia, a number of international governmental organizations such as the United Nations IUCN (the International Union for the Conservation of Nature), non-governmental organizations such as WWF (World Wildlife Fund) and WCS (World Conservation Society), together with the Royal Government of Cambodia are active in conservation efforts.

In Cambodia, the habitat of the dolphin extends from Cheuteal Pool just below the southern border of the Lao PDR to Kampi Pool near the Cambodian town of Kratie 190 km to the south (Beasley et al, 2003). Only the southern-most and northern–most pools are accessible by road. There are no roads or even motorcycle tracks running beside the river. An intensive dolphin research program has been conducted in the Cambodian Mekong River since 2001 and the latest findings by the Department of Fisheries suggest that the population now numbers only 80-100 individuals, with an annual mortality rate of about 14-18 individuals (2005 and 2006 respectively). Of particular concern is that infants and sub-adults are dying so that there is little recruitment to the overall population. While the dolphins probably migrate up and down this 190 km long stretch of the Mekong, their main habitat consists of nine deep river pools that have been declared protected areas by Royal Decree of February 2005 (see Maps 1 and 2). These are the last remaining pods of dolphins anywhere in the entire 3000 kms long Mekong River.

Figure 3.1   The Mekong River Dolphin (Orcaella brevirostris), Cambodia

Slide: Courtesy of Cambodian Ministry of Tourism, Phnom Penh

The population decline of the Mekong dolphin has been attributed by the Department of Fisheries in its 2004 report ("Cambodian Mekong Dolphin Conservation Strategy") to accidental and deliberate killing, gillnet entanglement, boat noise and collision, dynamite and electric fishing, over-fishing of prey species, disturbance by tourist boats, live capture, and pollution of the river. This report concludes that Cambodia is "nearing the last chance for the population to survive and the last chance for Cambodia to save one of its most important natural assets". There are 29 villages located on the banks of the nine pools and a further 75 impoverished villages spread out between the pools whose livelihood depends upon fishing. The village communities are one factor increasing pressure on the capacity of the dolphin to survive, but the fundamental needs of these people – which are also survival needs – must be taken into account.

Figure 3.2   Fishing is the Mainstay Activity for the River People (Their survival depends upon this resource)

Photographs: Trevor Sofield.

In recognition of the urgent need to conserve the Mekong River Irrawaddy Dolphin for the next generation, the Department of Fisheries has developed a dolphin conservation strategy. If there is to be any opportunity for the development of tourism activities in Cambodia based on the dolphin, as approved by the Royal Decree (2005), it is fundamental that this conservation strategy be implemented.

Any attempt to introduce dolphin-based tourism without ensuring the survival of the species in the first instance will result in wasted effort and wasted investment. The equation is simple:

> No conservation program = no dolphins = no attraction = no tourism or tourists = wasted investment

One of the deficiencies in this necessary effort to save the dolphin, however, is that in the Department of Fisheries exclusive focus on conservation it ignored a wide range of stakeholders, including the welfare of the village communities.

Stakeholder analysis was considered an appropriate methodology to provide an understanding of the complexities of this situation and was therefore utilised as a key component of the process. Unless a way could be found to bring all stakeholders to the point where they all had an interest in saving the dolphin, the conservation efforts would be negated. Since sustainability can only occur when outputs are predominantly convergent (Hardy, 2001), an innovative solution was obviously required in order to accommodate the multiple interests.

This was the point at which a tourism development solution offered the possibility of bridging the different interests of the stakeholders in a way in which conservation by itself could not. Out of this situation was therefore born the concept for a form of "soft adventure" tourism called The Dolphin Discovery Trail. When integrated with backward linkages into aquaculture and agriculture of the riverine village economies, soft adventure tourism offered the potential of bringing a wide range of conflicting stakeholder interests into a common, cooperative relationship. Because any activity which threatened the dolphin would destroy the very basis for sustainable tourism development, the foundation for the concept of the Dolphin Discovery Trail was therefore the conservation of the dolphin.

The concept of The Dolphin Discovery Trail was accepted by the Cambodian Government in 2005 as a way forward. In 2006 the UN World Tourism Organisation (UNWTO) reached an agreement with the Cambodian Ministry of Tourism and the Dutch agency, SNV, to transform the adventure tourism components of the concept into a tourism development project which is scheduled to commence in late-2007. Donors are still required to fund the backward linkages into aquaculture and agriculture.

This paper explores the dynamics of how adventure tourism integrated with aquaculture and agriculture could be utilised to operate as a mechanism to achieve "a middle way" and satisfy a wide range of development objectives based on conservation of the Mekong River dolphin.

3.2 Stakeholder Theory

An initial field trip by boat down the 200 km-long dolphin habitat of the Mekong River from Cheutreal to Kratie in 2005 revealed a very complex situation involving more than 175 stakeholders with very different interests. Stakeholder theory offers "a holistic approach or procedure for gaining an understanding of a system, and assessing the impact of changes to that system, by means of identifying the main actors or stakeholders and assessing their respective interests in the system" (Grimble and Wellard, 1997: 175). A widely accepted definition of a stakeholder is: "Any group or individual who can affect or is affected by a development and/or the achievement of an organization's objectives" (Freeman 1984, p.46). Mitchell, Agle and Wood (1997) identify narrow definitions of stakeholders that focus on the direct relevance of that agency or person to the core economic interest of a business or development, whereas broad views are based on the premise that a development or a business can be affected by, or can affect almost anyone.

The concept of stakeholder management hinges upon the notion of fairness: "Stakeholder management requires, as its key attribute, simultaneous attention to the legitimate interests of all appropriate stakeholders, both in the establishment of organisational structures and general policy and case-by-case decision making" (Donaldson and Preston 1995: 67). In other words, no one stakeholder should predominate — but in real life of course, the ability to exercise power and to draw upon superior resources vis-à-vis other stakeholders means that, in fact, there will be major or primary stakeholders, minor or secondary stakeholders, active and passive stakeholders, and those that affect other stakeholders vs those that are affected by other stakeholders (Clarkson 1995; Sofield, 2003). However, one of the benefits of utilising stakeholder theory is that it enhances prospects of an outcome which is sustainable. It facilitates the identification of differences in opinions, interests and needs and as Hardy (2001) noted, interaction that allows convergent and divergent opinions to be managed. It improves the assessment of social and political impacts of policies and projects. It is relevant for identifying multiple objectives and concerns and is therefore particularly useful when there are multiple uses and users of a resource. And it provides an efficacious way "in which the need and interests of people who are under-represented politically and economically can be highlighted" (Grimble and Wellard 1997: 178).

There are several reasons for carrying out stakeholder analysis (Grimble and Wellard 1997; Engel 1997; Röling and Wagemakers 1998):

- Empirically, to discover existing patterns of interaction;

- Analytically, to improve interventions;

- As a management tool in policy-making; and

- As a tool to predict conflict.

Grimble and Wellard (1997) underline the usefulness of stakeholder analysis in understanding complexity and compatibility problems between objectives and stakeholders. Stakeholder analysis is also derived from participatory methods that seek to integrate the interests and perspectives of disadvantaged and less powerful groups (Chambers 1997). The questions of who is a stakeholder and under what circumstances the opinions or knowledge of stakeholders count are common to both participatory research, and development and business literature.

While there are significant benefits in applying stakeholder theory to a development, there are problems. For example, in any given situation where does one draw the boundary since there are many backward and forward linkages from the front line sector into virtually all other sectors of the economy? How does one define community as a stakeholder? Is it just the local community within whose locality a development is to take place? Or should a wider community, for example, at the level of the population of a county, or a prefecture, or a province whose interests or resources may be affected by a particular development, be included? In addition the attempt to facilitate more transparent negotiation does not provide a panacea and bringing all stakeholders to the same table may result in more not less conflict. Differential power capabilities cannot be neutralized although they can sometimes be ameliorated.

Nevertheless stakeholder analysis is an appropriate methodology to assist in understanding a complex situation and it was therefore considered relevant in coming to terms with the intricacies of the situation surrounding the conservation of the Mekong River Dolphin. Grimble and Chan (1995) outline procedures for undertaking a stakeholder audit, as follows:

- Identify the main purpose of the analysis;

- Develop an understanding of the system and decision-makers in the system;

- Identify principal stakeholders;

- Investigate stakeholder interests, characteristics and circumstances;

- Identify patterns and contexts of interaction between stakeholders; and

- Define options for management of the resource;

- Formulating new strategies (if necessary) to improve stakeholder relations and therefore the sustainability of a development by meeting as many different needs as possible.

Armed with an understanding of individual stakeholder needs, interests and concerns, it might then be possible to formulate an integrated proposal that could meet the needs of multiple stakeholders and thus achieve a sustainable outcome. As Hardy (2001) emphasized, recognition of stakeholders and incorporation of their needs is essential if sustainability is to be realized.

An audit of stakeholders revealed the following principal actors:

National Governments:

Royal Government of Cambodia

Lao Peoples Democratic Republic The northern-most pool, Cheuteal, while located entirely inside Cambodia just south of the border with Laos, attracts significant numbers of tourists crossing the border from Laos because access is relatively easy from the Laotian side.

Provincial level Governments:

Steung Treng Province

Kratie Province and Kratie Municipality

District level Government:

Communes (District Administrations) x 27

Village Communities:

Active x 29 (those villages located around the nine pools, many of which were being engaged by NGOs to assist in conservation or scrutinized by big business because they owned the land that would be needed for hotels and resorts;

Passive x 75 (those villages which were located in between the pools inhabited by the dolphins and which were largely being ignored by the NGOs and business interests). Total: 104 villages, approximately 103,000 people (World Food Programme, 2004 estimate)

National Ministries:

Ministry of Agriculture, Forestry and Fisheries

Ministry of Interior

Ministry of Environment

Ministry of Public Works and Transport

Ministry of Tourism

National Tourism Authority (a semi-statuary body) The NTA was granted responsibility by the Government to manage dolphin ecotourism. It is headed by a senior minister who reports directly to the Prime Minister and not to the Ministry of Tourism and it was under his auspices that this author was requested to develop a strategy.

Commission for the Mekong River Dolphin Conservation This governmental authority was established in 2006 to oversee coordination of all matters pertaining to the dolphin, with dolphin tourism development, however, remaining in the hands of the NTA and the Ministry of Tourism.

Provincial Departments:

Line Departments of above ministries for Kratie and Stung Treng Provinces

NGOs

Nine NGOs including IUCN, WWF and WCS

Tour Operators:

Stung Treng x 2

Kratie x 2

Lao PDR x 4

Potential Investors in hotels/resorts:

Only two potential investors were identified, but it is likely that there are more.

Others (e.g., aid agencies x 6)

Mekong Wetlands Biodiversity Project, managing the Ramsar Site along the Mekong River in Stung Treng Province.

Grand Total of Stakeholders: 179.[1]

3.3   Stakeholder Analysis

Stakeholder analysis revealed that there was a very wide range of interests and positions, with different agendas being pursued by different stakeholders, as noted above. These interests ranged from narrowly-based conservationists focused solely on saving the dolphin at all costs at one end of the spectrum, with big business interests at the other end of the spectrum whose sole interest was in exploiting the dolphins for short term economic gain through mass tourism. In some instances there was not just opposition but hostility to other stakeholders. Extreme conservationists, for example, equated protection of the dolphins with no fishing, no access for tourists and no tourism and were prepared to undertake an international campaign to criticize the Cambodian Government for being a willing partner in commercial exploitation of the dolphin for tourism. At the other extreme, one business interest floated a proposal to capture dolphins for "tricks training" in a display pool at a casino. These stakeholders were on a collision course with each other.

Within the three tiers of government bureaucracy, different ministries and departments were equally divided and demarcation disputes over responsibilities were common. It is of interest that the Government itself recognized the problems of inter-ministry conflict as they defended their policy territories: thus by "Order of the Prime Minister on Mekong Irrawaddy Dolphin Conservation and Tourism Development," dated March 2005, the roles of the different ministries were clearly delineated and each Ministry was directed to cooperate with the others (Appendix 2).

A significant number of stakeholders held positions that were inimical to the continued survival of the dolphin. This number included not only short term business interests but paradoxically some of the conservation agencies who were contributing to the risk of dolphin extinction because they supported a ban on fishing. By prioritising the dolphins over impoverished villagers to the extent of threatening their livelihood, they were alienating many of the village communities whose survival depended upon fishing. These villages were presented with only dis-benefits in conserving the dolphin. While there were various plans to incorporate most of the 29 villages located around the nine pools in a range of activities such as dolphin ecotourism, the 75 other villages were being ignored. They thus had a vested interest in killing all dolphins as quickly as possible so they could continue to fish to put food in the bellies of their families.

---

[1] This survey is not comprehensive. It was restricted to an attempt to identify principal stakeholders only, i.e. those with a direct interest in dolphin tourism, or those such as the 75 villages who would be directly impacted by decisions related to dolphin conservation and protection.

At the international level, because there was relatively good road access from Laos to the border pool at Cheuteal and only very difficult access from Cambodia (and no Cambodian tourism traffic heading north to the border anyway), Laotian tour operators were taking tourists across the border by boat on dolphin-watching expeditions and then returning to Laotian territory. The Laotian tourism authorities had erected prominent dolphin direction signage 500 metres inside its border and constructed a permanent river pier but there was nothing to indicate to travelers that they were in fact crossing an international border to view the dolphins. No visas were issued because the Cambodian border post was located some 15 km away and Customs and Immigration had no water transport to check boats crossing into Cambodia from Laos. There was thus no proper border control and the operations were not regulated in terms of dolphin welfare – how close boats should go to the dolphins, whether they should feed them, what speeds they should travel, provision of encasings for propellers to prevent injury to the dolphins, etc. From the Cambodian side, the villagers of Cheuteal participated by providing extra boats and picnic shelters on a small island in the middle of the pool. The Cambodian Government wished to regulate these incursions across its borders but discussion with Laos was a stop-start affair with no resolution after several years, possibly because non-regulation favoured Lao tour operators.

Figure 3.3   Cheuteal Pool

Left: Dolphin Watching, Cheuteal Pool, Stung Treng, Cambodia; Right: Laotian signage for dolphin watching in Cheuteal Pool, Cambodia, located 500 metres inside Laos. Photographs: Trevor Sofield.

It needs to be emphasized that while stakeholder analysis proceeds by identifying common categories of stakeholders (such as government ministries or NGOs), there is not necessarily homogeneity or commonality of interests by individuals members of a stakeholder group. Indeed conflict between different members of the same stakeholder category can be as great or greater among themselves as with stakeholders outside their group and located in other categories. Hardy (2001) in a study of stakeholders associated with a major tourism development in north Queensland, Australia, noted that there was significant heterogeneity (positional differences) among members of the same stakeholder category.

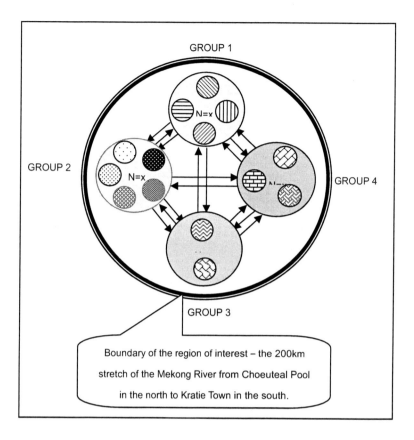

Figure 3.4   Heterogeneity of Individual Stakeholders whin the Same Category

Source: After Hardy, 2001

Stakeholder analysis revealed that four major deficiencies needed to be addressed:

- The emphasis on only the nine pools left more than 130 km of the river habitat unattended;

- If tourism developments were located only at key points along the river (e.g. at the nine deep pools), this fragmentation and piece-meal approach would not facilitate conservation efforts of the total habitat, and uncontrolled development in between those areas could increase the risk to the dolphin;

- A mechanism was needed to involve the 75 villages not located on the banks of the pools to have equity in any tourism development so that an interest in ensuring the continued survival and the welfare of the dolphins could be fostered; and

- The economic and political power of big business interests needed to be channelled into productive long term sustainability rather than a destructive short-term approach to dolphin ecotourism .

The strategy also needed to attempt a synthesis of several Cambodian Government policy objectives such as:

- appropriate forms of tourism development;

- environmental conservation;

- poverty alleviation, e.g. through community-based tourism;

- ecologically sustainable development;

- diversification of rural livelihoods and rural incomes;

- decentralization; and

- provincial development, amongst others.

Incorporating these objectives into a tourism strategy provided opportunities of enhancing the possibility of achieving outcomes which would be mutually beneficial to a range of interests and stakeholders.

3.4   A Solution – The Dolphin Discovery Trail

The Royal Government of Cambodia has a strong legislative and regulatory framework within which to operate for the protection and conservation of the dolphin, as evidenced by the following documents:

- Royal Decree on Determination of Protected Areas and Conservation of Dolphin (February 2005)

- The Order of the Prime Minister of the Royal Government of Cambodia on the Mekong Irrawaddy Dolphin Conservation and Tourism Development (March 2005)

- Guidelines No. 01 Jor Bor of 5 March 2005 regarding the Mekong Irrawaddy Dolphin Conservation and Tourism Development

- The Order of Senior Minister Veng Sereyvuth, Chairman, National Tourism Authority, on the Establishment of Offices and Working Groups at Kratie and Strung Treng Provinces for the Mekong Irrawaddy Dolphin Conservation and Tourism Development, 18 March 2005

- Ministry of Agriculture, Forestry and Fisheries, Department of Fisheries: Cambodian Mekong Dolphin – Management Strategy, October 2004

- Report of the Cambodia – Lao PDR Transboundary Workshop for the Conservation and Management of the Mekong River Irrawaddy Dolphins, 7-9 December 2004, Stoeng Treng, Cambodia

However the intent of these Government initiatives requires support by strong action and constant monitoring in their implementation if they are to be effective in protecting the dolphin.

The concept that was advanced to contribute to resolving some of the issues – the Dolphin Discovery Trail – was designed to support both conservation efforts and appropriate forms of tourism concurrently with a partnership between both conservation agencies and the tourism industry on the one hand, and to synthesize a number of RGC policies to assist in achieving outcomes that were mutually beneficial to a range of interests and stakeholders on the other. Poverty alleviation was a central consideration. According to the World Bank (2006), the poverty headcount for 2004 was estimated at 35 per cent, that is, one third of the Cambodian population was estimated as living below the national poverty line. Poverty in Cambodia is overwhelmingly a rural phenomenon as the vast majority of the population lives in rural areas. The region encompassed by the Mekong River dolphin habitat experienced pronounced poverty severity with more than 26,000 villagers living on less than US$ 0.46c per day (World Food Programme, 2004).

The basic proposal was to develop a non-vehicular trail for walking and cycling along the banks of the Mekong River from the Lao Border, (Cheuteal Pool) 190 km south to Kratie called the Dolphin Discovery Trail. This would allow an integrated comprehensive management regime for the entire length of known Mekong River dolphin habitat to be undertaken, which would maximise conservation efforts while minimising potential adverse impacts on the dolphin, and replace the fragmented focus on only the nine pools. The Trail would therefore introduce tourists not just to the dolphins but to "The World of the Dolphins"; to traverse the full distance would take 10-15 days.

A trekking and cycling trail would require every tourist to pass through every village at a leisurely pace. Thus, every village would have the opportunity to set up appropriate forms of tourism services and facilities – lodges, tea houses, refreshment kiosks, traditional wooden boat scenic tours, bicycle hire, sale of local handicrafts, restaurants, guiding around local attractions, etc. A significant contribution to poverty alleviation would therefore be a key objective (Sofield et al, 2004) and such a Trail could recruit the riverine inhabitants as active participants in the conservation efforts to save the dolphin because they would have a vested interest in its survival. This initiative would require capacity-building and HRD among village communities, expanding employment opportunities to new areas requiring new skills.

Figure 3.5   The Dolphin Discovery Trail Would Pass through All 104 Villages along the 200km Dolphin Habitat Stretch of the Mekong River.

Photographs: Trevor Sofield

Because tourism is a service industry, it is particularly adapted to training women (thus promoting gender equity), youths (thus making a contribution to chronic under-employment and un-employment in many rural areas), disadvantaged minorities and the physically disabled. Hospitality training, guiding, and cultural activities would be a particular focus, together with a range of opportunities in supporting ventures needed to provide essential goods and services for tourists. Through the tourism supply chain, there is significant potential to promote backward linkages into agriculture and thus assist in diversifying agricultural production and income generation through the sale of produce to tourists and tourism operations (Sofield, Fleming & Phan, 2005). Such linkages would have the added advantage of increasing food security and simultaneously lessening dependency upon wild fish stocks in the Mekong. Accordingly, the Strategy also proposed the establishment of market gardening, fish ponds in every village and each household being given 20 fruit trees. Since this initiative would require new skills, the Dolphin Trail Strategy proposes an aquaculture and agricultural extension service to provide assistance in these new forms of agricultural activity. In 2006, an American NGO began work with the first ten villages north of Kratie to introduce fish ponds and aquaculture. Through such linkages, combined with the establishment of cottage industries and handicrafts and lodging and hospitality, the Trail could make a direct contribution to poverty alleviation, and it is this aspect of the proposal that has formed the focus of the UNWTO proposal developed by SNV.

Additional rationale behind a non-motorised trail is that the noise, dust, pollution from vehicle exhausts and the inevitable mass tourism of tour buses would be a direct contradiction of nature-based tourism built on the conservation ethic and undermine the attributes of an ecotourism experience. Its actual physical design would require an environmental assessment, especially in terms of erosion prevention.

The semantics used to describe the trail – discovering the world of the Mekong dolphin – are important from two other perspectives. The first is that visitors travelling the route are automatically immersed in the world – the ecosystem – of the dolphin. Even if they do not see a single dolphin, they would have entered its very special world and become familiar with its habitat. Their satisfaction levels would be enhanced by actual sightings but their expectations of a special experience would have been met by simply living in the dolphin's unique world for a week or more. Through associated interpretation, education and awareness building, visitors and residents alike would be introduced to the need to safeguard the entire habitat in all its diversity. Visitors would leave Cambodia enriched, with an understanding of the needs of the dolphin for its protection, conservation and continued survival – something that is not part of the current Cheuteal Pool experience. Current dolphin "ecotourism" is not ecotourism but simply exploitation of a product (i.e. dolphins) for profit with no input into conservation of the dolphin. It simply focuses on sightings of the mammal itself while the essential linkages into its ecosystem are ignored. It is commoditization without conservation.

A second important touristic aspect of the nomenclature for Cambodia is that at present the country is a single image destination – Angkor. Once tourists have "done" Angkor, they leave. The ALOS (average length of stay) is only 3.1 days. But dolphins have a global image that extends far beyond Cambodia, an image which regards the mammal as highly intelligent, loveable, capable of forming close relationships with humans, an image that is positive and supportive of their well-being. In terms of marine wildlife tourism, dolphins, together with whales, seals and penguins, are the most widely known and popular of the marine charismatic mega-fauna. Most people would probably be unaware that Cambodia has these mammals. If therefore, dolphin tourism was developed appropriately in Cambodia, within several years it would have the potential to raise Cambodia to a two-destination image in the eyes of the travelling world. There would be two main reasons to visit Cambodia and dolphin tourism could thus contribute to extending the average length of stay of visitors, with concomitant benefits economically and nationally. However, it also needs to be recognized that dolphin tourism could not (and should not) be perceived as an opportunity to develop "another Siem Reap". It does not have the capacity to sustain mass tourism, although it could capture a sizeable niche market in addition to the trekking/adventure market.

The Dolphin Discovery Trail could also contribute to improving relations with Lao PDR through cooperation in cross border tourism to Cheuteal Pool. Under the Mekong Tourism Development Program, Cambodia and Lao PDR have already agreed in principle to a joint tourism development venture based on visitation to the Pool. The ADB has provided seed funding for this development and this could form the opening stage in development of the Trail.

Figure 3.6   Stung Treng RAMSAR site

Photographs: Courtesy of Ministry of Tourism, Cambodia and Trevor Sofield

The content of the Dolphin Discovery Trail is not limited to dolphin ecotourism. Rather, it is envisaged as multi-faceted Soft Adventure Tourism because it incorporates three main streams:

- Nature-based tourism where the tourist is introduced not only to the dolphin but holistically to the riverine ecosystem with its myriad animals, birds and flora through a trekking/cycling/river boating experience;

- Cultural tourism because trekkers and cyclists would pass through many villages, observing the rural way of life of river residents, staying overnight in other villages and seeing many aspects of village activities as they went along the trail; and

- Heritage tourism because the trail would provide access to temples, pagodas and other heritage/historical sites along the way.

A tourism factor analysis would need to be conducted over the 190 km-long route. This is a kind of audit, designed to identify all significant resources along the trail and then to assess their role for tourism attractions and/or activities. It is best accomplished by a multi-disciplinary team because of the diversity of resources that must be analysed and assessed. Some resources might need protection and be designated as off-limits to tourists (e.g. fragile wetlands or the breeding habitat of particular birds or animals). Others might form a key component in the trail, such as forests where varieties of flora and fauna can be observed. Significant ancient or historical built heritage such as temples, pagodas, forts and other constructions, could be identified and assessed. Local cultural assets and activities drawn from everyday life would be included, as would any special events or festivals. Vantage points and lookouts could be identified for construction of viewing platforms, tea houses, refreshment kiosks or pavilions for shelter. Appropriate places for small river piers could be located. Dangerous sections of the route would be listed for diversion.

The Stung Treng Ramsar Site offers the possibility of a combined ecotourism and cultural tourism experience. In 1999, a 37 km stretch of the Mekong river from about 5 km north of Stung Treng town to the southernmost point of Cheuteal Pool about 3 km south of the Lao PDR border (with 500 m on each side of the river) was designated as a Ramsar reserve ("wetland of international importance" under the Ramsar Convention). The site covers an area of 14,600 hectares. The Mekong River channel forms one of Cambodia's six major zoo-geographic boundaries and the Ramsar site has a great diversity of vegetation including one of Cambodia's largest stands of riverine or gallery forests, extensive evergreen forests and bamboo forests, and is surrounded by semi-green forests and deciduous dipterocarp forests (Try and Chambers 2006). It is the habitat for the four "flagship species of the Mekong Wetlands Biodiversity Project" (MWBP), the Mekong dolphin, the Sarus crane, the Mekong giant catfish and the Siamese crocodile. In terms of birdlife, with 231 species recorded (almost half the total for Cambodia) it is one of Cambodia's most important avifaunal regions (Birdlife International 2003). More than 40 mammal species have been recorded, including the Asian elephant (endangered), leopard (vulnerable), sun bear (rare, declining), sambar deer (hunted), the longtailed macaque and pig-tailed macaque, both locally vulnerable (Vong, 2004). Vong also recorded 43 reptiles and amphibians, including water monitor lizards, pythons, cobras and turtles, and 167 species of fish. The Ramsar site is being managed by the MWBP and an ecotourism plan is being formulated (Try and Chambers 2006). There are 21 fishing villages with a population of 13,000 living inside the Ramsar site boundaries and the prospects for poverty alleviation through the Dolphin Discovery Trail are strong.

3.5 Eco-Lodges and Resorts

Up-market resort tourism could be encompassed to some extent by providing motorised access to perhaps two of the nine pools, where strict controls over human/ dolphin interactions could be introduced and exercised. Eco-lodges for the upper end of the market could satisfy market demand for this segment of travellers provided that their construction was carried out under a strictly controlled environmental management building code. Such a code would need to include – but not be limited to – provisions for closed sewage systems to prevent any pollution of the waterways; solid and liquid waste management disposal systems that ensured no pollution of groundwater or the river; controls to prevent erosion of the river banks and surrounding countryside; and strict controls over the size and types of boats that might be allowed for river viewing of the dolphins.

Again the rationale for such provisions is clear: any activity which results in increased danger to the dolphins would simply hasten their extinction, and investment in tourism services and plant would result in financial loss. Cambodia would risk international condemnation for contributing to the demise of the dolphin instead of to its survival with potentially adverse impacts on its entire tourism industry and therefore the national economy. But eco-lodges that were constructed to best international practice for sustainable nature tourism, such as some of those in fragile environments in Australia, would have the opposite effect and win Cambodia international plaudits (e.g. the Daintree Ecolodge, north Queensland, which has won numerous awards for its environmentally sensitive design, management and involvement of the local Aboriginal community).

To be consistent with the adventure/nature based tourism of the Dolphin Discovery Trail, roads for motorized access to the pools and eco-lodges should not connect directly into the Trail or use sections of it; they should simply link into the existing road system, not proceeding north or south of the pools. Only walking paths or boardwalks should be constructed along the banks of the pools: roads for motorized vehicles should not be constructed in order to maintain the integrity of the natural experience that would form the basis for eco-lodge dolphin tourism.

While such upper-end tourism is often criticised for adverse impacts on the environment and because it is regarded as inconsistent with local living standards, what is often overlooked is the fact that, when properly managed and controlled, it can be harnessed to make a significant contribution to poverty alleviation (Sofield, 2005). This is because it has the capacity to employ many more people than small village-based ventures; and through its need for a wide range of goods such as agricultural produce, handicrafts and so forth, it can provide a new market for adjacent communities where previously none existed. Training programs in local village communities to help meet a resort's labour force needs assist this process.

There is no incompatibility between market segments for a tourism venture that has the capacity to attract and satisfy both backpacker demand at one end of the spectrum and five star resort tourism at the other. Angkor is proof of that: it attracts not only backpackers but elite travellers and all market segments in between. In terms of wildlife tourism globally, many destinations are extremely expensive (e.g. the Galapagos Islands, the gorillas of Uganda, Antarctica, etc.) and dolphins have also proved their capacity to satisfy this market with ocean dolphin tours in many parts of the world. In Australia, ecotourism based around the tropical rainforest and crocodiles has aided isolated communities and Aboriginal communities to benefit from the income-generating power of resort tourism (e.g. Kakadu National Park). Many tourists to eco-attractions are motivated by a keen understanding of conservation and the spending power of the upper end of the market can be captured for poverty alleviation and support for environmental causes with appropriate forms of ecologically sustainable tourism development. This has been the experience of many eco-lodges in African countries, for example (Ashley, Roe and Goodwin, 2001).

3.6   Agricultural Diversification

The introduction of tourism into villages along the route provides the opportunity to address visitor needs for food, as well as accommodation and other services, and this offers the prospect of building backward linkages into agriculture and aquaculture. Such linkages would have the added advantage of increasing food security and similarly lessen dependency upon wild fish stocks in the Mekong. Accordingly, the Strategy also proposed the establishment of market gardening, fish ponds in every village and each household being given 20 fruit trees. Since this initiative would require new skills, the Dolphin Trail Strategy proposes an aquaculture and agricultural extension service to provide assistance in these new forms of agricultural activity. In 2006, an American NGO began work with the first ten villages north of Kratie to introduce fish ponds and aquaculture.

3.7   Summary

Stakeholder theory provided a relevant methodology to analyse the complexity of the situation regarding the conservation of the Mekong River dolphin. That analysis produced the information necessary to formulate a strategy that offers a mechanism to satisfy multiple interests and move away from dissonance to convergence in a sustainable way. The mechanism that grew out of stakeholder consultations – the proposal for soft adventure tourism – also has the capacity, if implemented appropriately, to find a balance between conservation of the dolphin and the needs of impoverished communities residing along the Mekong. The Dolphin Discovery Trail could achieve a diversity of objectives that include:

- Contributing to poverty alleviation by developing appropriate forms of tourism in many small villages along the route – lodges, tea houses, refreshment kiosks, small boat scenic tours, bicycle hire, sale of local handicrafts, restaurants, and cottage industries;

- Assisting in the conservation of the endangered Mekong River Dolphin;

- Aiding the diversification of rural incomes through tourism micro-ventures;

- Developing backward linkages into agriculture to support rural livelihoods with potential to also develop agri-tourism;

- Introducing ecologically sustainable development for isolated rural communities;

- Capacity building and HRD, with programmes able to target women (gender equity), youths, disadvantaged minorities and disabled persons;

- Encouraging and supporting the protection, preservation and conservation of cultural, natural and environmental heritage through tourism;

- Extending and developing a variety of new tourist destinations along the proposed Trail;

- Expanding the international image of Cambodia from a one-attraction destination – Angkor – to a duality by taking advantage of the global image of dolphins; thus

- Providing a quality experience additional to Angkor able to attract a broader range of visitor market segments (wildlife tourism) to Cambodia;

- Increasing visitor numbers and revenue by extending the average length of stay of international visitors through marketing the Dolphin Discovery Trail;

- Working towards cooperation with Lao PDR in terms of both dolphin tourism and dolphin conservation efforts;

- Developing upper market wildlife tourism through a limited number of eco-lodges, thus simultaneously making another contribution to poverty alleviation and quality tourism; and

- Contributing to the development of two of Cambodia's less developed Provinces through the provision of infrastructure for tourism.

The future of the Mekong River dolphin now rests in the hands of the many stakeholders, to which must be added the UN World Tourism Organisation. UNWTO has accepted the challenge by establishing The Mekong Dolphin Discovery Trail – Poverty Alleviation through Tourism Development and Conservation of Mekong River Dolphin and Its Habitat Project under its global Sustainable Tourism for Eliminating Poverty (ST-EP) Foundation in association with the Cambodian Ministry of Tourism and the Dutch development assistance agency, SNV.

Appendix 1

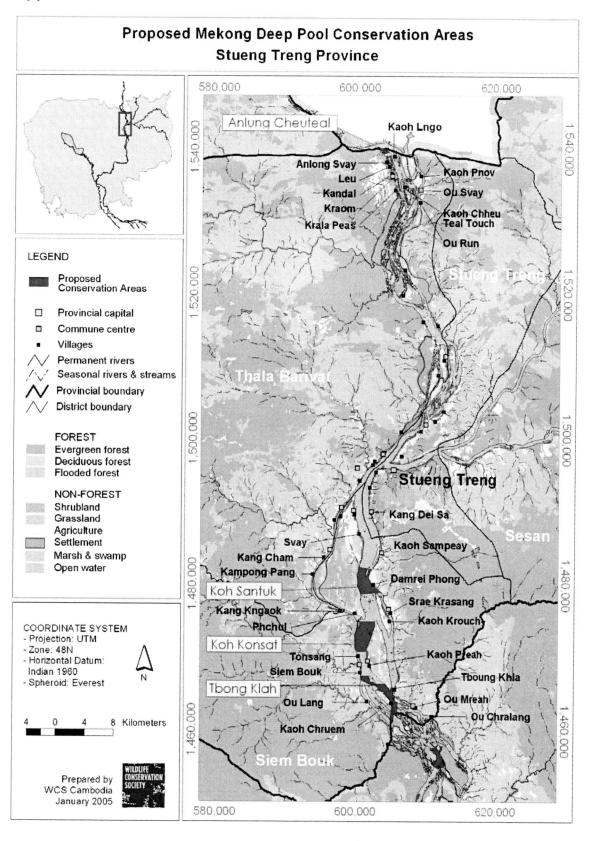

Proposed Mekong Deep Pool Conservation Areas
Stueng Treng Province

LEGEND

- Proposed Conservation Areas
- □ Provincial capital
- ▫ Commune centre
- ▪ Villages
- Permanent rivers
- Seasonal rivers & streams
- Provincial boundary
- District boundary

FOREST
- Evergreen forest
- Deciduous forest
- Flooded forest

NON-FOREST
- Shrubland
- Grassland
- Agriculture
- Settlement
- Marsh & swamp
- Open water

COORDINATE SYSTEM
- Projection: UTM
- Zone: 48N
- Horizontal Datum: Indian 1960
- Spheroid: Everest

N

4   0   4   8   Kilometers

Prepared by
WCS Cambodia
January 2005

WILDLIFE
CONSERVATION
SOCIETY

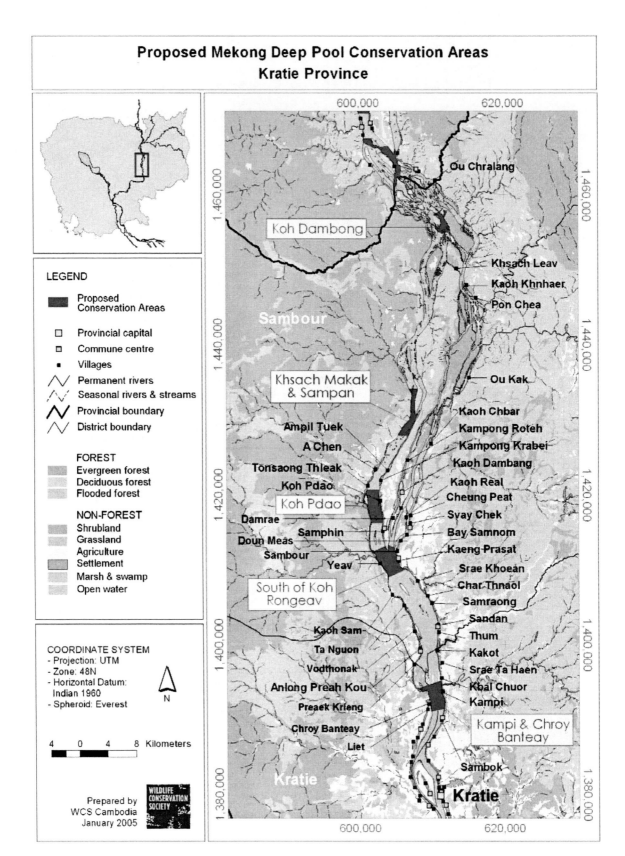

Appendix 2

The order of the Prime Minister of the Royal Government on Mekong Irrawaddy Dolphin Conservation and Tourism Development

- Ministry of Agriculture, Forestry and Fisheries has to co-operate with relevant agencies and provincial authorities to take restricted measures to ban all activities of all kind of nets, eliminate all illegal fishing activities such as electric fishing, dynamite fishing and bamboo and wood rafts which have been floating across the dolphin habitats from Kampi area of Kratie to Cambodian-Laos border of Stung Treng.

- Ministry of Public Works and Transportation has to study specific technique and educate all boat owners on how to protect propeller properly. Together with this, Ministry of Public Works and Transportation has to co-operate with all relevant agencies, Ministries and provincial authorities to install waterway traffic signboards and inform both fast speed and transportation boats which has [sic] been passing habitats to reduce speed and noise and also entirely ban waste oil draining into the river for environment preservation, particularly at the dolphin habitats.

- Ministry of Environment in collaboration with relevant Ministries and local Authorities have to take measures to educate local people on how to protect environment and urgently stop waste draining into the river, particular at the dolphin habitats.

- Ministry of Tourism has to pay a lot of attention and consideration on tourism guidance education and management and improve the quality of tourism service in these areas.

- National Tourism Authority has to co-operate with all relevant agencies to effectively advertise and educate all level of public mass and local communities. Along with this, National Tourism Authority has to co-operate with provincial authorities and relevant authorities to establish two offices in Kratie and Stung Treng for permanent leading mechanism and urgently create patrolling teams to effectively stop and crackdown all illegal fishing activities which cause the dolphin [to] die.

- Ministry of Agriculture, Forestry and Fisheries, Ministry of Tourism, Ministry of Environment, Ministry of Public Works and Transportation, all relevant agencies and Ministries, provincial authorities of Kratie and Stung Treng provinces have to increase attention to help Cambodian National Tourism Authority conserve Mekong River Dolphins and develop tourism activities from Kampi Dolphin Pool in Kratie up to Cambodian-Lao border to contribute to reduce the poverty of people.

- People who contravene this order will be responsible under law.

Having receive [sic] this order, Ministry of Agriculture, Forestry and Fisheries, Ministry of Tourism, Ministry of Environment, Ministry of Public Works and Transportation, Ministry of Interior, Ministry of National Defence, other Ministries and relevant agencies, National Tourism Authority, Governor of Kratie and Stung Treng provinces have to effectively follow this order.

References:

Ashley, C., et al (2001), 'Pro Poor Tourism Strategies: Making Tourism Work for the Poor. A Review of Experience', *Pro-Poor Tourism Report no 1*, Overseas Development Institute, International Institute for Environment and Development, and Centre for Responsible Tourism, University of Greenwich, London

Beasley, I., et al (2003), *Mekong Dolphin Conservation Project Report* submitted to James Cook University, Australia; Department of Fisheries, Cambodia; and the Wildlife Conservation Society, Cambodia Program.

BirdLife International (2003), *Directory of Important Bird Areas in Cambodia: Key Sites for Conservation*, Department of Forestry and Wildlife, Department of Nature Conservation and Protection, Birdlife International in Indochina and the Wildlife Conservation Society Cambodia Program, Phnom Penh

Butler, R.W. (1999), 'Sustainable Tourism: A State-of-the-art Review', *Tourism Geographies*, Grimble and Wellard, 1 (1), pp. 7-25.

Chambers, R. (1997), *Whose Reality Counts? Putting the First Last*, Intermediate Technology Publications, London.

Clarkson, M.B.E. (1995), 'A Stakeholder Framework for Analyzing and Evaluating Corporate Social Performance', *The Academy of Management Review*, 20 (1), pp. 92-117.

Department of Fisheries (2004), *Cambodian Mekong Dolphin Conservation Strategy*, Ministry of Agriculture, Forestry and Fisheries, Phnom Penh

Donaldson, T. and Preston L.E. (1995), 'The Stakeholder Theory of the Corporation: Concepts, Evidence and Implications', *Academy of Management Review*, 20 (1), pp. 65-91.

Engel, P. (1997), *The Social Organization of Innovation: A Focus on Stakeholder Interaction*, Royal Tropical Institute, Amsterdam.

Freeman, R.E. (1984), Strategic Management: A Stakeholder Approach, Pitman, Boston.

Grimble, R. and Chan M.K. (1995), 'Stakeholder Analysis for Natural Resource Management in Developing Countries', *Natural Resources Forum*, 19 (2), pp.113–124.

Grimble R. and Wellard K. (1997), 'Stakeholder Methodologies in Natural Resource Management: a Review of Principles, Contexts, Experiences and Opportunities', *Agricultural Systems*, 55 (2), pp. 173-193 (21).

Hardy, A.L. (2001), *A Troubled Paradise: Stakeholder Perceptions of Tourism in the Daintree Region of Far North Queensland, Australia*, PhD Thesis, School of Natural and Rural Systems Management, University of Queensland.

Mekong Wetlands Biodiversity Project (2005), Flagship Species of the Mekong — A Tool for Wetlands Ecosystem Conservation and Management, MWBP Fact Sheet, Phnom Penh

Mitchell, R.K., et al (1997), 'Toward a Theory of Stakeholder Identification and Salience: Defining the Principle of Who and What Really Counts', *Academy of Management Review*, 22 (4), pp. 853-886.

Röling, N., and Wagemakers, M. ed. (1998), 'Facilitating Sustainable Agriculture: Participatory Learning and Adaptive Management' in *Times of Environmental Uncertainty*, Cambridge University Press, Cambridge, UK.

Royal Government of Cambodia (2005), *Royal Decree on Determination of Protected Areas and Conservation of Dolphin*, Ministry of Environment, Phnom Penh

Sofield, T.H.B. (2005), *'Mainstreaming' Poverty Alleviation & Tourism – Exploring Links into Mass Tourism*, Keynote address, Third Global Summit of the International Institute for Peace Through Tourism, Pattaya, Thailand, 2-5 Oct. 2005.

Sofield, T.H.B. (2005), *'The Dolphin Discovery Trail' – An Introduction to the World of the Mekong River Dolphin*, Ministry of Tourism, Phnom Penh

Sofield, T.H.B, et al (2004), *Sustainable Tourism – Eliminating Poverty (ST-EP), An Overview*, CRC for Sustainable Tourism, Brisbane

Sofield, T.H.B., et al (2004), *Training Module for Agriculture. Community-Based Tourism (CBT) Training Module*, Centre for International Trade, UNCTAD, Geneva

Sofield, T.H.B. (2003), *Empowerment for Sustainable Tourism Development*, Pergamon, London.

The World Conservation Union (2006), *IUCN Red List of Threatened Species*, IUCN, Paris

Try T. and Chambers M. (2006), *Situation Analysis: Stung Treng Province*, Cambodia. Vientiane, Lao PDR: Mekong Wetlands Biodiversity Conservation and Sustainable Use Programme.

Vong, S. (2004), *Biodiversity Assessment of the Stoeng Treng Ramsar Site*, Final Report, Ministry of Environment – ASEAN Regional Center for Biodiversity Conservation, Phnom Penh

World Bank (2006), *Cambodia: Halving Poverty by 2015*, World Bank, Phnom Penh

World Food Programme (2006), *Cambodia: Annual Report, 2005*. WFP, Phnom Penh

World Tourism Organization (2006), UNWTO-STEP Project Proposal: Mekong Dolphin Discovery Trail – Poverty Alleviation through Tourism Development and Conservation of Mekong River Dolphin and Its Habitat, Prepared by Anne-Marie Makela, SNV and MOT, Phnom Penh, Cambodia.

Yuksel, F., et al (2004), 'Stakeholder interviews and tourism planning at Pamukkale, Turkey', *Tourism Management*, 20 (3), pp. 351-360.

Chapter 4 ——————————————

Community-based Tourism Planning in Klong Khwang, Thailand

4.1   Introduction

The emphasis on public participation, brought about by changes to the 1997 Constitution (Council of State of Thailand 1997), has created a significant interest in local level planning initiatives in Thailand. Moving from a top down model of planning and decision-making has required officials and communities to develop the capacities enabling local communities to become an effective part of the planning and development process.

With the potential for quick economic gain, ecological, social and cultural goals may be sacrificed by shortsighted and damaging tourism development schemes – ultimately harming both communities and tourists alike. There is growing recognition that public involvement is essential to ensure sustainable tourism development. How this should occur is still relatively unknown; a search for practical approaches to allow for community-driven tourism development is ongoing.

As part of the process of testing new approaches, a range of community-based tourism planning and management methods were established in the community of Klong Khwang in Thailand. This chapter describes and analyzes how the principles of local determination and participation in tourism development were positively introduced and implemented. The success of the initiative has been recognized by senior government officials in Thailand and by APEC (Hatton, 1999).

4.1.1   The Nature of Tourism

Tourism is a social, economic, and environmental activity. While tourism is most often seen as economic in nature, it also has a number of non-economic objectives and benefits ranging from social (e.g. educational and recreational activities) to environmental (e.g. conservation of natural resources) and cultural (e.g. sharing of cultural traditions and events) objectives.

Tourism is a socio-economic phenomenon comprised of the activities and experiences of tourists and visitors away from their home environment which are serviced by the travel and tourism industry and host destinations. The sum total of this activity, experience and services can be seen as the tourism product. This is why understanding the interrelationships among the several parts of the system enables all tourism stakeholders to both improve planning and management effectiveness in order to assure the likelihood of success and therefore benefit the poor.

Essentially, the tourism system can be described in terms of the concepts of supply and demand. The planning of tourism should strive for a balance between demands (market) and supply (development) (see for example Gunn, 1979; and Gunn & Var, 2002). This requires understanding, not only of market characteristics and trends, but also the process of planning to meet these market needs. Furthermore, the context of the supply and demand sides needs to be carefully monitored and managed, i.e. the ecological, political, social, cultural, and other factors in the external and internal environments of the visitor demand and destination supply components must be carefully considered Often, tourists from generating markets are identified as the demand side, and the supply side includes all those programs, attractions, and land uses that are designed and managed for the visitors. These supply side factors may be under the control of private enterprise, non-profit organizations and/or governments. New and innovative forms of partnerships are also evolving to handle the challenge to ensure the sustainable development and management of tourism-related resources.

Hence, the supply and demand side can be seen to be linked by flows of resources such as capital, labor, goods, and tourist expenditures into the destination, and flows of marketing, promotion, tourist artifacts, and experiences from the destination back into the tourist generating regions. In addition, some of the tourist expenditures often leak back into the visitor-generating areas through avenues such as repatriation of profits to foreign tourism investors and payment for imported goods and services to provide to the tourists in the destination.

The dynamic nature of tourism systems makes it critical to be scanning the external and internal environments of the destination on a regular basis and to be prepared to make the necessary changes to ensure a healthy and viable tourism industry. The tourism system is not only dynamic but also complex due to the many factors and sectors that are linked to the provision of the tourist experience and the generation of tourism revenues and markets.

4.1.2 Sustainable Tourism and Community Planning

Since the Bruntland Commission Report (World Commission on Environment and Development, 1987), more and more communities and planners have begun to take into consideration sustainable development principles as they prepare plans and policies for future development. While there is still a great deal of rhetoric associated with sustainable development, some of the principles are now having an impact on how communities approach their planning and development process.

The tourism community over the last decade also adopted sustainable tourism practices. It is clear that sustainable tourism and sustainable community planning have the very same objectives. These principles include the following factors:

- Participation: Residents of a community must maintain control of tourism development by being involved in setting a community tourism vision, identifying the resources to be maintained and enhanced, and developing goals and strategies for tourism development and management. Residents must participate in the implementation of strategies as well as the operation of the tourism infrastructure, services and facilities.

- Stakeholder Involvement and Cooperation: Tourism initiatives should be developed with the help of broad-based community input. Cooperation between local attractions, businesses, and tourism operators is essential given that one business or operation can be directly affected by the performance or quality of another. Harmony is thus required between the needs of a visitor, the place and the community. This is facilitated by broad community support with a proper balance between economic, social, cultural and human objectives.

- Monitoring and Evaluating: There is a definite need for the impact assessment of tourism development proposals to distinguish between plans which encourage mass versus quality tourism. The capacity of sites must be considered, including physical, natural, social and cultural limits. Tourism planning must move away from a traditional growth-oriented model to one that focuses on opportunities for employment, income and improved local well-being while ensuring that development decisions reflect the full value of the natural and cultural environments. Tourism development must provide quality employment for community residents. The provision of fulfilling jobs must be seen as an integral part of any tourism development at the local level. There should be codes of practice established for tourism at all levels national, regional and local. Guidelines must be established for tourism operations, including requirements for impact assessment.

- Training and Promotion: Sustainable tourism development requires the establishment of education and training programs to improve public understanding and enhance business, vocational and professional skills especially for the poor and women. Such development involves promoting appropriate uses and activities that reduce poverty and draw from and reinforce landscape character, sense of place, community identity and site opportunities. Sustainable tourism development also has to provide for intergenerational equity with equitable distribution of the costs and benefits of tourism development occurring among both present and future generations.

It is important to note here that we are now at a stage in community planning and tourism development where the challenge is to ensure that sustainable tourism principles are actually implemented. The case study discussed in this chapter has attempted to incorporate as many sustainable development principles as is possible. The authors are of the opinion that it represents a good example of sustainable development. The merits of the case were also recognized by the APEC Tourism Working Group when it examined various community planning initiatives in Asia (Hatton, 1991).

4.2   Study Background

In 1998, the authors became involved with the community as members of the Canadian Universities Consortium Urban Environmental Management Project (CUC UEM), based at the Asian Institute of Technology (AIT) in Bangkok, and funded by the Canadian International Development Agency (CIDA). Prior to choosing Klong Khwang, the Project, in cooperation with the Tourism Authority of Thailand, assessed a number of communities where sustainable tourism planning and participation processes could be implemented. The criteria for selecting a community included

- Tourism potential

- Community receptivity to tourism development

- Political support

- Accessibility

Klong Khwang was chosen because it had the potential, motivation and capacity to be part of a demonstration project experimenting with a variety of community development approaches within a tourism development setting.

In the beginning, the project team's role was to provide technical advice and support. The community would be responsible for managing the process and eventually developing the tourism plan. Unlike other aid initiatives, the project provided little financial support to the community, which raised the funds to implement plans. This was a unique situation for government officials; typically, foreign governments provide capital and operating financial resources.

The project team included Thai professionals and expatriates with backgrounds in tourism planning and management, architecture, and urban environmental management. Day-to-day discussions were the responsibility of members of the Thai team and community. The expatriates provided technical advice/direction and developed a strong relationship with the village headman and other community members. A capacity-building exercise was also part of the project designed to ensure tourism and other local officials were updated regularly on the demonstration project's approaches and lessons learned through publications, briefing notes, manuals and videos (Jamieson, 2001a, 2001b).

4.2.1 Tourism in Klong Khwang

Klong Khwang is in the Province of Nakhon Ratchasima (Korat) in the northeast region of Thailand. It is 30 minutes by automobile west of Korat, the province's capital city (Figure 4.1 for contextual map.) The village belongs to the Sema Tambon (sub-district), which includes 13 villages and the Amphoe District of Sung Noen with a population of 75,000. The village has about 100 households and is led by a headman elected by the community.

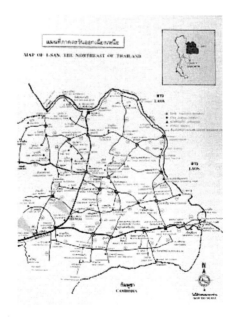

Figure 4.1   Map of the Region of Klong Khwang

Klong Khwang's economy is based on agriculture; rice is the main crop. In order to generate additional income, the community identified tourism as a potential source of economic development. The village normally hosted small groups of local tourists who came to pay their respects to the Reclining Buddha, the Stone Wheel of Thamma and visit an archaeological site near the community. These were identified as Klong Khwang's main tourism attractions (Figure 4.2).

Figure 4.2   Tourism Attractions

Due to limited tourism activities in the community, in 1999 when the project started visitors typically spent only an hour visiting Klong Khwang and contributed to the temple about 10,000 Baht (US$ 250) per month (statistics provided by village headman). Funds were used primarily for the maintenance of the community's temple (Wat). Klong Khwang community, led by an enthusiastic and capable headman, was convinced tourism could increase income, job opportunities and improve villagers' quality of life. The community did not have a defined concept of tourism development and decided a plan had to be developed to increase visitors' experiences and generate extra income while not damaging its environment or the social and cultural characteristics.

4.2.2 Key Actors in Community-based Tourism Development of Klong Khwang

Support for the planning process came from a number of key actors including the village headman, community committee, Sub-district Administration Organization, community co-operative, provincial government offices and the Tourism Authority of Thailand. It is important to note that not all of these stakeholders worked together at the same time.

Village Headman and Community Committee

The headman, responsible for villagers' quality of life, is elected every four years. His main role in relation to the community-based initiative was to provide tourism information to villagers, solicit their views and encourage them to participate in the planning process. The community committee helps the headman with a variety of village activities.

Sub-district Administration Organization

This local government body was responsible for providing basic facilities and infrastructure in the area including local roads, electricity, telephones, water supply and solid waste management.

Community Co-operative

The co-operative was locally formed to work on the development of local products e.g. agricultural products and souvenirs. Most members are women and elderly people.

Provincial Government

At the provincial level, two main organizations are involved – the Non-Formal Education Center and the Office of Skill Development. They mainly provided training to enhance the skill and knowledge of community members in product development.

Tourism Authority of Thailand (TAT) Regional Office

The TAT central office provided advice to CUC UEM in selecting a community as well as providing ongoing support and advice throughout the planning process. The TAT regional office helped the community in marketing and promotion of the area including producing brochures and providing directional signage in and around the village.

International Organization

The Canadian Universities Consortium Urban Environmental Management Project (CUC UEM) worked with the community from the inception of the planning and development process. It provided technical assistance and support for Klong Khwang during the planning process. The Project encouraged the use of a number of participation techniques designed to encourage the villagers' involvement in developing a community-based tourism plan.

4.2.3   Approaches and Activities for Community Participation

At the beginning, the community had little knowledge about tourism. A number of awareness and involvement techniques were used to ensure the community played an integral role in the ongoing development process and that future actions met residents' expectations. Approaches ranged from public consultation techniques and focus groups used in similar situations to an integrated simulated tourism experience during the planning stage by CUC UEM. The techniques were adapted to the community's particular characteristics and capacity levels.

Public Consultation

Throughout the planning process CUC UEM held regular tourism planning meetings with the village headman and committee. The intent initially was to determine why the community wanted to develop tourism, the type of tourism products which could be offered to visitors, the expected benefits of tourism and the level of tourism the community could absorb. At first, villagers thought a tourism plan would be developed for them (a common practice). Over time, this perception changed and the villagers realized the importance of their involvement in the overall decision-making process.

The community was encouraged to define its own tourism vision. As part of that process, a map of local resources and infrastructure facilities was produced that identified tourism resources and involved the community in the planning process.

Visualization techniques were used to provide residents with a look at how proposed revisions would affect their village. It also helped the community "see" the future utilizing a user-friendly medium. This open visual process proved to be the most effective communication method. This approach has been used for more than 100 years by anthropologists and psychologists working with indigenous communities whose literacy skills were not high - See for example, techniques for fieldwork by Bronislauw Malinowski (1922) on the Trobriand Islands, PNG. The importance and methods of using visualization techniques in tourism research generally and CBT was well described by Pearce (1996).

A series of focus group discussions and interviews were conducted to give the community input into tourism development and guidelines for decision-making. This process was facilitated by the village headman who had a clear vision for the community and provided direction and support to other members. The community had strong views about the areas and kinds of activities they wanted to open up to visitors. In some cases, suggestions came directly from the community; at other times, the project team discussed/modified and then adopted ideas (based on community acceptance) in the community's overall tourism vision. The community was guided by principles put forward by the King's Project (RDP, 1997). Figure 4.3 illustrates the nature of the tourism products identified by the community.

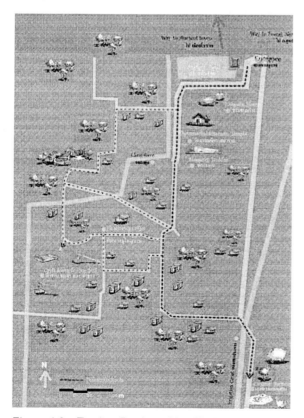

Figure 4.3   Tourism Products Identified by Klong Khwang Community

The headman assumed leadership of the process and was involved in describing the advantages/disadvantages of tourism and proposed activities for the community. There was general agreement that tourism was a desirable path for development; however, at the beginning, some villagers were concerned that it was not appropriate to make money from using the Buddha and temple. The headman explained to the villagers that this money would be used to protect and enhance the community's cultural and religious resources as well as contribute to increasing the income of the local people.

The community was introduced to a number of potential tourism and community development initiatives; creating an information center, providing parking, developing agricultural products and souvenirs, and establishing a savings group. See Figure 4.4 for examples of public consultation situations.

Figure 4.4   Public Consultations

Simulated Tourism Day

In theory, effective community participation is an essential principle of sustainable development. However, it is often one of the most difficult tasks to carry out in practice. To build community readiness and the capacity to embrace tourism, Klong Khwang villagers, with assistance from the project team, conducted a full-scale simulated "mock tourism day."

The event had three objectives. It was designed primarily to provide villagers with an opportunity to experience a large volume of visitors and learn to deal with a variety of tourism and resident issues. It also tested first-hand the community's infrastructure from a visitation perspective and evaluated the attractiveness of the site as a tourism destination. Finally, it allowed residents to decide whether they wanted to accept and develop tourism as a village activity over a longer period of time.

In the mock tourism exercise, a multinational group of 40 volunteers assumed various tourist roles. The day's program and activities were effectively developed by the village headman and community members, including providing English-speaking tour guides, planning a sightseeing itinerary and serving a buffet lunch prepared by the women'sgroup. See Figure 4.5 for scenes from the mock tourism day.

An evaluation confirmed the "tourists" had an enjoyable and educational day and, more importantly, the community experienced the demands and opportunities associated with hosting a group of tourists. The tourism day provided opportunities for determining the feasibility of large tour groups, timing of visits, adequacy of existing facilities and infrastructure, including waste management, location of toilet facilities, distribution of economic benefits and influence on daily community life.

Figure 4.5   Mock Tourism Day

One major finding was that a restaurant for tourists, run by local people, might not be feasible if it depended on volunteer labor. The women realized that in addition to their agricultural activities in the community and taking care of family needs, they had little time to take on new responsibilities. If a restaurant were to be developed, it would have to be staffed by paid employees and could not be seen as an additional responsibility for women in the community.

4.3   Klong Khwang Tourism Plan Development

Experiences have shown that tourism destinations must develop appropriate organizational structures, carry out a range of planning and design activities, be deeply and directly involved in marketing the destination and view product development as an essential element in the overall tourism development process (e.g. Jamal and Getz, 1995; Murphy, 1985; Sofield, 2003).

With the assistance from the CUC UEM Project, Klong Khwang developed a community tourism plan that proposed tourism development scenarios involving different levels of activity from minimal intervention to large-scale tourism initiatives. The community proceeded with a moderate scale model for tourism development that would produce modest numbers of visitors. It was felt this moderate level of development would position tourism as a seasonal activity separate from, and for the most part, not disruptive to the community's existing agricultural base. Villagers believed this would be least intrusive on the community and provide much-needed income at certain times of the year.

It was recognized that this modest approach required a much lower level of resident involvement and a smaller financial investment. This kind of tourism development also considered the limited carrying capacity of the community, budget realities, the committee's modest economic goals and the need to protect Klong Khwang's agricultural base. Tourism was not seen as lacking in value or importance but simply reflecting only one component of the community's overall development objectives.

The Tourism Plan

Following the preparatory stage, a detailed tourism plan was developed by the community with the assistance of CUC UEM. A summary of the community-based tourism development plan is presented in this section (The full plan document can be found at www.integrationmgt.com). A number of plan components are briefly covered here to provide a sense of the overall direction adopted by the committee to use tourism as a cultural and economic development tool. These components are in Figure 4.6.

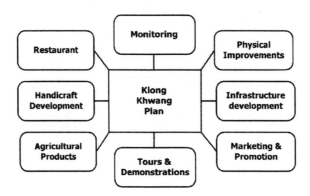

Figure 4.6   Tourism Plan Components

Handicraft Development

Women and older people in the village were interested in making handicrafts (e.g. mat weaving) as a source of extra income. However, there would be a need for assistance in developing products to meet market standards and demands. Examples of local handicrafts are outlined in Figure 4.7.

Figure 4.7   Local Handicrafts

Promotion and Development of Local Agricultural Products

The community was convinced an opportunity existed to develop additional income by producing new agricultural products and adding value to those currently grown in the community.

Tours and Demonstrations

The community saw the possibility of raising money through tours and exhibitions. Demonstrating traditional lifestyles, e.g. weaving, could be incorporated into an overall visitor experience to provide tourists with a glimpse of traditional ways of life in this part of Thailand. Tour guides would have to be trained, some would have to learn English, and there was a need to develop guiding skills. This was seen as a way for younger people in the community to earn extra income and develop new skills and knowledge. A small charge would be levied for these walking tours and demonstrations.

Marketing Plan and Promotion Strategy

The community felt visitation level objectives would not require a significant marketing initiative or ambitious promotional efforts. TAT could work with the community to identify specific target groups and initially raise the community's profile in Korat. This would ensure that, at various times of the year, there would be sufficient tourism numbers to justify community investment and provide reasonable financial returns.

The project team helped Klong Khwang develop marketing and promotional materials, e.g. brochures and postcards. Local officials were responsible for supplying information, e.g. key points of interest in Klong Khwang and text for print materials. The plan recognized the need for an information kiosk located in a prominent position to provide visitors with information, such as the history of the reclining Buddha, the Wheel and the village itself.

Infrastructure Development

The community acknowledged it would have to provide sufficient toilets, drinking water for visitors and effective directional signage. Security and medical services would also be required for larger events.

Physical Improvements

To make the community more attractive to tourists and facilitate visitor activities, a number of physical changes were proposed to the plan, including improving the entry to the community (Figure 4.8). It was also proposed that the area near the Wat be improved to provide a resting and meeting place for tourists and community residents.

Figure 4.8   Improvements to the Plaza Area and the Wat Village Entrance

Part of Klong Khwang's tourism product is its traditional village character. As incomes rise and tastes change, the physical form of the community might also change when new housing and building materials are introduced. If these changes were to alter the character of the community, a large part of the tourism appeal of Klong Khwang would be lost. This produced a great deal of discussion. To maintain the existing character – an important community objective – some form of development controls would have to be put in place. Figure 4.9 demonstrates how original materials could be reintroduced to maintain the traditional community fabric.

Figure 4.9   The Use of Traditional Materials and Form

Monitoring

With the help of TAT and local district officials, it will be necessary for Klong Khwang to monitor the impact of economic, physical, environmental, social and cultural issues every year. The community, with the support of the project team, has developed a series of simple indicators which can be easily monitored. These are described in further detail later in the chapter.

4.4   Plan Implementation

4.4.1   The Implementation Framework

After the tourism plan was developed at the end of 1999, Klong Khwang began to implement the plan on a gradual, measured basis. On their own, they have sought assistance and support from various organizations such as the provincial government offices. Some major achievements are discussed below.

Organizational Structure

As the plan was being implemented, the village headman commented, "A plan is a bridge for the future."   He and the community recognized that to implement the tourism plan and strengthen local people's involvement in managing tourism activities, an appropriate organizational structure was required. From the beginning of the planning process, the community set up a tourism committee to serve as an advisory board for tourism-related development activities. It included a monk, a teacher, volunteers and an appointee who would look after the interests of the monastery. The committee, functioning in a businesslike manner, helped to guide tourism development and the community.

Establishment of Community Co-operative

According to the moderate tourism development model adopted by the community, a co-operative was established with a small investment of 9,400 Baht (US$ 240). It consists of five working groups: production, marketing, finance, auditing and sales. Each group selected a head and the village headman acted as chairman of the co-operative. The objectives of the co-operative are to: 1) generate additional income for villagers from tourism; 2) reduce the number of unemployed people; 3) promote Klong Khwang village and local goods made from agricultural products.

In 2000 the headman reported that the cooperative had 60 members with 25% participating in group activities. To encourage members to work, there is an agreement that anyone who regularly participates gets a 75% dividend every month – those who do not work get 10% annually. 15% of the profits go to the saving co-operative fund which provides loans to co-operative members and assistance for medical expenses or funeral ceremonies.

Product Development

Training in agricultural product development has been provided by provincial government agencies, e.g. the production of banana chips or banana candy. Profits from the sale of these local products are around 12,000 Baht (US$ 300) per month. To maximize profit, all efforts are made to primarily purchase raw materials locally from Klong Khwang villagers (statistics provided by village headman).

A limited amount of souvenir production generates about 10,000 Baht (US$ 250) a month (statistics provided by village headman). Due to a lack of human resources, villagers who do not make souvenirs themselves hire others to do the work. The headman encourages and trains unemployed villagers to do this job. See Figure 10for examples of local products. Although the income generated from the sale of local products appears to be small, it is an important source of extra income for the residents.

Figure 4.10   Local Products

Facilities, Services and Infrastructure

Road connections to Klong Khwang have been improved, providing good access to the community; a new parking area has been identified to avoid any damage from vibration to the Reclining Buddha. Public telephones and washrooms have also been provided. With support from TAT, there is now signage in Thai and English from the main road right into the village. The community did not want to provide home stays or build guesthouses because of the potential adverse social and cultural impact.

Environmental Protection

The tourism development approach adopted by Klong Khwang was designed to create minimal environmental impacts to the community. For example, Klong Khwang realized that with the increasing number of vehicles coming into the village, the vibration from these vehicles might damage the Buddha; therefore a new parking area was identified that would avoid any damage to the Reclining Buddha. Other impacts from increased solid waste or wastewater would be minimal given that Klong Khwang does not provide accommodation or restaurants to the visitors. There is very little noise pollution due to the short periods of time tourists are in the community.

Income Distribution

One key concern with tourism development is that economic benefits are often not distributed in an equitable manner. In Klong Khwang, donations are directed primarily to improvements and the maintenance of the temple and its facilities. Profits from agricultural products are equally distributed through the co-operative to members (as mentioned earlier). Net profits from the sale of souvenirs are given to villagers and the co-operative. This example of managing profits/income is an excellent model for income distribution. From the beginning, the community was less concerned with individuals benefiting from the development process and more interested in ensuring the entire community would profit once tourism activities took place.

Monitoring Tourism Impacts

One problem associated with tourism development is that often resources are not devoted to monitoring activities (Jamieson, et al, 2000). It is important that Klong Khwang monitor the success or failure of its management strategies. Without this activity it will be very difficult for Klong Khwang to determine its ability to meet future challenges. Simple monitoring indicators developed by the project team were presented in the Klong Khwang tourism development plan (See Table 4.1; Cf. Jamieson and Sunalai, 1999).

Table 4.1   Monitoring Indicators

Issues	Monitoring Indicators
Economic	▪ The amount of money the community obtains from tourism is categorized by these following items: 　-　Donations 　-　Food and drink 　-　Souvenir sales 　-　Sale of agricultural products 　-　Walking and demonstration tours 　-　Jobs created by tourism activity
Physical	▪ Damage to the reclining Buddha. ▪ Whether grass and foliage is getting trampled or destroyed. ▪ Damage to the roads/parking lot caused by buses and other vehicles.
Environment	▪ Problems with solid waste. ▪ Problems with wastewater. ▪ Noise pollution from tourists and buses. ▪ Air pollution from buses/vehicles.
Socio-cultural	▪ Changes to the behavior of the community. ▪ Changes in housing styles ▪ Changes to the dress of the local people.

After one year of tourism plan implementation (end of 2000) the project team came back to the community and discussed the monitoring of tourism impacts in Klong Khwang with the headman. Simple methodologies to collect information involved observation, discussion with the headman and interviewing the community members. Based on the monitoring indicators presented in Table 4.1, the following are the results of tourism impacts on the Klong Khwang community.

- Economic impacts: Based on data collected by local people, the number of tourists increased from 1,100 in 1999 to 3,000 visitors per month in 2000, that is, 36,000 for the whole year with associated increases in the income of local people.

- Physical impacts: Currently the negative physical impacts from tourism development can be kept with the accepted level because of the gradual and careful process adopted by villagers.

- Environmental impacts: Since negative impacts either from the disposal of solid waste or dealing with wastewater can be managed by the informal treatment facilities at this stage, if tourism levels increase, formal infrastructure initiatives will have to be taken. The headman has been active in encouraging villagers to reuse and recycle materials to reduce the amount of waste being generated within the community and to earn extra income from selling recycled products.

- Socio-Cultural impacts: From the village headman's point of view, the community is now more positive toward tourism. The community is friendlier and provides information to tourists. Modes of dress have changed; residents wear Thai clothes more often than before. There are also indications that the villagers are working together more co-operatively, given the type of tourism planning process that is in place in the community.

4.4.2   Management Issues/Barriers

While the experience has been positive, there are ongoing issues. It is too early to determine the willingness and ability of the villagers to continue sustainable control and management of the tourism process. This will require ongoing community guidance and support.

Initially it was thought very little marketing would be required; it is now clear the community must develop a set of marketing and promotional tools to position their product in a more effective way. An important issue is how to position and promote a community like Klong Khwang. Currently, promotion is mainly by word of mouth. Responsible government agencies like the regional office of the Tourism Authority of Thailand or the provincial government must support Klong Khwang as one of the destinations on the Korat tourism circuit. The community cannot function alone as a destination but must be seen as part of a larger series of activities. This was stressed in the recommendations of the CUC team to the community.

Given the community-driven nature of the process, the community is learning to determine its own activities as it gains experience. There are other competitive destinations in the region and therefore a need exists to professionally develop the tourism product in order to continue to attract sufficient income. There is also a need for professional advice on how to develop new markets for both agricultural and handicraft products.

4.4.3   Lessons Learned

Klong Khwang has been recognized by the Nakhon Ratchasima provincial government as an excellent community-based initiative and is becoming well-known to other communities in the province. The headman has been invited to talk to other communities on how to get villagers involved in community activities and how to strengthen their unity in working together to improve their quality of life through tourism development. Klong Khwang also accommodates a number of study tours from within the country and outside Thailand.

It was acknowledged by all major stakeholders that the technical assistance provided by national and local governments and the project team was instrumental in ensuring important issues were identified, technical advice and direction were available to committee members, and an overall understanding of community-based tourism was established. The community was receptive to accepting technical advice and, most importantly, committed to a planning process. In addition to assistance from outsiders, the success of community-based tourism development in Klong Khwang was due to a committed and high quality of leadership. The process would not have worked without the headman's ability. His vision and commitment to make the community a better place was clearly an important ingredient. While this type of leadership may not always exist, developing such capacities and commitment are essential. It takes time and effort but undoubtedly pays off in the long term.

Another lesson learned is that if communities are to assume responsibility for their futures, they need time to develop the necessary skills and knowledge and recognize the importance of sustainable approaches to community development. Traditional classrooms for education and training may not be required; informal discussions and meetings with focus groups, walking around the village to identify issues and tourism products, and using maps and other visual illustrations as guides for physical development are more effective.

An approach taken during the process to allow all community members to think independently about issues (not driven by political forces) resulted in a constructive process of information and skills development. It may not always be possible to replicate this situation, but independent teams, unconstrained by governmental structures and policies, are best suited to work with communities and help them achieve their objectives.

Another major reason for the success of the planning initiative was that the community realized the importance of a sustainable planning process. It is interesting to note that the community is following through closely on the plan it developed because community members feel a strong sense of "ownership." This leads to a high commitment to tourism activities and ensures success. An "outside" plan would probably not have achieved the same level of success.

Capacity-building was also seen as a key factor and it occurred at a number of levels, including improving the project team members' abilities to increase the community's capacity to manage its own affairs. One interesting result of the process is that the village headman has now become increasingly recognized by various governments and organizations as someone who can articulate a sustainable process of community-based tourism planning and development. He is a living example of the ability of communities to manage their own affairs if they have access to technical advice and support. For example, the headman was a guest speaker, along with academics and professionals, at a major international conference on community destination management.

If the planning process is to succeed, the major actors must be able to think "outside the box." For example, the notion of a co-operative was not originally seen as part of the overall implementation process, but the community was adamant about the need for such an approach. It has turned out to be one of the most important tools for ensuring equitable distribution of tourism resources.

The use of simulation and visualization techniques proved to be successful. Technical assistance projects should adopt similar approaches, especially if they are dealing with communities that are visually oriented. This approach is also suggested by Edelheim and Ueda (2007).

The final lesson learned is that the nature of the community's values and spiritual way of life was essential in producing a plan with an equitable distribution of resources. The project team initially approached the community planning situation as one where individual efforts would be encouraged and recognized. It became clear that the community, based on its Buddhist and rural way of life, saw things quite differently. The notion of sharing and commitment to the community's spiritual and cultural resources was therefore seen as a priority.

4.4.4 Applicability to Other Communities in Asia and the Pacific

Given the multiplicity of different factors and forces at work in any community tourism development process, it is obvious that the Klong Khwang process described above cannot be entirely implemented in another situation. The authors' work in similar situations in several other countries has demonstrated that the importance of incorporating sustainable tourism principles as guiding elements in any planning process is essential. Without a careful implementation of these principles, it is not likely that a community will be able to achieve a sustainable tourism plan and development process.

The authors would argue that the overall process employed provides an excellent framework for the structuring of a tourism planning and development process. However, it is clear that each community must develop its own set of organizational and management strategies that consider the full range of stakeholders who have an influence on the eventual tourism product. The tourism planning process should adopt a comprehensive approach concerned with a detailed inventory and assessment process, the incorporation of pro poor tourism concerns and the development of destination plans that include visitor management strategies. It is clear that marketing information and promotional capacities are essential and any tourism development process must ensure that there is coordination between the various tourism initiatives taking place within the community and its original context.

One of the deciding factors in how successful a community can be in its tourism planning and development is clearly on the level of support it can receive from various governmental and non-governmental organizations as well as technical assistance agencies. Without this type of support it is almost impossible to understand how a community, without the necessary resources, can achieve a sustainable tourism product.

Finally, it is absolutely essential that communities do not adopt tourism as a major engine of economic growth at the expense of their traditional ways of income generation. Tourism by its very nature is cyclical and is very vulnerable to events outside of the control of the community. The impacts of the tragedy of September 11th in the United States, the Bali bombings, the SARS epidemic of 2003 and downturns in the world economy are all warning signs that communities must adopt tourism as one of their sources of economic development. The case study developed within this chapter clearly demonstrates how a community chose to add to its economic activity, build on its traditional activities yet still achieve the benefits of tourism development.

4.5 Conclusion

In assessing the success of the community-based tourism initiative in Klong Khwang, it is useful to identify the internal and external forces essential to the development process. A number of external forces helped support the process of community involvement and plan development including the interest and support of the Tourism Authority of Thailand, the support of the district government and the work of the project team. Without them it would not have been possible for the community to succeed.

While these forces have been influential, the internal workings of the community have been the key to success. The headman's leadership, along with the willingness of the community to participate in the process and support the development of a sustainable tourism development plan, is seen as a significant dimension within the larger development process. The combination of internal and external forces has been essential to the overall effort. The 'local hero' the fundamental role of as the key driver of innovation is fundamental (Saperstein and Rouach, 2002).

Whether the Klong Khwang experience can be replicated as a "package" in other situations is uncertain; however, there is no doubt that many of the elements in this chapter are relevant to other community tourism planning situations. It is hoped funds will be made available for similar types of initiatives to allow officials and community members to develop our knowledge of community development and planning. Only then can we begin to fully understand the role of technical advice and innovative techniques in helping to support community-based tourism plans.

References:

Council of State of Thailand (1997), *Constitution of the Kingdom of Thailand*, Bangkok: Office of the Council of State.

Edelheim and Ueda (2007), 'On Effective Use of Simulations in Journal of Hospitality', *Leisure, Sport and Tourism Education*, 6(1).

Gunn, C.A. (1979), *Tourism Planning*, Crane Russak, New York.

Gunn, C.A. and T. Var (2002), *Tourism Planning (4th ed.)*, Routledge, New York and London.

Hatton, M.J. (ed.) (1999), 'Community-Based Tourism in the Asia-Pacific: Klong Khwang Village', *Planning for Tourism Development*, Asia-Pacific Economic Cooperation (APEC), the School of Media Studies at Humber College, Canada.

Jamal T.B. and D. Getz (1995), 'Collaboration theory and community tourism planning', *Annals of Tourism Research*, 22(1), pp. 186-204.

Jamieson, W. and P.P. Sunalai (1999), *Klong Khwang Plan, Training and Technology Transfer Program*, Canadian Universities Consortium Urban Environmental Management Project at AIT.

Jamieson, W., et al. (2000), *Local Level Planning for Sustainable Tourism Development*, Canadian Universities Consortium Urban Environmental Management Project at AIT.

Jamieson, W. (2001a), 'Interpretation and Tourism', *Community Tourism Destination Management: Principles and Practices*, in Walter Jamieson (ed.), Canadian Universities Consortium Urban Environmental Management Project.

Jamieson, W. (editor and participant) (2001b), *Recommendations for Sustainable Village Tourism Development for the Greater Mekong Subregion*, Training and Technology Transfer Program, Canadian Universities Consortium Urban Environmental Management Project at AIT.

Malinowski, B. (1922), *Argonauts of the Western Pacific*, Dutton & Co. Inc., New York.

Murphy, P. E. (1985), *Tourism: A Community Approach*, Routledge, London.

Pearce, P.L., G.M. Moscardo , and G.F. Ross (1996), *Tourism community relationships*, Pergamon Press, Oxford.

Royal Development Projects Board, Department of Technical and Economic, Cooperation and United Nations Development Program (1997), *Concepts and theories of His Majesty the King on Development*, 21 Century Co., Ltd., Bangkok.

Saperstein J. and D. Rouach (2002), *Creating Regional Wealth in the Innovation Economy: Models, Perspectives, and Best Practices*, Financial Times Prentice Hall.

Sofield, T. (2003), *Empowerment for Sustainable Tourism Development*, Elsevier Science Ltd, Oxford, UK.

World Commission on Environment and Development (1987), *Our Common Future (The Bruntland Commission Report)*, Oxford University Press, Oxford.

Chapter 5

The Successes and Difficulties of Advisory Work in Lao PDR: A Case Study "The Buddha Cave"

5.1 Background

5.1.1 SNV Netherlands Development Organisation

SNV is a development agency based in the Netherlands operating in over 30 countries in Africa, Asia, Latin America and Europe. SNV provides advice to organisations at their request, on how to improve their way of working so they are able to fight poverty more effectively. In Lao PDR, this work is conducted in several sectors, the main ones being: pro-poor sustainable tourism, non-timber forest products, governance, biogas, gender and small business development.

SNV Lao PDR currently provides technical assistance in the field of pro-poor sustainable tourism (PPST) to the government tourism offices in four provinces, with the aim of improving the capacity of these organizations and alleviating poverty by identifying pro-poor tourism opportunities (Ashley,2005). The main constraints of the tourism offices in Lao PDR are a lack of experience and knowledge of tourism issues, limited capacity of junior staff, low budgets for routine activities and sometimes poor motivation related to low government salaries.

5.1.2 SNV in Khammouane

In Khammouane province, SNV provides capacity-building assistance to the Provincial Tourism Office (PTO) by providing two tourism advisers, one international (the author) and one national adviser. The main work of the advisers has been to assist the Khammouane (PTO) with planning, developing and implementing new community-based tourism sites through the Mekong Tourism Development Project (MTDP) an Asian Development Bank funded initiative (Asian Development Bank, 2005); improving staff skills through training and coaching; and upgrading its information services. Based in the PTO, the advisers also interact and advise other tourism stakeholders inside and outside the province. One such opportunity in the province is the Buddha cave market where rural communities can directly benefit from tourism activities. Being based in Thakhek the SNV advisers were well placed to advise the authorities when the new Buddhist cave was discovered in April 2004.

5.2   2004: The discovery of the Cave[2]

Tham Pha (Buddha cave, Figure 5.1) near the Village of Ban Nak Khang Sarng in Thakhek district came into the news following the rediscovery of 229 ancient Buddha images in a small cave.

Figure 5.1   Bronze Buddha

Courtesy of Charles Ghommidh professor Montpelier University France

Local villagers traditionally collect food from the forests and hunt bats in rock holes and caves. Mr. Bounnong, a middle aged man from Ban Nak Khang, during the month of April 2004, entered the small cave opening (1.5 m), which lies 15 m from ground level on a 300 m cliff face. He had noticed bats entering the cave and decided to climb a vine to investigate. Passing through the small cave entrance he looked down into the cavern below using his headlamp and to his amazement saw a large Buddha statue. He then proceeded down into the cave and realized the there were over 200 Buddha statues ranging in size from 15 cm to the larger Buddha of approximately 1 m in height, all the Buddhas appeared to be made of bronze. (It is said that for two days he did not believe his eyes and in fact told no one of his discovery!)   Later he went back with a group of nine other villagers to confirm his findings. In early May 2006, local and district authorities were informed and came to the site to perform a religious ceremony. They ensured the security of these highly valuable items and that the Buddhas were not moved from their original positions inside the cave. In the following weeks, the news spread widely in Thakhek and to Vientiane and beyond. Thousands of people from all over Laos made pilgrimages to the cave and a temporary bamboo stairway was constructed.

The cave itself is quite beautiful and can be divided into three parts (See Figure 5.2 below). The first part is a large flat area where people now worship, the second is the location of Buddha statues of different sizes placed between limestone "rims" (grey calcified ditches) and the third part is behind the statues which extends into the cave gallery. The ceiling and walls of the cave are decorated with stalactites, stalagmites and "shields" forming a curtain behind the statues. The gallery part of the cave has exceptional natural beauty but is not open to the general public for safety and security reasons.

---

[2] General background information: Publication on the Buddha cave by the Culture and information department hakhek Khammouane province Lao PDR (translated by K. Khamlasy, edited by J. Burrows).

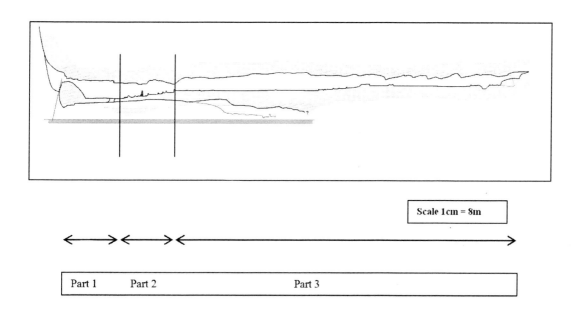

Scale 1cm = 8m

Part 1   Part 2   Part 3

Figure 5.2   Cross Sectional View of Tham Nong Pa Fa

Topography: C. Mouret, K. Khamlasy and C.J. Ghommidh 2004.

Currently the villagers are guarding the cave and supervise the visitors, but due to the initial large numbers, they were somewhat overwhelmed by the situation.

More recently, there has been assistance and guidance from local authorities and the tourism department on how they might manage the situation. The villagers have organised themselves to guard the cave (24 hours a day) and control the entry to the cave via a 15 m bamboo ladder. Inside the cave, guards are well-positioned to prevent members of the public getting too close to the Buddhas.

An entrance fee is now in place for visitors, which has somewhat controlled and limited the numbers of visitors that can enter the cave at any one time, reducing impact. There have been several official government visits to the cave and it is hoped that the relevant stakeholders will soon meet to discuss the future of the cave. The provincial tourism office has made a recent survey of the cave and believes the site has the potential to continue as a major tourist attraction for Khammouane Province, both for local people and foreign tourists. Initially there were rumours that the Buddhas might be removed for safekeeping to a museum in Vientiane; in part due to the efforts of the PTO and SNV's advisory services, the Provincial Government has now confirmed the Buddhas will remain in the cave and have created a committee to manage the cave for tourism purposes. The SNV Tourism Advisers based in Thakhek feel this was a wise decision as the Buddhas represent an important discovery for Khammouane and Lao PDR as a religious site, archaeological site and tourism attraction.

In the advisers' opinion, the Buddhas are well-protected at present by the community members. The Buddha cave also has the potential to benefit local people in the village of Ban Na Kan Sarng and the wider area of Thakhek as a source of long-term income from entrance fees, food stalls and accommodation. During the visit by the tourism office, SNV advisers were able to meet with the village elders and discuss some current concerns at the site. It was suggested that the current rope used in the cave to prevent visitors getting too close to the Buddhas be moved back one meter as there is an accumulation of Buddhist offerings and candle wax on the archaeological site (and the Buddhas). It was also suggested that the monks in the cave remove (move back) all Buddhist donations that have been placed on and around the Buddhas so as to preserve the original state of the cave when it was first discovered. There was also some discussion on the impact of candle smoke on the white cave walls, but it was agreed that this was a more difficult problem to address at present. The limestone formations within the cave are quite spectacular and add to the natural beauty of the cave.

Close to the cave, many stallholders from Thakhek started selling snacks and drinks; unfortunately, local villagers do not have the resources to set up such stalls, though it was suggested that they might sell in-season fruits from the village. The litter problem was also mentioned and there was advice that the village leaders discuss this problem with the stall holders; the recommendation from the adviser was that the stallholders do a daily clean up and take their rubbish back with them to Thakhek.

The village of Ban Na Kan Sarng has only been in existence for 30 years, so it is very likely that the cave has been forgotten for quite some time. At the foot of the cliff is a much larger resurgence cave called Tham Pa Pha (Pa Pha is a soft shelled turtle). It is possible to take boat rides into the cave during the dry season and visit a gallery inside. This cave has long been visited and contains a large lake which is also of interest for tourism purposes, as you can travel into this cave by boat for about 50 meters until it becomes too narrow to proceed further.

In 2004, things were happening very fast at an exciting time in Thakhek.

It was hoped that the final decisions made on the cave's development and management would involve discussions from several government departments including the culture and information and the tourism departments, both at the provincial and national level; and last but not least that the community of Ban Na Kan Sarng would have a say in how "their" cave was to be managed. Finally, it was also hoped that the advisory service provided by SNV Netherlands Development Organisation in Khammouane be well-used by local authorities.

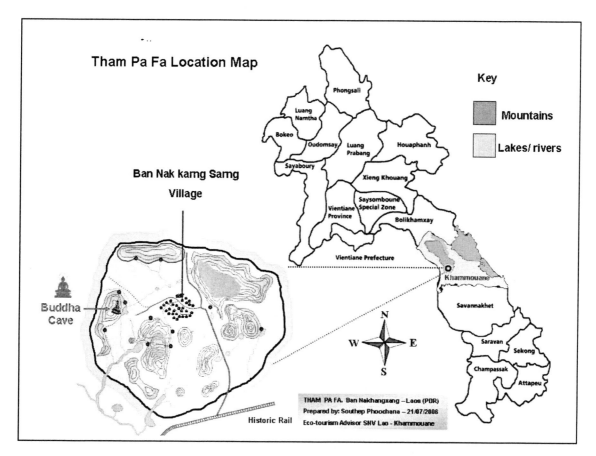

Figure 5.3   The location of Ban Nak Karng Sarng

Note: by Southep Phoochana SNV National advisor based in Khammouane provincial tourism offices Thakhek Lao PDR.

5.3   2006: Successes and Difficulties of Advisory Work

By 2006 SNV had provided advisory support to the provincial tourism office in Khammouane for almost three years. Since the discovery of the Buddha cave, quite a large amount of time has been devoted to advising on the Buddha cave tourism development. To date the main achievements are considered as follows:

- brochures for the Buddha cave produced in Lao and English;

- information signs produced for visitors in Lao and English;

- development of a CBT trek in nearby village;

- identification of new business opportunities in Buddha cave market;

- some awareness created of Buddha cave nationally and internationally;

- maps developed by French cave experts;

- advice on installation of a professional lighting system;

- training of village guides at cave and for local trek;

- boat rides for tourists developed in the lower cave;

- discussions with villagers to preserve/protect site;

- baseline studies on village income;

- editing of booklet for culture and information department.

Working at the provincial level, SNV advisers were well-placed to advise the tourism office and other stakeholders on Buddha cave issues. What influence advisers actually have is some times hard to judge, but it is clear that the expertise of SNV has been well-used in the cave's development, and without someone "on the ground" events may have taken a very different direction, particularly with regards to developments inside the cave. Villagers living near to the cave have taken great pride in managing the cave and providing different services to the visitors and have commented that "they appreciate the help with regards to protecting the cave as Lao people have not yet learned how to look after things."

As advisers, we learnt to realise that our influence is sometimes not that strong and that our advice might not always be taken. Though we have the "right to advise" through our memorandum of understanding with our clients, ultimately we are not the implementers of projects as such; SNV's mission statement states that "SNV is dedicated to a society where all people enjoy the freedom to pursue their own sustainable development."

Our clients have to make the best decisions based on the information available to them, or in some case they may not simply agree with the advice of the foreign expert: after all, they have the right to manage their own resources. Of course, this is their choice and the advisers have to come to terms with such eventualities. Building strong relationships and trust with partners are particularly important as a way to gain respect and influence with our clients, and this takes time. When the cave was discovered, the advisers had already been in the province for over one year and felt comfortable in giving clear advice and recommendations to the relevant parties.

Particularly key to this was an SNV-funded study tour to Vietnam several months prior with several members of the culture and information office, who later were to become major players in the decision-making and development of the Buddha cave.

Unfortunately, in the development field, local partners may sometimes expect some kind of financial reward/benefit from project donors. SNV has taken a brave move from being a project implementer to being a provider of an "advisory service". SNV advisers come with only small budgets which are specifically for activities related to capacity-building purposes. With regards to the development of the Buddha cave, it appears that most of the costs of building infrastructure so far have come from the revenue from ticket sales. In the advisers' opinion, more influence is often gained if "you are paying" for the development or costs of infrastructure. By not doing this you may in fact have little influence, but on the other hand development is likely to be small scale and have more local ownership and pride. It was, however, decided that a small contribution could be made from SNV with regards to installing a professional lighting system and some information signs and this token contribution has, in the advisers' opinion, been well received by the authorities and villagers.

Over the last two years, there has been a lot of effort and advice given to the various stakeholders involved in the development of the Buddha cave, the following points are considered as successes so far:

5.3.1   Tourism Office Involvement

On our first visit to the new attraction with the vice director of the tourism office, he was very resistant to even meet villagers to discuss issues at the cave. The culture and information office was the major player at that time and the Buddha cave was not considered as a tourism issue. Incredible as it might seem, the first official survey by government officials did not include a representative from the tourism office! Through the encouragement of the SNV advisers, the provincial tourism office have become more proactive and the vice director eventually joined the Buddha cave committee which is the steering committee for the cave. By advising the vice director, the input of the SNV advisers can be voiced at steering committee meetings. SNV is looking closely at finding a way to directly advise the committee itself and is proposing to explore the idea of the Buddha cave committee becoming an SNV client.

5.3.2   Daily Removal of All Buddhist Offerings by Villagers

When the cave was first discovered, Buddhist "flower baskets" and candle wax were accumulating in worryingly large amounts on and around the Buddhas. The advisers quickly recognised this as a potential threat to the site and have worked to put systems in place with the villagers to protect the Buddhas. Candle-burning was prohibited in the cave quite early on, as the smoke was blackening the white walls and increasing temperatures in the already confined air space. Due to poor air flow in the cave, it is also likely that candle-burning might reduce oxygen levels: a balance had to be found between Buddhist traditions and protecting the site.

Local people like to place offerings directly next to the Buddha statues; the security guard facilitated this but offerings quickly began to accumulate to a point where they were obscuring the view of the Buddhas. As people were coming from all over Laos with offerings, it was not possible to deter this tradition. A compromise was reached with the guards where they agreed with the advisers to clean away all religious donations at the end of each day; some are taken to the local village temple. By doing this, the "archaeological site" remains relatively clear of modern religious donations and the Buddhas remain in a condition very similar to those in which Mr Bounnong first saw back in April 2004.

A barrier was also constructed through SNV support which is designed in such a way as to encourage visitors to place their offerings on the structure while not obscuring the view of the statues. The barrier also serves as a security measure, preventing visitors from actually touching and hence damaging the Buddhas (or indeed as protection from potential theft resulting from international demand). The advisers have noticed that during quiet times, the guards do open the small door in the barrier for the occasional visitor to pray directly in front of the large Buddha, and there has to be a balance in everything (a very Buddhist treatise!), in this case between tradition and security. It has also been noticed that incense sticks are still lit, but only for a few seconds after which they are extinguished.

Movement of artefacts themselves was also initially a problem. There has been much discussion with the villagers with regards to the importance of not moving the Buddhas from their original positions.

During early visits, it was noticed that several ancient iron bowls and ceramic vases had been moved so that visitors could place their donations into them. The villagers were asked to replace these but said that people preferred to use the old bowls (400 years old). Due to the local wishes and the extremely bad condition of these bowls, it was agreed that they remain in use; however, the ceramic vases were returned to the original position to prevent potential damage.

5.3.3   Tourist Information and Signs

Signs have been developed with visitor guidelines for the cave.

Larger signs directing people form Thakhek to the Buddha cave area are yet to be finished due to costs (some signs do exist in Lao script). The SNV advisers are hoping for some financial support from the Mekong Tourism Development Project (Thavipheth and Schipani, 2007) to complete this important activity, as it is essential that signs are in English, Lao and Thai if the Buddha cave is to be successful in attracting more international visitors. Some previous advice about the location of signs and their design was given to the provincial authorities but no follow up as such was taken due to financial restraints.

With regards to information signs at the cave, SNV has met and discussed with several government departments and the cave committee to develop guidelines for visitors to the cave. The final "Buddhist rules" developed were used to make two signs, one is located in the market area and the other near the cave entrance. These simple wooden boards are in both Lao and the English language. Hopefully, this information will help visitors understand the importance of protecting the site.

Local students at the vocational technical school in Thakhek were given the task of producing the signs. The visitor guidelines are considered as an important step in protecting the cave, particularly with regards to setting limits for the number of visitors for reasons of safety and comfort, and the no candle and incense burning policy. Due to poor air circulation in the cave, it is possible that a large number of persons in the cave at any one time might contribute to a change in temperature and moisture levels, which may be detrimental to the bronze Buddha statues.

5.3.4   French Survey and Mapping of the Cave

French caving expeditions have been visiting Khammouane Province for several years; in fact, they visited Tham Pa Pha (the water cave below the Buddha cave) in the 1980s but did not venture into the cave above.   When the Buddha cave was first discovered, SNV made contact with a French team led by Mr. Claude Mouret. The SNV advisers asked if they would be interested in visiting and accurately mapping the cave and giving any recommendations to the local authorities with regards to preserving/protecting the cave. Key to gaining full access to the cave was a strong relationship with the culture and information office developed with the SNV adviser on the recent study tour to look at show-cave tourism in Vietnam. The Thakhek Buddha cave was accurately mapped and the location of the Buddhas was recorded. It was, however, also discovered that the cave floor is only 25 cm thick in certain places. This information was presented to the provincial authorities and contributed to guidelines being developed for cave visitors. The water cave below the Buddha cave was also surveyed and mapped; the cave was found to be interesting enough to develop boat rides for tourists, which is now very popular with visitors and increases the attractiveness of a visit, as well as providing an additional source of local income. Also during this survey, we were able to gain permission to photograph the Buddha statues (prohibited to the general public). These photographs have been very important for developing brochures and other promotional materials for a new Tourist Information

Centre in Thakhek. Photography is not allowed in the cave, which is rather unusual in Laos and Thailand. There are security concerns, but more realistically it seems that the culture and information office have seized this opportunity to sell posters and VDC's outside the cave. Due to the small size of the cave and the praying of visitors, perhaps this was indirectly a wise decision and has helped to maintain the ambiance of this religious site.

5.3.5   Professional Lighting System Installed

Initially, a series of fluorescent lights were placed in the cave for the visit of a local television crew. These lights unfortunately caused algal growth on the cave walls and the lights themselves were rather unsightly. The lights remained in the cave for quite some time before the SNV advisers were able to identify a technician with experience in developing lighting systems for tourism purposes from the German Development Service (DED), actually based in Thakhek at the vocational training school.

In early October 2005, a multi-stakeholder group travelled to the Buddha cave to discuss (and demonstrate) the positioning of a new lighting system. Those attending were members of the cave sub-committee, culture and information department, village elders, tourism office, German Development Service (DED) adviser and SNV advisers. The groups were able to decide and agree upon the type of lights and appropriate positioning of the lights within the cave. Later in October, students from the vocational technical school in Thakhek constructed and installed the lights with assistance from the DED and support from SNV. The lights installed are low wattage cool white spotlights. Recently, a back-up system has been installed, as during power cuts the generator being used was found to be incompatible with the electronics in the low wattage bulbs. The result is a professional lighting system which is perhaps the best in Laos in a Buddhist cave. The SNV adviser considered this "activity" one of the particular "success stories" at the Buddha cave, which covered a variety of important aspects:

- Capacity-building of local people through meetings and discussion, bringing groups together that do not normally cooperate (tourism and culture and information).

- A joint cooperation between SNV and DED, and involvement of the vocational training school electrician students who gained some practical experience in setting up lighting systems for (caves) tourism.

- Improvements to a tourist attraction that is becoming internationally known and is likely to attract many more foreign tourists to the province. It's important that the visitor attraction is well done and attractive.

- The previous lighting system was actually damaging the cave (possibly the Buddhas also) by encouraging green algae to grow on the white cave walls. By using cool white bulbs with low wattage we have now eliminated this problem.

5.3.6   Placing Crushed Rock on Cave Floor

This was prevented by the advisers by reporting this to the provincial authorities. During a routine visit to the cave, it was noticed that a new stairway was being built inside the cave and gravel from another source was to be placed on the cave floor. The advisers discouraged this for two reasons: firstly, following a survey of French experts, it had been discovered that the cave floor was only 25 cm thick in some places, the added weight from gravel might contribute to a collapse of the cave floor (also the reason for reducing visitor numbers); secondly, as the site has archaeological importance, foreign materials should not be brought into the cave. Following our concerns and advice, only locally made mats have been placed on the floor and visitor numbers have been restricted to 30 at any one time.

5.3.7   Business Opportunities and Micro-Finance Activities

In March 2006, SNV advisers facilitated a business opportunities exercise at the Buddha cave market, it was concluded that business activities were limited to the sale of mainly local food and non-timber forest products. There were a variety of reasons why the villagers seemed not to have maximised the opportunity to sell more products to the daily visitors: a lack of expertise and knowledge; seasonality of products (and a preference to sell them in Thakhek); lack of micro-finance opportunities; and being already busy providing other services to the cave (flower baskets, selling tickets, security guards, boat service). This situation was further explored in September 2006 when micro-finance advisers met with the villagers to explore some opportunities identified particularly with regard to transportation services and the sale of souvenirs. SNV is keen to maximise the expertise of its different advisers using "cross-cutting" themes.

5.3.8   Community-based Tourism Trek (CBT)

When the cave was discovered, the MTDP was already developing CBT treks in the Province of Khammouane. Following surveys, it was found that the forests and other caves in the area were interesting enough to develop a CBT trek to the Buddha cave. This response to demand for adventure tourism has made the "Buddha cave trek" particularly popular. The trek involves local village guides who focus the tour on the use of local forest products for food and medicines. Tourists also spend some time exploring the Tham Paseum cave where they swim the first 20 meters into the cave. After visiting the Buddha cave, tourists take a boat ride in the water cave. Finally, visitors return to the village for a traditional Baci ceremony to wish them good luck on their onward journey. The price paid by tourists also includes a contribution to a village development fund. These treks are led and managed by a Thakhek-based English speaking eco-guide unit. Advertising is done locally, at the national level and internationally, particularly with Thailand where religious tourism is an important business.

In its first year, from March 2005 to May 2006, 30 treks to the Buddha cave were sold by the eco-guide unit based in Thakhek with 84 tourists participating. This generated a direct income of US$ 500 for the villagers of Ban Nakarn Sarng. Though this amount is small compared to total income gained at the cave, the amount is likely to increase as the cave becomes better known to international visitors. Figure 5.4 below illustrates the distribution of the income gained from selling two treks.

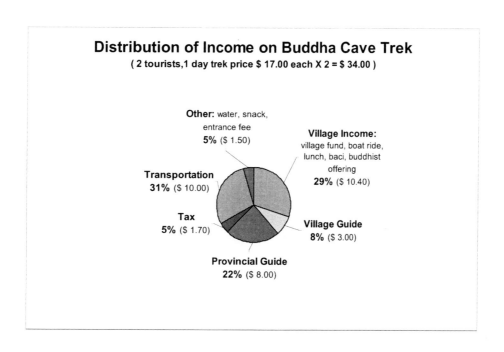

Distribution of Income on Buddha Cave Trek
(2 tourists,1 day trek price $ 17.00 each X 2 = $ 34.00)

Other: water, snack, entrance fee
5% ($ 1.50)

Village Income:
village fund, boat ride, lunch, baci, buddhist offering
29% ($ 10.40)

Transportation
31% ($ 10.00)

Tax
5% ($ 1.70)

Village Guide
8% ($ 3.00)

Provincial Guide
22% ($ 8.00)

Figure 5.4   The Distribution of the Income Gained from Selling Two Treks

5.3.9   Zoning Activity

Most recently, as part of the MTDP project, a heritage and zoning plan has been developed for the cave area (Thavipheth and Schipani, 2007). Zoning is particularly important when developing a tourism attraction. Discussions have been held and maps produced to show current land use activities in the area. The local market was in fact moved back 500 m away from the foot of the cave entrance. However, the reasons might relate more to the annual flooding of the area during the rainy season which makes visiting the cave only possible by a short boat ride. This both generates more income for the villagers and perhaps, in reality, has prevented any new development near to the cave.

5.4   Difficulties of Advisory Work – Advice Not Taken

5.4.1   Concrete Stairways Constructed Outside and Inside the Cave

It was strongly suggested by the advisers that the authorities consider the use of materials other than concrete for constructing the stairways inside and outside the cave (wooden or steel structures). Despite tourism department lobbying, other materials were not considered and the advisers were not able to influence the decision to build a concrete stairway inside and outside the cave. With regards to the outside stairways, the Buddha cave committee decided this would be the most appropriate material and that it would be "the same colour as the rock". This is actually true, though the structure does not really fit in well; however, it is not tied into the cliff and in all practicality this is perhaps the cheapest and safest way to allow visitors to enter the cave. Many of the visitors are elderly people.

The advisers have also recently been asked to assist with installing more lighting on the stairs inside the cave for safety reasons. With regards to the stairways inside the cave, the advisers were able to prevent this stairway being tied into the cave floor, which could have caused a collapse!

5.4.2 Gong Inside the Cave

Despite several requests to remove a gong inside the cave to a new location, this has not been done. Vibrations could potentially cause a rock or stalactite fall. It seems the monks do not want to remove it and the advisers have now suggested that the gong not be used by the general public but by monks only – or it could be relocated in the cave away from the general public. Obviously this situation is quite difficult to solve as, at the end of the day, the cave is a religious site!

5.4.3 Removal of Buddhas for "Water Splashing"

Six ancient Buddhas were removed from the cave for New Year celebrations in 2006 and placed in a (fairly secure) cage for "water splashing" (part of the traditional "cleansing of sins" ceremony to mark the Lao – and Thai – new year at the start of the rainy season in which worshippers gain merit by washing the Buddhas). This was reported to the provincial authorities and it appears permission had come from the Governor! Despite communism, Lao PDR remains a deeply Buddhist country. Again, this is an example of how tradition might be damaging to historic artefacts. Some of the Buddhas chosen were actually wooden with gold leaf paint aged 400 yrs. Perhaps the use of wooden gold-painted Buddhas 400 years old for this purpose was rather unwise, although it does raise the issue of when does a (living) religious object (to be used) become a (dead) museum artefact?

The advice for next year is, if this activity is to continue then only the bronze statues should be used, or better still make some replicas as the originals should ideally not be removed for the cave.

5.4.4 Clean up of the Area

There remains a litter problem at the cave area; although this situation has improved, it seems to be a national problem. Recycling is done in Thakhek by some families and litter containers have been provided. However, the annual monsoon rains and flooding in the area seem to be the current (and traditional) method to clean away rubbish on an annual basis.

5.4.5 Life Jackets Not Used for Boat Rides

Originally provided by PTO for the boat rides in the cave, life jackets appear not to have been looked after and are not always used. It has now been recommended that life jackets be rented for a small fee, which will encourage the villagers to look after then and gain a small income for the rental service.

5.4.6 Environmental Problems

A variety of environmental problems have occurred from the number of visitors to the cave over the last two or so years. Initially, there was a huge litter problem, but most of this was washed away by the monsoon rains of 2005! Now there are some litter containers but, as of yet, no persons employed to collect the trash. There has been some discussion with the sub-committee with regards to recycling the trash locally, but this has not yet started. Initially, no toilet facilities perhaps led to local contamination of ground water; however, the vast amount of rainfall perhaps solved this problem on an annual basis. Toilets have now been constructed but there are only two for the 200 visitors per day.

Deforestation has also been an issue: to build the new road it was necessary to clear considerable amounts of secondary forest and local villagers also used many trees for constructing new stalls in the market despite that fact that cutting is not allowed in this area.

5.4.7   Ticket Sales

Tickets have been sold at the Buddha cave since June 2004 (Kip 2,000 per person). They were introduced by the Thakhek District office. Initially, it was difficult to determine where this income was going, but it appears that the money has been used by the authorities for developing basic infrastructure near the cave (stairways), road improvements to the cave, several bridges and toilets. Ten per cent of the ticket money goes directly to villagers as payment for work in the various service groups; this has now been increased to 20%.

The advisors had suggested to the authorities that it would not be unreasonable to charge Kip 5,000 to foreign visitors and even charge a small fee for photography but this advice has yet to be taken on board, though they did like the idea.

Though the advisers cannot take any credit for the money gained through ticket sales, promotional activities certainly contribute to the increase in international visitor numbers. A study by Caroline Ashley in December 2005, gives some indication of the income that has been generated by tourist spending at the cave. The study noted, for example, that the income from ticket sales is only 16% of total tourist spending at the attraction with other money being spent at the market stalls around the site. Hence, it has been projected that an increase in sales at the market will considerably increase village income. This point is indicative of the importance attached to ongoing SNV activities to identify other business opportunities at the cave market as a tool for poverty alleviation in the rural area near to the cave.

Table 5.1   Total Tourism Earnings around Buddha Cave

Total paying tourists to date, mid 2004 to December 2005 (US$)		54,300
Estimated paying tourists per year	approx	40,000
		US$
Current estimated spend per tourist		1.2
Sales of candles and incense		0.56
Entry ticket		0.20
Parking fees		0.01
Boat fees		0.00
Donation and sponsorship		0.13
Food, snacks, medicines		0.30
Total		1.20
Source: village chief data for June to December 2004, except for food/snacks which is a current estimate from December fieldwork		
Total estimated village income per year		48,000
If expenditure per tourist can be increased to potential village income per year from 40,000 tourists		80,000

Source: Information from Caroline Ashley's visit to the Buddha cave in November 2005.

With regard to advice not being taken, it is worth mentioning that sometimes the advisers have to come up with an alternate strategy or compromise to solve a particular problem. On occasion, we have to come to terms with the fact that we cannot always influence a decision and in some cases that the local way of doing things might be better or "the preferred way." This is particularly true when we are dealing with religious traditions unlike our own; it is indeed a learning process.

5.5   Indirect Effects of Advice

Initially security was the biggest concern with regard to the Buddhas remaining in the cave, particularly because many of the Buddhas are very small and could be easily hidden in a pocket or bag. At other cave sites in Lao, sadly the theft of Buddhas by or for tourists is a major problem (although it has long been illegal to export a Buddha from Lao PDR). It is the national policy for treasures of the nation to be moved to the national museum in Vientiane for security purposes. Though the advisers were not directly involved in the decision to keep the Buddhas in the Khammouane, strong lobbying by director of tourism may have carried some weight. Fortunately for Khammouane, the decision was made by the Governor to keep the Buddhas in the cave. Perhaps the location and access to the cave itself has made securing the site relatively easy. What influence the tourism director had on this decision is not known, but prior to the meeting he was strongly advised by SNV that keeping the Buddhas in situ was important for the province and could bring substantial benefits to the nearby villages and the provincial capital of Thakhek (14km away).

5.6   Conclusion

The Buddha cave is currently the most visited tourist/religious attraction in Khammouane Province with approximately 200 visitors per day (mainly Lao visitors). The number of international visitors is increasing (particularly Thai). The site has special importance to the Lao nation and is an important archaeological/religious site that needs to be well-protected. There are a variety of issues/problems yet to be solved mainly relating to the environment near the cave. The cave's rural location means that local villagers have been able to take advantage of an opportunity to increase local income. A market has developed near the cave providing an opportunity for local villagers to sell their wares; mainly foods and refreshments are being sold, but also a substantial amount of non-timber forest products are now on sale. The sellers were initially all from Thakhek, but now, two years on, it seems that all sellers are from the local village of Ban Nakarn Sarng. Villagers seemed to have almost naturally taken to this opportunity to provide services to visitors. Efforts are underway to encourage other villages nearby to also sell products in the market (such as candles, incense sticks, souvenirs, handicrafts and local weaving) through micro-finance support for small business ventures.

Villagers from Ban Nakarn Sarng take turns at working at the cave. There are a variety of jobs and quite a few villagers are present at any one time. Security guards, ticket sellers, boat owners, renters of Lao sin skirts (visitors must be modestly dressed to enter the religious site), makers and sellers of flower basket arrangements, baci ceremonies and local guides for the cave. The income from these different activities and the Buddhist donations of money are compiled daily then counted and secured in a safe in the village (it is said that five keys are necessary to open this safe!).

At present, 10% of the total income from ticket money goes to the villagers, the remainder to the Buddha cave development fund which has financed most of the infrastructure to date. Villagers have recently made a request for 20%, which has been approved by the Buddha cave sub-committee. The income from ticket sales needs to be well-managed and transparent.

There is also the potential to increase the number of international visitors to Thakhek (itself a charming but largely undiscovered French colonial-style town on the banks of the Mekong) as the cave becomes better know nationally and internationally. The attraction itself is fairly unique and, although the idea of finding new caves with such a large quantity of Buddhas in the future seems rather remote, it is not impossible.

No doubt the cave is likely to see many new developments in the future and SNV is continuing to provide input on a proposed site master plan. Hopefully, with SNV's continued presence in the province, the local authorities will further benefit from the team's advisory expertise.

Advisor perspective

The Buddha cave will surely see many more developments over the coming years.

The advisor concludes that, although being in the right place at the right time was important, tourist attractions will develop in their own way with or without outside help from development organisations.

One of the biggest lessons learned and one of our suggestions is that tourism advisors should perhaps focus on existing tourist attractions rather than developing complex CBT models that often fail once the advisory assistance has gone, particularly those that did not involve the private sector from the onset.

Looking for pro-poor tourism opportunities at existing tourist attractions can give rise to increased income fairly quickly for local communities. One important factor is that tourist numbers are generally already high and it is simply a matter of identifying new business opportunities for the villagers. In this case study, villagers quickly saw the opportunity to sell their wares and a market developed, which continues to be a major source of income to the villagers today.

We should also take note that most visitors to the Buddha cave are local people rather than foreign visitors. Even though the spending power of local people is quite low, what matters is the total amount of money spent at the attraction which, in this case, is high due to sheer numbers of visitors.

Perhaps the importance of a religious attraction should also not be overlooked in that the same people visit several times on religious days or festivals, not just once, which is often the case with other types of attractions.

Finally, without well-established and trusting relationships with stakeholders, it unlikely that advisory influence can be gained, particularly at the government level. Developing such relationships takes time and the SNV strategy of placing advisors with a main client for a period of several years is a long term strategy that gives the advisor time to develop acceptance and trust and gain influence, something that perhaps a short term consultancy cannot achieve.

References:

Ashley, C. (2005), 'Evaluation of PPST in Asia December 2005', in Acksonsay Rattanavong, *Tourism impact study in Khammouane and Luang Prabang.*

Ashley, C. (2005), *Participation by the Poor in Khamouane Province Tourism Economy: Current Earnings and Opportunities for Expansion*, ODI-SNV paper, ODI, London.

Asian Development Bank (2005), *Mekong Tourism Development Project, Lao PDR*, (online), available: www.adb.org/Documents/LAO/Mekong Tourism/default.asp (1-4-2007).

Chapter 6

Community Tourism and Broad-based Local Development: The Case of Doi Village, Thua Then Hue Province, Vietnam

6.1 Community Tourism and Broad-based Local Development

6.1.1 Community Tourism: Potentials and Pitfalls and the Need for Community-based Development

Community-based Tourism (CBT) is an approach to tourism development that puts local people at the forefront of decision making regarding how tourism is planned, developed, and managed in their communities. This approach also aims to increase income earning opportunities, and support sustainable development while contributing to the creation of high quality, authentic and diversified tourism products. While the principle objectives of a CBT initiatives are often to enhance local economic benefits supporting cultural and environmental conservation, CBT initiatives can also be effective in supporting enhanced local governance capabilities and social capital development at the community-level.

Local cultures, natural resources, and historical artefacts are not only potential resources for tourism development, they are also local resources shared by all members of a community. Developing these resources in an appropriate manner for tourism purposes requires broad engagement and collaborative decision making by community members, and consequently, provides an excellent rallying point to initiate grassroots democratic decision making processes. The Community-based Tourism approach is not only effective in supporting these necessary decisions relating directly to tourism development, but also provides a platform for supporting community-based decision making relating to more generalized community development issues. The community-based approach also helps to ensure local "ownership" and endorsement of tourism development, equitable distribution of cost and benefits from tourism development including targeting poverty reduction when present.

6.1.2 Community Tourism as a Tool for Rural Development and Poverty Reduction

When appropriately managed, community tourism can provide a range of development benefits to communities, especially in poor or disadvantaged areas. Tourism is often well suited to remote areas populated by people from poor or disadvantaged backgrounds who also share distinctive cultures and attractive natural settings. The potential benefits presented by community tourism development are many, including enhanced livelihood opportunities for unskilled or semi-skilled workers, especially women and youth who may otherwise face limited occupational opportunities. Tourism spending can help stimulate new economic growth and contribute to local economies through the high multiplier effect. The initial infrastructure requirements of tourism development can also serve to improve the physical community infrastructure (such as sanitary and hygienic water supply and latrines) often lacking in many rural communities.

6.1.3   Sustainable Tourism and Local Communities

Equitable sharing of costs and benefits is at the foundation of supporting broad-based community development through tourism. What impact the introduction of tourism will have on hosting communities is largely dependent upon the level of community participation in the planning and management of tourism in their communities. Where tourism is not managed in an equitable and participatory way, financial and power disparities will be exacerbated. Such situations typically occur when only a few families, or groups from outside the community, are the main beneficiaries while the community as a whole provides the attraction and bears much of the costs, and only a minority reaps the benefits. The exploitation scenario is more common where community tourism is developed and controlled by non-resident interests or the local elite. The scenario of vitality and sustainability is most likely to be achieved when community tourism is planned and managed with the support, participation, and approval of hosting communities, ensuring that tourism is consistent with community values and aspirations and the costs and benefits are equitably distributed. Achieving equity and guarding against a scenario of exploitative development again demands community-based management of tourism development.

Such a situation is not only in the best interest of the community, but is equally important to all other stakeholders concerned with sustainable development, including tourism businesses and local governments.

Poverty alleviation is also recognized as a significant objective of sustainable development that engenders important considerations and opportunities in the context of community tourism. Compared to alternatives options tourism can provide more accessible development opportunities for the poor. Fewer tangible assets are required to partake in tourism income earning opportunities such as guiding or cultural performances. Tourism is also well suited to provide opportunities for typically more marginalized or disadvantaged groups such as minorities, women and youth. Incorporating poverty reduction objectives and strategies into community tourism development will make significant contributions to improving the quality of life for many while supporting social inclusion and broad-based appreciation for the development process.

It must also be understood that tourism is far from a panacea for poor rural communities. Not all locations are capable of attracting tourism. Neither is tourism equally well suited to all communities (i.e. hosting travelers is part of the heritage of some ethnic minority groups, while to others it is an unfamiliar and awkward experience). At best, tourism should serve development in a supplemental fashion and target broad-based community development.

6.2   Community Tourism Development in Vietnam

6.2.1   Tourism Development, Communities, and Poverty Reduction in Vietnam

Vietnam has experienced steadily increasing tourism numbers for more than a decade (Jerome, et al. 2006). In 2006 3.5 million international and 17 million domestic tourist trips were made. Vietnam is now expecting to receive 5. 5 million to 6 million international visitors in 2010 when domestic tourism numbers expected to reach 25 million to 26 million. The boom in the tourism industry presents both challenges and opportunities for Vietnam's continued development. While the economic growth is indisputable, questions have emerged as to whether or not the benefits from tourism development are equitably distributed, and if the resources upon which tourism is dependent are being managed in a sustainable manner.

The Government's commitment and progress in pursuing the MDG (Millennium Development Goals) provide ample opportunities to integrate tourism development as a supporting strategy. Tourism has recently been allocated a stronger mandate in the new National Social Economic Development Programme. A number of other tourism initiatives at the national level further indicates the government's desire to chart a sustainable path for the tourism industry as a whole. These include the recently revised National Tourism Master Plan that includes a mandate to support sustainable development and poverty reduction, a National Tourism Action Programme that cites "ensuring sustainable growth" as a main objective, and the new Law on Tourism that strongly emphasizes sustainable development, cultural resource conservation, and support for tourism development in disadvantaged and remote regions and includes a specific article on Community Participation in Tourism. The Government has also committed itself to a policy for the "Socialization of Tourism" in order to spread tourism development benefits throughout a wider segment of the population. In 2004 a Ministerial Conference on Cultural Tourism and Poverty Alleviation was held in Hue, Vietnam. This resulted in the Hue Declaration of Cultural Tourism and Poverty Alleviation, whereby the Ministers of Tourism agreed to a range of policy approaches and actions to address poverty through tourism.

The clear government commitment, related policies and programs as well as recent events provide strong indications of commitment and opportunities to pursue sustainable tourism development that contributes to cultural conservation and local community development. While conditions are forming to achieve these objectives, further efforts are still required to continue awareness raising and sectoral coordination, coupled with creating more mechanisms for supporting local involvement in tourism development,   closer integration of tourism development planning and local social economic development, and resource conservation policies and planning. Community-based development approaches and mechanism are still very much in the developmental stages in Vietnam where most government supported development interventions still reflect a centralized and "top-down" approach.

6.2.2 Poverty Reduction, Cultural Conservation, and Other Development Challenges and Opportunities for Community Tourism

Rural poverty in Vietnam is predominantly concentrated in the North West, the Central Highlands, and some coastal regions. These areas also feature beautiful mountainous and coastal settings and are recognized as areas of high tourism development potential.   These areas are also inhabited largely by Ethnic minority groups. Vietnam is blessed with rich and diverse cultural resources that are keystones of the country's strong tourism assets. In addition to the historical and creative cultural resources are the magnificent living cultures of the 53 different Ethnic Minority groups that live within Vietnam. Ethnic minority cultures feature prominently in Vietnam's tourism products and in tourism promotional material of the country. While rich in cultural heritage and diversity the Ethnic minority groups remain amongst the poorest and most disadvantaged populations in the country. Poverty, settlement programs, and pressures to integrate into mainstream society have put many cultural societies and their traditions under severe stress. In this context, community tourism development has the potential to make significant contributions to reducing poverty and enhancing livelihoods for some of the country's most disadvantaged groups, while proactively securing and conserving rare and unique local cultures.

6.2.3   Introduction to the Roles of SNV

SNV is a Netherlands-based, international development organization that provides advisory services to organizations in developing countries to support their fight against poverty. SNV works worldwide with 1.300 organizations in 27 countries in Africa, Asia, Eastern Europe, and Latin America. In Asia, SNV is active in Nepal, Bhutan, Lao PDR, Cambodia, and Vietnam. SVN has been supporting sustainable tourism development since the early 1990s, and in Viet Nam since 2001. In 2004 the Pro-poor Sustainable Tourism (PPST) programme was formed to meet the expanding interests in this sector. The main mission of the PPST is to fully utilize tourism as a development tool in supporting the Government of Viet Nam in achieving the Viet Nam and Millennium Development Goals. SNV achieves these objectives through providing technical assistance and capacity building support to local agencies and organizations such as government departments, tourism business associations and tourism training institutions and through the support of other development partners that include the UN-WTO, ADB and other UN agencies.

6.3   Community Tourism and Broad-based Local Development

6.3.1   The Case of Doi village

Doi village, is located in Thuong Lo commune in Nam Dong District of Thua Thien Hue Province, approximately 60km from Hue City. Doi village is nestled in a scenic mountain valley and adjacent to Bach Ma National Park. The residents of Doi village are of the Katu Ethnic Minority group, originally the masters of the upper source of the Huong River who practiced shifting cultivation in primary forest. Today, the total population of approximately 37,000 Katu people have largely been "settled" into permanent hamlets and have struggled to adapt to livelihoods based on sedentary, subsistence farming. These drastic changes in livelihoods have had devastating effects on the Katu's traditional culture.

Thuong Lo commune is made up of four hamlets consisting of 101 households wherein 506 people live and is considered to be amongst the 10% of the poorest communes in Vietnam. Doi village is one hamlet of Thuong Lo commune comprised of 26 recently resettled households located in a shallow valley. The inhabitants of Doi village are primarily young families whose traditional family lands are no longer sufficient to support another generation of families so they required resettlement in a previously uninhabited area. The quality of the agricultural land here is very poor and all families need to supplement agricultural incomes through the extraction of forest resources. Families in Doi village are amongst the most disadvantaged in the commune, and in this sense can be considered as "the poorest of the poor".

6.3.2 The Doi village Community-based Tourism Initiative

In July 2003, SNV and the Tourism Department of Thua Thien Hue Province entered into a partnership to support Community-based Tourism (CBT) development in Thua Thien Hue. The goal of the project is to utilize CBT development to address poverty reduction, sustainable livelihood enhancement, and other rural development objectives. After an extensive assessment process SNV and the Tourism Department with the agreement of the community of Thuong Lo commune/Doi village launched the Doi village Community-based Tourism Initiative in February 2004. The project was designed to support key locally identified development objectives including expanding local economic opportunities, revitalizing threatened cultures, increasing awareness of sustainability issues, improving local governance, and providing a genuine and high quality experience for visitors.

6.3.3 Project Activities

Activities carried out over the first 18 months of the project represent both planned activities as well as important activities that were identified through the community-based development process. A synthesis of project activities is documented below in chronological sequence except where otherwise mentioned.

6.3.3.1 Awareness Raising

As the hamlet had no previous experience with tourism is was necessary to raise awareness within the community of the potentials of tourism development: including potential positive and negative impacts, a comprehensive understanding of what is involved in hosting tourism, and what realistic expectations to expect from tourism development. Providing this level of awareness was a fundamental necessity to ensure informed decisions that would be required for participating community members throughout the development process. Awareness raising activities included community-level seminars and discussion sessions and study tours with other communities involved in tourism. The exchange visits for community participants to other community tourism projects was effective in providing important "first-hand" learning experiences that included insights gained through the experiences of other communities and included topics such as tourism impacts and local management issues that later proved invaluable. These exchange visits were also effective in creating motivation and creating momentum for the project since participants recognized that if other communities could effectively engage in hosting tourism, then so could they.

6.3.3.2 Community-based Planning

An APPA (Appreciative Participative Planning and Action) approach was taken to build upon the community's current strengths and assets in identifying community tourism development potential and interests as well as to develop action plans to bring these potentials into reality through an informed decision making process. Participating community members were made responsible for deciding what forms of tourism development would be pursued, the level that tourism activities would infiltrate community life, how many and how often tourists would visit their village, how tourism activities would be managed, and how tourism's costs and benefits were to be distributed. Through the "discovery" phase of the APPA process it became apparent that there was still a great interest and enthusiasm for the Katu culture amongst the young families participating. Accordingly, cultural tourism was identified as a preferential strategy for achieving local development objectives. The APPA process also identified guided tours to a nearby waterfall, and providing food to visitors as preferential activities with good tourism development potential.

6.3.3.3 Community Organization

Community organization was conducted through extensive local discussions that led to the establishment of three Tourism Service Teams; one for Cultural Performances, one for Waterfall Guiding and Management, and one for Food Services. Participating community members selected what teams they preferred to join. It was also agreed that the formation of a Community Tourism Management Board would assist in coordinating and integrating local tourism activities within the community. It was decided that the initial Community Tourism Management Board should consist of the Village Head, one representative from each of the Tourism Service teams, and an accountant. It was also agreed that the Community Tourism Management Board would meet on a regular basis whenever issues affecting the larger community and other important decision needed to be made. It was recognized that while the formation of this Board was required for the initiation of the project, after one year of activity and experience an election involving the wider community would be held to elect a Board through a democratic process.

6.3.3.4   Equitable Sharing of Benefits

Participating community members were also responsible for determining how the benefits from tourism activities would be distributed. This was a more complex and challenging decision. The project provided the advice that in order to ensure that tourism was managed equitably and sustainably at the village level households not directly participating in tourism activities should still be entitled to some of the benefits from tourism development as they also were members of the community, and owners of the cultural resources that would be attracting tourists. Initially some members of the Management Board were requesting a larger allocation from the tourism revenues for board membership and administration activities. After some thoughtful discussions and deliberations it was decided that the Management Board would reduce the amount they would receive and that a greater proportion of tourism revenues would be allocated to the Community Development Fund specifically to capture some of the tourism revenues to be allocated for initiatives that would benefit the wider community.

6.3.3.5   Entry Point Activities

As mentioned previously, through the "discovery" phase of the APPA process it became apparent that there was still a great interest and enthusiasm for the Katu culture amongst the young families participating; they all still spoke Katu, some could even remember songs, however none of them still had their traditional clothes, nor musical instruments needed to engage in cultural activities – in their own words, they were "too poor" to practice their cultural heritage. Small investments were made to jump-start the product development phase, and demonstrate commitment to, and results from, the project in order to further galvanize community involvement. One of these small investments included providing the Cultural Performance Team with the materials required to create traditional costumes and musical instruments that they previously could not afford. This activity was effective in enhancing participants' belief in the project objectives and was absolutely necessary for the Cultural Performance Team to get started.

6.3.3.6   Training

Together with awareness raising, training and skills development were a very important cross-cutting component of most project activities throughout the project development and implementation process, and was provided for by a number of different sources. Training of the Cultural Performance Team on traditional dances and songs was provided on a volunteer basis by village elders. Training for responsible environmental management was provided by staff from the adjacent Bac Ma National Park. Training for safe food preparation, hosting skills, and basic accounting skills was provided through Hue Tourism College that had become very interested in supporting the project.

It was clear that to maximize local participation in tourism some specific training would be needed. Most of the community participants had only finished some lower levels of formal education, they were also very busy with their daily lives and although extremely enthusiastic, they could not realistically participate in any formal tourism training program. Special training needed to be developed and tailored to meet local requirements and capacities. It was pragmatic training; a focus on vocational skills training that would provide local participants with the specific skills needed to participate in tourism. It was also recognized that a significant portion of the training needed to take place in the community as most participants could not afford the time or money to study outside of the community.

Development of the training programs considered all these issues, as well as how to maximize the knowledge, skills and resource already available in the community. Existing training curricula were adapted to focus on the primary skills and concepts needed and more formal classroom education techniques were replaced with more opportunities for discussion and group learning activities.

It was also seen as necessary to transfer the lessons learnt in the classroom setting to the village setting where they would actually be put into practice by the participants.

With great innovation, the Hue Tourism College came up with a unique and specialized training program for village participants that included:

- Basic understanding of tourism concepts:

- The importance of sustainable tourism development and the important roles for local people to participate and benefit from tourism development,

- Visitor reception and hosting skills,

- Hygienic food preparation and presentation,

- Basic small business skills.

The training also took on a Training the Trainers approach, where training participants would also be coached to become trainers themselves to pass their learning experiences on to other community members interested in participating in tourism at later dates.

6.3.3.7   Construction of the Community House

One unanticipated request that came forward from the community was for the construction of a traditional community house. While the initial project budget did not account for such an expense, it was seen as an important initiative that deserved to be pursued. The Community House came to fruition through the combined efforts of the District Authority's contribution of timber, some financial support from SNV (approximately 30% of total costs) and most of all, from the community themselves. Each household collected two cubic meters of locally available thatch for the roof of the house, members of the Fatherland Front provided the labor for the foundation and floor, the Youth Union provided labor for the construction of the walls and roof. Through this process the community assumed rightful ownership and great pride in this community resource that would not only facilitate hosting tourists but also would become an important focal point for the community's cultural revitalization and enhanced local governance and pride.

6.3.3.8   Product Testing and Refinement

Several months of attention was directed to product testing activities that included numerous practice sessions of the Cultural Performance Team, cleaning and organizing management for waterfall area, hosting representatives from local tour operators on FAM trip visits, and even some "voluntourists" to test the developing tourism products and identify areas where the tourism products could be further improved and refined.

6.3.3.9   Partnership Building

Partnership building was pursued throughout the project development and implementation process. Effective partnerships were instrumental in the project's quick development on a very modest budget. Specific partner contributions include:

- Nam Dong District People's Committee: Subsidized timber for the Community House and administrative support for the project.

- Hue Tourism College: Provision of subsidized training of local participants.

- Bac Ma National Park: Provided training on responsible environmental management.

- Dong Kinh Tourism Company: Provided the right tourist experience.

Six months after the project commenced Doi village was ready to host their first group of tourists. The project had developed relations with Dong Kinh Tourism Company, a Japanese joint venture tour operator that was featuring one week cultural tours to Hue. In addition to the historic cultures of Hue City the tour company wanted to offer an authentic experience with ethnic minority culture in a one-day outing. As a socially responsible business, Dong Kinh was interested in making donations to the community as an expression of appreciation for the experience provided by the villagers. After community consultations it was decided that these donations should be distributed amongst the poorest households in the commune and should comprise clothing, supplemental food, and school supplies for the children.

6.3.3.10   Democratic Elections

After the first year of tourism activities a community election was held to reformulate the Community Tourism Management Board. These elections were very well attended (98 of 110 households participated) with a significant percentage of women actively involved. The elections were preceded by a statement prepared by the Management Board detailing the activities and results of the first year of the initiative and outlining the intended actions and results for the forthcoming year. Households had been provided with a set of suggested criteria for making their nominations of candidates, of which there was a total of 9 for the five positions available. In response to seven candidates receiving a larger proportion of votes, the community decided that the size of the Management Board be increased to 7 positions. The results of the election were 5 new individuals attaining membership of the Board with two remaining from the original Board. An initial shortcoming of this result was the loss of 3 original Board members who had gained and contributed significantly in the project. This occurrence was examined in post elections discussions and it was decided that these past members would play important advisory roles to the Board, and that another Board election would take place in one year's time. Although these results of the election did not meet with the initial expectations of the project team it was important that the community as a whole participated in the elections activities in an open and transparent process.

6.3.4   Results to Date

The Doi Village Community-based Tourism initiative has proven effective in applying a community-based planning approach to tourism development that has achieved broad-based community development benefits. While the project featured the creation of new jobs and income earning opportunities for some of the poorest people in the district, and at the same time an important opportunity to salvage and restore cultural traditions of song, dance and handicrafts that were eroding as a result of the pressures of poverty, a range of equally important development results were also achieved.

6.3.4.1   Cultural Revitalization

This project contributed significantly to cultural revitalization in this ethnic minority community where traditional cultural activities had been abandoned for many years. Village elders note that traditional dance and music performances have returned to the community for the first time in approximately 10 years. Many community members attend the cultural performances, often in traditional dress. Two children's cultural performance teams have been created solely on the community's own initiative. Other cultural activity in the village has increased including weaving and musical instrument making. Cultural activities have been re-established with different generations involved, and are practiced for both tourism and non-tourism purposes.

6.3.4.2   Poverty Reduction and Diversified Income Earning Opportunities

Through project activities 58 in a village of 110 HH (including women and youth) have new sources of non-farm incomes directly linked to tourism. While these are not fulltime, nor fully sufficient, wage earning activities, they do provide very valuable supplemental income sources very important for people living below or near the poverty line.

6.3.4.3   Increased Market for Local Products

Local economic earning opportunities have been diversified directly through tourism purchases and through the provision of inputs for hosting tourists, including value added sales of honey and handicrafts. The multiplier effect of tourism generated revenue is further stimulating local economies.

6.3.4.4   Gender Equity

Gender equity in the community has been strengthened as a majority of those receiving incomes from tourism activities are women, as well as key positions on the Community Tourism Management Board being held by women.

6.3.4.5   Reduced Vulnerability

Contributions and savings in the Community Development Fund were allocated to help rebuild several houses belonging to poorer families that were damaged as the result of a small typhoon that struck the area.

6.3.4.6   Benefit Sharing of Voluntary Donations

In addition to the Community Development Fund, tourist donations of books, food, and clothes have been distributed to the poorest households not participating directly in tourism activities. These non-monetary benefits are regularly mentioned with appreciation by the local community.

6.3.4.7   Enhanced Local Governance Capacity

Traditional systems of local governance are merging with new structures designed to promote an equitable distribution of tourism benefits, and more open and inclusive decision making processes. The establishment of a locally elected Community Tourism Management Board has helped to support equitable, community-based tourism planning and provided an opportunity and platform to engage in other local governance activity. Processes of consensus-based decision making is now established and community meetings are now held in the new Community Cultural house – a more neutral and democratic setting.

6.3.4.8   Enhanced Local Governance, Social Capital and Community Pride

Participating community members are now responsible and confident in making decisions regarding tourism development. This confidence and experiences has facilitated a more pronounced role and participation of community members in other issues relating to community life that require decisions to be made.   Familiarity with, and endorsement of, consensus-based decision making is now becoming the norm. The community organization activities have facilitated broader and more direct participation in community development discussions that have further contributed in strengthening the sense of pride and self determination in the community.

Community-based tourism development has also led to the revitalization of local cultural traditions and performances that in turn has resulted in a greatly strengthened sense of community pride, and a strong enthusiasm for sharing their culture with visitors has developed. The community has started hosting neighboring communities for special cultural occasions in addition to tourist visits. The Community Cultural House now provides a neutral and democratic setting for holding community meetings. It is seen as an asset that is collectively owned by the community to which all have equitable access. Pride and confidence resulting from the success of the tourism project have provided community members with greater social capital as they are now more confident in making decisions that affect their community.

6.3.5   Applicability to Other Communities in Asia and the Pacific

Generalizations:

- Different factors and actors in each context. Contexts naturally vary; each will be unique and require special attention.

- Differing levels of development and maturity of the "enabling environment"

- Availability of resources, capacities and partnership opportunities

- Community-level work requires significant investment of time. Local participation and external support.

- Mutual learning needs to be incorporated in the development approach and methods.

Specific Recommendations:

- Focus attention on working with, and building upon, community strengths as a means of addressing development challenges.

- Adaptations of general models and approaches to the realities of each project context will be necessary

- Stakeholders engagement and cooperation is essential. The cross-cutting, multi dimensional nature of tourism requires that development not take place in isolation, but through effective partnerships. Examples could include: 1) Local authorities in creating regulatory context and support through linking other relevant development initiatives and creating a supportive enabling environmental; 2) Tourism businesses, particularly in product development and promotion, but also training and even small scale investments; 3) Development partners that could included local and international development agencies, donors, and public sector development programs; and 4) Human resources development: specific trainings necessary for involvement to tourism to skills required for making complex decisions that not only involve tourism management but also community development implications.

- Effective community engagement is absolutely essential in creating, and benefiting from, enthusiastic local participation and local ownership of the project process and results. This in turn contributes to: 1) Enhanced responsibility, commitment to the process; 2) Broader integration of tourism benefits into the wider community; and 3) Higher quality, more authentic tourism products and experiences.

6.4 Conclusion

The Katu people of Vietnam were once feared as powerful warriors and jungle hunters who have recently settled into farming lifestyles that present poverty-level living conditions with limited income earning options, weakened social structures, and threatened culture. Yet through community-based tourism, one village at least has been developed enhanced income earning opportunities for more than have is population, strengthened local governance and social capital, and revived their rich cultural heritage. The Doi Village Community-based Tourism Initiative has helped to create new jobs and income earning opportunities for some of the poorest people in Vietnam, and at the same time provide opportunities for them to practice once again important cultural traditions of song, dance and handicrafts that were eroding as a result of the pressures of poverty. The result of this community-based development approach is an authentic and high quality tourism experience that is provided through the community with pride and enthusiasm.

Today, Doi village provides a rare opportunity to experience and participate in traditional cultural activities such as singing and dancing, appreciate the fine weaving and local cuisine, and even spend the night in a traditional Katu community house.

References:

Agrusa, J., J. Tanner, and J. Dupuis (1999), 'Determining the potential of American Vietnam veterans returning to Vietnam as tourists', *International Journal of Tourism Research*, 8(3), pp. 223-234.

Chapter 7 —————————————————————————

Success of Chuncheon Puppet Festival in Korea and Local Community's Active Participation in Chuncheon City, Korea

7.1 Introduction: An Overview of the Problem at the National Level

Community participation has become an umbrella term for a supposedly new genre of tourism development process. Not surprisingly, to propose a development strategy that is not participatory is nearly reactionary. Major aspects of development intervention, research, planning, implementation and control, have been reoriented in order to make them more participatory (Tosun, 2000). Community participation is to design 'development in such a way that intended beneficiaries are encouraged to take matters into their own hands, to participate in their own development through mobilizing their own resources, defining their own needs, and making their own decisions about how to meet them' (Stone, 1989). This implies that community participation as a development strategy is based on community resources, needs and decisions. Hence, community is the main actor in the development process. On the other hand, the concept of community participation is seen as a powerful tool to educate the community in rights, laws and political good sense (Low, 1991).

In the 21st century, major tourism leaders in the world have recognized the importance of the high value-added culture industry. They are making efforts to change the traditional cultures of the local areas tourism resources and to develop the related areas into a strategic industry. With the advent of a full-scale local autonomy, provinces and metropolitan cities in Korea have recently promoted various cultural tourism events that were traditionally run by the Korean Central Government. Citizens are becoming more aware that the development of the local cultures and the local tourist industries lead directly to the nation's overall development of culture and tourism (Formica & Uysal, 1996). Unfortunately, even though those world-class cultural tourism events held in Korea did become global festivals with their ideology – thus enabling countries to exchange culture and various cultures and get together – the reality is that not as many foreign tourists participated in the events as was expected (Byun, 2001). This is contrary to the country's aims to promote global tourism through cultural festivals (Mihalic, 2000; the Ministry of Culture and Tourism, 2004).

After a period of electing local authorities directly, many cultural tourism events in Korea were developed and many of them became success cases, thus bringing about various positive effects in such areas as the local economies, social and cultural development and the environment. However, many provinces are competing with each other far too aggressively and are ignoring the pure functions of those festivals; this generates conflicts between the local areas and residents. Furthermore, because many of them have similar themes and copy each other so intently, there are growing dysfunctional problems, such as overlapping investments and wastage of the country's funding by producing many repetitive, rather than unique, local culture events. This makes it clear that there is a need to reconstruct our cultural tourism industry.

The local festival is the most typical local cultural event in Korea. But more than 70% of these festivals do not have specific aims and motivations. Most of them have been held from the mid-1990s when the local autonomous system was launched in the country. The most important of several problems for the local cultural events are the quality issues of timing, venue and the uniqueness of the programs.

The timing depends on the convenience of the local authorities: more than 70% of the festivals are held in September and October (The Ministry of Culture and Tourism, 2005). They are generally driven by government agencies and have simply replaced the old government-run events. Of the venues, more than 90% are playgrounds, parks, riverside highlands and civic halls, which do not respect the uniqueness and characteristics of each local festival (The Ministry of Culture and Tourism, 2004). More than 85% of them have a public agency as their main stakeholders (The Ministry of Culture and Tourism, 2004). As a result, most festivals are scheduled in the autumn season at sports complexes mainly for the convenience of the public sector agencies. Each local festival includes many different kinds of typical national folklore events that do not necessarily represent the local uniqueness. Therefore, the motivations for the local cultural events are heavily conventional and homogenous: they are usually succession of local culture, traditional folklore representation or people harmony. The events should really be held in a sacred venue, with a separation from the routine life to attract people through their curiosity, sacredness and unique local motivation. The local festivals can be competitive and attractive when their original meaning is preserved within its own authentic culture. Most of the events in Korea are provided for its own convenience, the timing is concentrated in the peak-season, staff are not professionals and with frequent changes, and particularly the route for the participation of local community residents is blocked by the over-control of the public sector agencies.

7.2 The background of the Main Case: Tourism Development Process and the Basic Profile of the Chuncheon Puppet Festival in South Korea

The Chuncheon City in Korea had faced financial difficulties in managing the Children's Hall in 1989. The City had entrusted the management of the Hall to one of the local entrepreneurs – the Barunson Co. The private company had developed various cultural art programs to operate the Hall efficiently with the local community residents. Several local academics and puppet industry professionals had proposed to the company and local community leaders the hosting of a puppet festival. The offer was accepted, an executive committee was composed, and the initial planning was set up and implemented in 1989.

The Chuncheon Puppet Festival is an international puppet festival event that has been held every year in Chuncheon, Korea since 1989. It started as a local cultural event and has been steadily developing as an international cultural art festival. There are several distinctive characteristics about the festival. First, rather than being managed by government agencies of the city of Chuncheon, it is planned, operated, managed and financed by the local residents of the city and a local entrepreneur. This involvement has been maintained and encouraged with several hundred volunteers from the local high schools and colleges every year being involved in the festival. Second, it has maintained the single genre of a cultural art festival with puppet performances that are based on modern cultural art. It is different from other local general festivals that lack such unique figures. Third, it has helped children to undergo an interesting cultural experience in the local environment, and has been aimed at developing a puppet show that is different from other festivals that focus mainly on merely commercial profits. The festival is planned to remain as a cultural event especially for children in respecting its motto 'Dream for children, love for all'. Fourth, the main stakeholders of the Festival have not been changed ever since it was launched in 1989. Thus, the basic characteristics of the Festival have been maintained. This is different from many other festivals in the country that have been discontinued due to serious discords and conflicts between main driving forces of festivals. Fifth, it is regularly hosted every August, which is an off-season for festivals in Korea. This was decided by the local community residents and has been highly successful because it is a school holiday season in the country. Finally, it has been a model of a successful local festival and has demonstrated that a centre for culture of the country could move to decentralized areas that had previously been concentrated in the capital city area of Seoul (Lee, 2007). Figure 7.1 is one of the posters of the annual Festival and Figure 7.2 shows a picture when children meet with one of characters of the puppet shows during the performance.

Figure 7.1   A Poster of the Chuncheon Puppet Festival

Figure 7.2   Children Meet with One of Puppet Show Characters

In 1989, the Chuncheon Puppet Festival had less than 100 participants from 14 local performance groups at only one venue (the Childrens' Hall). These numbers had increased by 2006 to more than 1,000 professional participants from seven overseas theatre companies, 40 local performance groups and 31 amateur theatre groups at more than 10 venues all round the Chuncheon City. The city with a population of 200,000 has more than 100,000 visitors during the festival. Table 7.1 shows how the festival has grown from 1989 to present day,

Table 7.1   Development of the Chuncheon Puppet Festival

Year	Number of performing companies	Number of performed shows	Length of festival in days	Total number of attendees
1989	15	40	4	7,500
1990	23	63	5	10,000
1991	33	64	5	16,500
1992	39	64	5	16,500
1993	43	68	5	23,500
1994	51	68	5	23,107
1995	53	71	5	44,523
1996	60	110	5	56,867
1997	61	117	5	55,600
1998	67	121	5	54,265
1999	65	148	5	54,942
2000	67	149	6	80,973
2001	64	235	7	91,528
2002	65	172	8	107,743
2003	79	240	10	124,000
2004	72	226	10	130,500
2005	76	200	7	101,413

There are many background conditions that have made the Chuncheon Puppet Festival successful over the years. These have been, (i) steady financial support from a local entrepreneur (Barunson Inc.) from the first year of its planning and operation, (ii) diverse types of local community organizers and professional groups in puppet performances designing and managing the festival, (iii) active participation and support from local community volunteers in Chuncheon area, (iv) strong promotion of the event in the consumer market from different types of local mass media, and (v) constant interests and practical support for the event from the local public sectors of Chuncheon City.

7.3   Issues in the Case

Mann (2000: 25) suggested ten principles for community-related tourism.

- Community tourism should involve local people. That means they should participate in decision-making and ownership, not just be paid a fee.

- The local community should receive a fair share of the profits from any tourism venture.

- Tour operators should try to work with communities rather than individuals. Working with individuals can create divisions within a community. Where communities have representative organisations these should be consulted and their decisions respected.

- Tourism should be environmentally sustainable.   Local people must benefit and be consulted if conservation projects are to work. Tourism should not put extra pressure on scarce resources.

- Tourism should support traditional cultures by showing respect for indigenous knowledge. Tourism can encourage people to value their own cultural heritage.

- Operators should work with local people to minimise the harmful impact of tourism.

- Where appropriate, tour operators should keep groups small to minimise their cultural and environmental impact.

- Tour operators or guides should brief tourists on what to expect and on appropriate behaviour before they arrive in a community. That should include how to dress, taking photos, respecting privacy.

- Local people should be allowed to participate in tourism with dignity and self-respect. They should not be coerced into performing inappropriate ceremonies for tourists, etc.

- People have the right to say no to tourism. Communities who reject tourism should be left alone."

Mitchell and Reid (2001) have proposed a framework for community integration in tourism planning and management. The theory is that a tourism integration process for a given community should be linked to three critical parameters: (1) community awareness, (2) community unity, and (3) power or control of relationships, both local and external. Awareness, unity, and power for a certain tourism sector comprise an integration triangle and form a necessary part of the community's rise to self-reliance and local control. These variables are principally endogenous (factors internal to the community), but they will also be influenced by the exogenous environment (factors outside the community).

Chuncheon is located in the most populous area in Korea by the upper stream of the Han river; this has kept it from being industrialised by large-scale factories. Therefore, the Chuncheon residents have suffered and felt discriminated against because their region has been isolated and has not been developed for centuries. But now, they have a strong pride as residents of Korea's proto-typical cultural city, mainly because of the Chuncheon Puppet Festival.

This was confirmed by a nationwide survey by the Korean Government in 2002. When the residents were asked what should be the best strategic direction for Chuncheon City in the future, 34.7% answered, a culture/art-oriented city, in comparison with a sophisticated industry-focused city (17.8%), and a tourism-focused city (15.7%). This example of strong local pride and cultural consciousness was derived from the series of cultural events initiated by the Chuncheon Puppet Festival. There are four international performing cultural festivals in Chuncheon that have been hosted annually, the Mime Festival, the Animation Festival, the Chuncheon International Theatrical Festival and the Puppet Festival. Educational institutes have been opened in recent years, including the Puppet Theme Park, the Puppet Play sample market, and the Puppet academy. Several different sizes of public performance halls have been opened; Chuncheon now has the highest level in the country of the ratio of population-to-seats in the performing theatres. The Ministry of Culture and Tourism in Korea designated Chuncheon as an official city of culture in 1995 on the basis of the successful achievements of the Chuncheon Puppet Festival.

Chuncheon residents have escaped from the defeatism of the past of being an isolated region lacking local development. There are 'new' residents in the city who initially came to Chuncheon as a professionals or students in different types of cultural events in the city. Many of them work as operating staff in related events, with ordinary citizens serving as voluntary staff – with the highest voluntary rate in the Korea. Chuncheon should be an example of successful community participation with a high rate of volunteering that helps increase local competitiveness and local innovation.

There have been diverse socio-cultural effects of the Chuncheon Puppet Festival. These include the following: it (i) improves the local image of Chuncheon City; (ii) enhances the local affection of the local residents; (iii) promotes the local cultural art; (iv) improves the quality of life through the local residents' participation in high-profile cultural event activities; (v) protects and strengthens the local cultural resources; and (vi) promotes cultural exchange between regions and countries. By hosting a cultural art festival, the festival not only facilitates cultural exchange but also assists the event to keep developing and evolving, thereby investing in its own longevity. Many cultural art stakeholders from other regions have participated in the Chuncheon Puppet Festival, consequently contributing to the spread of the puppet show and human resource exchange. As a result, professional puppet show personnel have been trained and educated in the local Chuncheon area by one who works in the Festival as an executive member.

The Chuncheon Puppet Festival in Korea is regarded as a Mecca for puppetry. It is one of the most renowned puppet performance festivals in the world. Its facilities, such as the Chuncheon Puppet Theater (opened in 2001) and the Chuncheon Puppet Museum (established in 2004), are considered state-of-the-art pioneers in showcasing various events as well as puppet shows. The Chuncheon Puppet Theater is the largest puppet theater in the country with a main performance hall (497 seats), open air performance hall (200 seats), and tent performance stages. Figure 7.3 shows the Theater during the Festival in 2006.

Figure 7.3   The Chuncheon Puppet Theater during the Festival in 2006

The festival also has hosted the Puppet Theater Market since 1999 which efficiently connects supply (performing companies) and demand (groups who want performance) in the puppet-performing industry. With its meticulously-prepared parade at the opening ceremony, the Chuncheon Puppet Festival has offered aficionados a great opportunity to appreciate a variety of unique presentations, such as the invited performances, the general participation, the free participations and street performances.

The Chuncheon Puppet Festival has been recognized as a successful local event in Korea. However, there are still several tasks required to improve the Festival as a purely local community' festival, (i) there should be more exchange of human resources among the festival executive members, community associations, and the Chuncheon Civic Government; (ii) the local Chuncheon residents must have full control of the festival; and (iii) the network for the local cultural trust should be established by cultural art professionals, the local residents' organizations, the puppet show professionals and the public agency staff.

There are the necessary conditions to achieve these tasks. First, complete financial security and independence is required. The budget for the cultural sectors needs expanding to help Chuncheon maintain its reputation as 'The Cultural City'. Profit-creating programs need to be designed and the puppet show operating fund should be secured throughout the whole year. All kinds of souvenirs should be made and commercialized, celebrity puppets should be manufactured and sold, royalty income from character-making cannot not be ignored, and the diverse distribution of tickets needs to be developed. Secondly, the cultural infrastructure should be improved. The efficient linkage with other fields should be fully developed. The adjacent tourist sites, cultural relics, restaurants, accommodations, entertainment facilities, accessible roads and joint-marketing need to be developed for the mutual benefit of all concerned for the success of the puppet festival.

7.4 Conclusion

Murphy (1985: 151) argues that "community involvement in tourism planning and development can result in a shared vision and that by focusing on the community's heritage and culture in the development of the tourism product, destination distinctiveness can be created". Simpson (2001) agrees that residents who concur with tourism goals set for their region will be equally happy with the outcomes that ensue, which in turn helps to achieve sustainable tourism and sense of place (cited in Fallon and Kriwoken, 2003: 292). As for socio-cultural measures, perceptions and attitudes towards the local tourism industry and perceived community or individual participation should be enhanced with community integration. Attitudinal responses of local residents, industry players, and tourists alike for a given destination area can be assessed over time (Mitchell and Reid, 2001: 119).

Kirschenblatt-Gimblett (1998: 73) state that "Cultural festivals and community fairs add vitality and enhance the tourist appeal of a destination. Cultural festivals and events can become the quintessence of a region and its people". Carlson (1996) provides an interesting analysis of the significance of performance in cultural events. He argues that performance implies not just doing things, but self-consciousness about doing and re-doing, on the part of both performers and spectators. He continues saying that performers and audience alike accept that a primary function of this performing activity is strongly cultural, the exploration of self and other, of the world as experienced, and of alternative possibilities.

Local cultural events can be attractive tourism resources when there is a strong harmony among the visitors, the event organisers, the tangible products and the local community (residents) that gain from the socio-cultural effects. The tangible products are composed of festivals, event programs, entire event packages and tangible merchandise that are available during the events. The local uniqueness needs to be secured to have cultural art events successfully developed as a tourist attraction. There also should be a logical and scrupulous preparation in the design, implementation, operation, and support systems. Unfortunately, the financial support for the local events from the central and provincial governments has previously been applied over too many small events across Korea, and with only a limited budget.

In conclusion, there are requirements for the local cultural events to be steadily improved for the economic, social and cultural effects in the local areas. First, the local community and private sectors should be the leading stakeholders in the local events with the public agencies needing only to focus on a supporting role. In the first place, the local festivals should be designed, celebrated and enjoyed by the local residents. The tourists tend to visit these local events when the local community residents participate and enjoy them first. Secondly, there should be financial independence. Various profit-creating businesses closely linked to the event need to be developed. The local entrepreneurs prefer to invest their funds in the local events in which the local residents have an interest and enjoy. Thirdly, the regular cultural events in the local areas need to be provided for throughout the year. The all-year-long performance hall could be one of the ideal infrastructures in this. Fourthly, the back-up facilities and products for tourism development should be secured by including restaurants, historical cultural relics, accommodation, entertainment facilities and so forth.

The general problems for the event industry regarding community involvement in Korea are: (i) the lack of a professional education institute for the event industry; (ii) unclear motivations and themes for the events; and (iii) the lack of responsibility by the main stakeholders. Notwithstanding these negative issues, the local cultural events have a great potential for contributing to the local economy and the socio-cultural benefits of all if they are operated with local residents' interests and participation, as can be seen in the Chuncheon case.

References:

Andereck, K. L. and Vogt, C. A. (2000), 'The relationship between residents' attitudes toward tourism and tourism development options', *Journal of Travel Research*, 39(1), pp. 27–36.

Byun, W. H. (2001), 'Evaluation and comparative analysis of tourism impact of Gyeongju Culture Expo', *Tourism and Leisure Research*, 13(1), pp. 23–41.

Carlson, M. (1996), *Performance: A Critical Introduction*, Routledge, London.

Fallon, L. D. and Kriwoken, L. K. (2003), 'Community involvement in tourism infrastructure: the case of the Strahan visitor centre, Tasmania', *Tourism Management*, 24(3), pp. 289–308.

Formica, S., and M. Uysal (1996), 'A Market Segmentation of Festival Visitors: Umbria Jazz Festival in Italy', *Festival Management and Event Tourism*, 3 (1), pp.175-82.

Kirschenblatt-Gimblett, B. (1998), *Destination Culture: Tourism, Museums and Heritage*, University of California Press, Berkeley.

Lee, S. H. (2007), *Annual Report of Chuncheon Puppet Festival in 2007*, Chuncheon Puppet Festival Foundation, Chuncheon.

Low, N. (1991), Planning, Politics and the State: Political Foundations of Planning Thoughts, Unwin Hyman, London.

Mann, M. (2000), *The Community Tourism Guide*, Earthscan, Kent.

Mihalic, T. (2000), 'Environmental management of a tourist destination: a factor of tourism competitiveness', *Tourism Management*, 21(1), pp. 65–78.

Mitchell, R. E. and Reid, D. G. (2001), 'Community integration: island tourism in Peru', *Annals of Tourism Research*, 28(1), pp. 113–139.

Murphy, P. (1985), *Tourism: A Community Approach*, Methuen, London.

Simpson, K. (2001), 'Strategic planning and community involvement as contributors to sustainable tourism development', *Current Issues in Tourism*, 4(1), pp. 3–41.

Stone, L. (1989), 'Cultural cross-roads of community participation in development: A case from Nepal', *Human Organization*, 48(3), pp. 206–213.

The Ministry of Culture and Tourism in Korea (2004), *Local Festivals in Korea*, The Ministry of Culture and Tourism, Seoul.

The Ministry of Culture and Tourism in Korea (2005), *Annual Report on Tourism Trends in Korea*, The Ministry of Culture and Tourism, Seoul.

Tosun, C. (2000), 'Limits to community participation in the tourism development process in developing countries', *Tourism Management*, 21(6), pp. 613–633.

Design for Intervention

Chapter 8

The Stakeholders' Collaboration towards Community-based Tourism: The Case of GTNP, Mongolia

8.1 Background

Community-based tourism (CBT) seeks to increase local people's involvement and stewardship of tourism at the destination. One of the key issues of CBT is to designate the local stakeholders, especially local community involvement, within the network of community-based tourism planning, to establish an integrated process to ensure key stakeholder interest. Indeed, bringing various stakeholders and interests together is quite complicated, especially in the case of developing countries. This paper explores the above-mentioned issues, particularly to reveal the stakeholders' interests to collaborate in order to establish CBT. This case study is of Gorhi-Terelj National Park (GTNP), one of the first tourism destinations of Mongolia, located a mere 60-80 km to the northeast of the capital, Ulan Bator.

As a land-locked country between giant neighbors Russia and China, Mongolia was isolated from most of the world for nearly 70 years until 1990, when democratic forces brought an end to the centralized political system. After the breakdown of the former planned economy, the Mongolian authorities began implementing wide ranging programs of monetary, fiscal and structural reforms designed to reduce the role of the public sector and to promote rapid development of the private sector.

The process of creating a market economy in former socialist countries has proved to be complex. The social costs of transition have been higher than anticipated and in Mongolia in many ways absorbed by traditional livelihoods. The people dependant on nomadic pastoralism doubled or tripled over the first ten years of transition. Facing an enormous amount of economic and social problems, the national government emphasized international inbound tourism as a promising strategy in the national poverty alleviation plan and in its attempt to reduce the chronic imbalance between national income and expenditures.

The major potentials of Mongolia for a successful international tourism development are its beauty of unspoiled landscapes as well as cultural heritage, in particular by the today's pastoral nomad tradition. The majority of international tourists who visit Mongolia do not just expect beauty of landscape. They seek unaffected pristine nature, authentic and genuine culture. Especially, most Western tourists are attracted by Mongolian nomadic lifestyles. These mobile people on horseback who live in gers (yurts) caused the Chinese to build the Great Wall of China. While the Great Wall has become an archaeological wonder over the last 2000 years, the Mongols are still on horseback, still living in gers, still livestock breeders.

Mongolia has one of the largest grasslands for common grazing in the world. More than one third of the population directly relies on nomadic pastoralism for their livelihood. Almost every aspect of Mongolian society has been shaped by pastoral nomadism, an ecological adaptation that makes it possible to support more people in the Mongolian environment than would be true under any other mode of subsistence. Pastoralism is a complex and sophisticated adaptation to arid environments marked by extreme variability in temperature and precipitation on time scales ranging from days to decades and permits societies to exploit the variable and patchy resources of the steppe. The key to pastoralism is mobility, which permits temporary exploitation of resources that are not sufficient to sustain a human and herbivore population for an entire year (Fernández-Gimenenz, 2001).

The value of the pastoral life is kept by Mongolian herders from generation to generation and it is still continued in the daily life of today's nomads. The nomadic community is organized around pasture capacity, water and accessibility of water sources (wells), kinship and tribal relationships. Basically, traditional herding groups are found at two levels in the nomad community, as follows:

- The "hot ail", or nomadic herding camp which is a basic traditional independent unit of livestock production, consisting of 4 to 20 households (ails). Ail is a household living in a ger [nomadic tent]. Customarily the hot ail is composed of relatives and kinship relations with an acknowledged leader who is usually the most experienced male leader. The number of households of hot ails varied according to natural conditions and pastoral capacity.

- The "neg nutgiihan" or "neg goliihon" is a neighbourhood group [composed of 4-to-20 hot ails]. This group inhabits a specific pastoral area and is made up of households that have herded together for generations (Germeraad, 1996:33).

Furthermore, the communities in Mongolia are various in terms of population, practice, cultural meanings and geographic-living circumstances. Each community should decide what kind of tourism can be best suited to their own identity and specialized habitat. For example, some of the communities are already used to rudimentary forms of tourism business while other communities are not involved yet. Some areas – such as the Gobi – have fragile water supplies or lack camel herds. Other places, such as those near the Siberian north, have some 3800 rivers, abundant water (sometimes flooding) and sufficient numbers of camels. There are quite a few sensitive tourist attractions in each community, but they are not really managed or controlled by the local people. Therefore, Mongolia is an interesting case to study concerning stakeholder collaboration towards community based tourism.

Mongolian tourism is still in a phase of growth which regulates itself. It is still in a phase of an emerging destination as TV documentaries and photo articles spread images of Mongolia around the world. Worldwide interest is thus increasing. It is a summer destination with unique features and characteristics. It is likely to continue to grow for several more years. With the sole exception of the year 2003 when the SARS epidemic in China hampered all tourism in Asia, Mongolian tourism has had a growth rate of some 20% per annum (Mongolian tourism Board, 2005), without any major marketing efforts. World tourism is estimated to double by the year 2020(World Tourism Organisation, 2000). Mongolia will be no exception. Currently tourism in Mongolia generates 10% of GDP, which is the world average.

8.2   Tourism Development in the GTNP

The GTNP has been one of the traditional tourist destinations in Mongolia since socialist times; therefore, one third of all foreign tourists usually visit this National Park while they are in Mongolia (Figure 8.1).

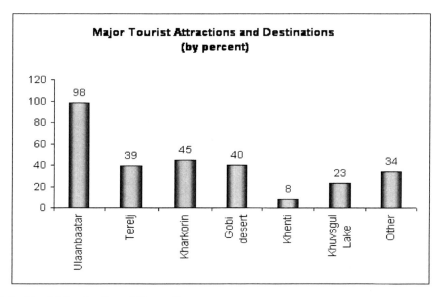

Figure 8.1   Major Tourist Destination of Mongolia

Source from Mongolian Tourism Board (MTB), 2005.

GTNP is about 65-80 km from the capital of Mongolia, Ulan Bator. This National Park (NP) is attractive due to its unique landscape, its geological richness, such as gold, and its proximity to Ulaanbaatar. This makes GTNP popular for the domestic as well as for the international visitor both on short and long stay package tours and is one of the top destinations in Mongolia for tourists. GTNP is adjacent to Khan Khentii Strictly Protected Area (KKSPA); therefore, the National Park is administered by KKSPA.

Gorhi Terelj comprises a surface area of 2,930 km^2 and was officially declared a National Park in 1993 (see Figure 8.2), mainly because of its scenic beauty and its traditional use as a tourism destination both by Mongolians and foreigners from former socialist countries (Myagmarsuren, 2000). In Mongolia, the management and administration of Protected Areas exists in a vertical hierarchy. That means a protected area is directly managed by the Central Authority of Protected Areas, which is one of the agencies in the Ministry of Environment. Therefore a local protected area is totally independent from the Local Government. This creates certain gaps and uncertainties for local people in terms of the legitimacy, every day issues and social problems, such us education and other managerial things between the protected area and the Local Government. Since 1993, Gorhi-Terelj received 'National Park' status according to Mongolian law, and the main goal of the Park Administration was formulated as 'to be responsible for all issues in the territory of the National Park' (Annual report of Park Administration, 2004). The structure of the Park Administration is the following:

Central Office and 7 different local branch Offices. The staff of the central office is: Director-1, senior specialist-1, specialists-6 (2 out of this 6 are self earned salary), accountant-1, bookkeeper-1 and 2 drivers. Totally 36 rangers are working through the branch offices together with officers, specialists and researchers. The annual budget (2004) for the joint management of GTNP and KKSPA is MNT[3] 13 million (US\$ 16,250) [Tugrik is a name of Mongolian currency]. Ten million Tugrik have been assigned by the government, 2 million Tugrik are from tourist entrance fees in Gorhi Terelj and 1 million Tugrik is from other land-use fees in 2000 (Annual report of KKSPA, 2005).

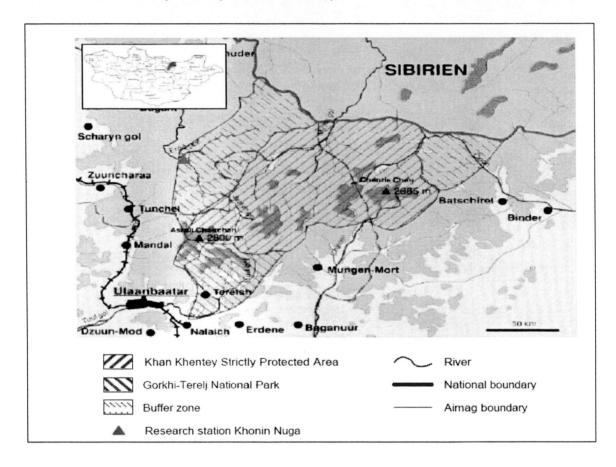

Figure 8.2   Physical Map of Gorhi-Terelj National Park

A typical tour program in GTNP starts from the entrance gate to the National Park. Here foreigners pay US\$ 3 for entrance fee per person and US\$ 5 per vehicle. They can either visit directly on their own or through advanced arrangement with tour companies. As they enter the national park, they usually drive to find one of the previously booked tourist camps. Some people prefer to find an attractive welcoming local family who can host them in their satellite ger accommodation[4]. From the entrance gate, there is only one narrow paved road. During the drive various kinds of natural landscape with striking geological features, clear rivers, steppe valleys, forests and unique rocky mountains, gers of nomad people going about their daily life, and herds of camels, yaks, and horses can be seen. After 15 minutes' drive from the entrance gate, the first tourist camp is reached. Tourist camps are situated at a distance of 1-2 km from each other. It is interesting that traditionally dressed local people stand near the road with horses, camels or yaks and when they see a tourist's car, they wave and smile at them. These people are either new herders or local herders who offer to visitors any local services, such as the experience of riding a horse, yak or camel; guiding, local food or lodging. They try to catch those who visit the National Park for the first time and those who are looking for cheaper services than the tourist camps. Many domestic

---

[3] MNT = Mongolian togrog which is the Mongolian currency.
[4] An additional ger built next to the family.

visitors prefer to stay in a satellite ger of local people while foreign adventure tourists, mostly Western backpackers, like to stay with local people.

Once the tourists arrive at a tourist camp or local family, they are always welcomed by the camp staff. Sometimes guests have an opportunity to choose their own ger, but in most cases they stay in a pre-selected ger. The traditional Mongolian ger and its furniture gives an impression of nature, a feeling that the visitor is a part of the world; looking at the blue sky from the ger may provide a strong impression of being close to nature.

Tourists have various opportunities to do different activities during their stay in the ger camp; however, they should be aware that the camp staff should arrange any service or activity. Most tourist camps are resort camps, which provide entertainment, sports, games and dancing services.   Tourists can expect here a Western style of equipment, except in the Mongolian traditional ger. There are Asian and Western cuisines, electricity, modern shower and toilet amenities. For these reasons, Asian (Japanese, Chinese and Korean) tourists and Western leisure-oriented tourists prefer to stay in the ger camp, whereas adventure tourists and domestic visitors mostly stay with local families which then gives them the opportunity to participate in the daily life of local people.

The park has a variety of accommodations, some of which were built in socialist times. At present, there are two hotels (with a total of 160 beds, plus another 160 in adjacent gers and cabins), four camps for children and youth, and one research and education facility of the National University. Public recreational and interpretative infrastructure is rare. According to the annual report of Park Administration of KKSPA (2005), 40 tourist camps received permission to run a 'tourist camp' service within the National Park. The number of visitors to Gorhi Terelj in 2004 was estimated at 52,000 by the Park. Of these 45,000 were Mongolians who have traditionally used the area as a summer holiday destination and for day and weekend trips from Ulaanbaatar. The remaining 7,000 visitors were foreigners, many of them businessmen who come for a one-day excursion from Ulaanbaatar. The problem is that the number of visitors is not clear anymore, because in 2004 according to the same report, around 14,700 foreign tourists stayed at tourist camps.

Tourism is already a major source of income for local people in Gorhi Terelj. The northern section of GTNP is relatively untouched, whereas the southern zone along the major road to Terelj village is considerably disturbed by activities of the local population as well as by recreational and tourist activities. Residents in GTNP originate from different places as a consequence of contemporary international tourism development since 1990. Numerous rural people in Mongolia were interested to settle down in the National Park because of its close location to Ulaanbaatar and the possibility of a better livelihood based on employment in and income from tourism Many of them were previously marginalized nomads Therefore, many residents inside the Park are not native inhabitants of GTNP and their culture has been modified to accommodate necessary adjustments with the tourism sector.

The number of local people who live within the NP is not stable. On one hand, nomad people always move according to pastoral availability. On the other hand, statistics are not well developed, especially for nomadic migrations. There are around 25 hot ails living in the National Park, according to annual report of Park Administration of KKSPA (2005). That means there are around 3000 people living locally in GTNP. Out of this figure, more than 2,000 people live in the relatively small area of Terelj village where most tourist camps are situated.

8.3   Problem Statement

In the current situation, GTNP faces several problems; these especially became clearer around 2000. In Mongolia, the first decade after democratization in 1990 saw the beginning of international tourism flows throughout the country. During that time, everybody involved in the tourism sector in GTNP had the basic aim of developing tourism in that area. Their aim was to test all profitable outcomes from tourism which might result in earning more income, increasing employment, and provide new faster development of the infrastructure in the National Park area. Stakeholders were satisfied with the way tourism developed in GTNP and how tourism contributed to local community development. Specifically, income derived from entrance fees which were increased annually; income from visitors, land use tax from tourist camps and local people was satisfactory to the Park Administration. Visitors who enjoyed the NP were satisfied with the quality of landscape and services. Tour operators were satisfied by sending their clients to the park. Local people were employed in tourist camps and most tour programs provided various ways of involving the local people. Tourist camps were happy with the limited number of camps and increased numbers of visitors, as well as with the quality of sightseeing for clients. Thus, the relationship between local stakeholders was good as long as tourism numbers were limited. The conclusion is that the emergence of truly international tourism was a "wheel" of integration among those stakeholders. However, this situation changed because of problems which relate with how tourism was allowed to be developed spatially in the NP.

The GTNP did not establish a clear tourism policy and strategy at the local level by consensus with stakeholders. Therefore, this park was not ready for any unintended or unexpected impact from tourism development. The Park Administration established a tourism development paper, but it only referred to Tourist Camp and Tour Operators' functionality. The Park Administration gave numerous licenses to those who wanted to establish a new tourist camp or a resort with no understanding of carrying capacity. Indeed, the Park Administration had no experience with tourism development in the National Park area, or with various impacts and threats arising from tourism on environmental, socio-cultural and economic levels. And they also had a lack of management and planning regarding how to develop tourism within the Protected Area. One of the essential problems is that there are no co-ordination and integration mechanisms between the tourism sector and local development. The lack of management induced a lack of co-ordination and integration between traditional stakeholder groups, such as nomad hot ail groups and tourism-based new stakeholders, such as Tourist camps and Tour operators. Therefore, there was a gap between nomad society and tourism sector stakeholders in then current policy papers and management practice.

The next problem addresses the pastoral land use among local stakeholders. The Mongolian Government privatized all state-owned herds after the end of the socialist state, granting ownership to the nomads. Thus, nomads have a high interest to increase the number of their herds, because herds represent traditional forms of wealth. But pastoral land and water/wells, which are an essential and inherent part of the nomad economic and social system, were not regulated or privatized. Therefore, conflicts with regard to pasture land and water accessibility emerge between different nomad hot ails and herders' group. But state-based lands have been given to tourist camps for lease and even now some lands are legally privatized to tourist camps. The Park Administration simply wanted to gain more income by distributing numerous licenses for land use to those who established new tourist camps. The usage of pastoral lands and drinking water, which are core elements of the rural community, was not arranged (neither privatized nor by leasing) by law to nomads although all herds are privatized. Nevertheless tourist operators have been setting up their camp on pastoral lands and organizing various itinerary programs through these lands. Thus, the access by different interest groups to pastoral lands creates a conflict between local stakeholders.

Gradually the number of local people with their herds and the number of tourist camps have increased in the National Park. Moreover, as noted above, many country people from various places in Mongolia settled in the National Park. This sudden jump in numbers caused overcrowding in the National Park and started to have negative effects on the tourism-based stakeholders and nomad families alike.

The number of tourists to GTNP has increased over the years. Since Asian tourists like to make short day tours in Mongolia, most tour companies offer Gorhi-Terelj as a suitable destination for day trips and short over night trip requests. At the same time, tour operators still sell their traditional programs to the Western market and Gorhi-Terelj is seen as a traditional package destination. Thus the number of Western tourists has not decreased. Additionally, the number of domestic travelers, especially from local residents of Ulaanbaatar, increased until recently. But the numbers are now decreasing.

Currently, the trend in GTNP is that established tourist camps and resorts want to further invest to build more luxury buildings and facilities especially catering to identified needs in the Asian market. The location near the capital is one of the reasons why new modern urban development is growing in the National Park. In the beginning, local people were very enthusiastic about this and saw it as a source of employment; however, gradually employees came from Ulan Bator and not from the local community. The number of newly established constructions increased. The pressure on the local community increased. Thus, current overdevelopment is also one of the problems in this National Park. The national Park Administration has been too weak and has allowed this to happen.

The tourist camps and most tour operators seemingly are profit-driven, pushing their businesses for more. The Park Administration just passively involves itself in this process by charging taxes, though not much more than this. The condemnatory and distrustful passive way of communication among the local stakeholders does not allow the establishment of a common objective, interest or desire for cooperation. At the same time, tourism in Gorhi-Terelj National Park is erratic, because everybody wants to do something only for their own short-term goal.

The consequence of these problems leads to more and more conflict among local stakeholders, especially between local nomad stakeholders and tourist-based stakeholders. Almost all of the tourist camps have a problem of littering, fire-wood and payment of electricity to the PA. Tour operators have problems with environmental pollution and overcapacity through their itinerary-based routes. So, some of them try to find environmentally friendly tour packages, for example hiking, horse riding, camel riding and camping. But the lack of know-how with regards to sustainable traveling technology of these tour programs produces several problems, like littering, four wheel drive impacts and the shortage of drinking water on the pastoral land of the nomads. Every stakeholder believes that other stakeholders are producing problems that affect them and they try to solve their problems without asking support or solution from the others. Especially, empowerment of local people by other stakeholders is missing.

Therefore, tourism development in GTNP requires re-identifying appropriate local stakeholders who are based on the local community identity and establishing sufficient policy and management to reinforce mutual collaboration between these local stakeholders. Otherwise, problems for the local communities will increase and deepen.

- Research Question: The research question of this paper is formulated as follows: What are the positions to the collaboration of key stakeholders in order to support CBT?

8.4   Research Methodology

For this research both quantitative as well as qualitative data were needed. The research started by collecting quantitative data and statistics which relate to tourism development in Mongolia and GTNP which were provided by the Mongolian Statistics Enterprise and the Mongolian Tourism Board (MTB). It was also necessary to collect descriptive data from local stakeholders and ascertain their opinion, behavior and impressions concerning collaboration. On the other hand, this research required qualitative data, as for example, to gain insight into issues surrounding the willingness to collaborate between the stakeholders and consider issues of overgrazing, overcrowding and environmental damage. These data were collected in the form of snowball interviews with the Park Administration and the local herder people. Questionnaires were distributed by the Managers of Tourist Camps, Tour Operators and the Park Administration. It was impossible to have (one-to-one) interviews with all the people who worked in the above organizations. Therefore, a random sample was taken from the total target group. Interviews were conducted among key stakeholders who represented institutional and private sectors, such as:

- Government sector: Staff of the National Park Administration (6 respondents);

- Private sector: 1) Tourist Camps Staff (36 respondents); 2) Tour Operators Staff (22 respondents).

Interviews were undertaken with 25 local herders, 14 male and 11 female. Twenty per cent of the interviewees had lived temporally in GTNP during the summer in the last 2 – 4 years, 35% of the interviewees had settled permanently in NP around 6 – 10 years ago and another 45% had been living for more than 10 years in the National Park.

8.5   Tourism in the GTNP/Stakeholder Analysis

According to the analysis, the Park Administration holds the legal power; tourist camps and operators have the market, the service and the economic power; and the local people control the socio-cultural resources via local know-how. Therefore, all four are to be considered as key stakeholders at GTNP.

Key stakeholders (n-80) think that tourism affects the National Park more negatively (68%) than positively (32%) (Figure 8.3).

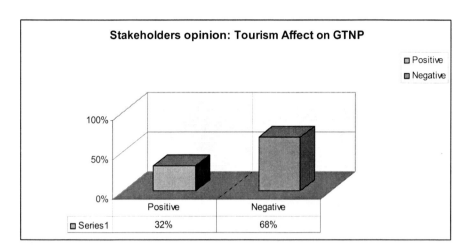

Figure 8.3   Effects of Tourism on GTNP

As discussed above, stakeholders were satisfied in the beginning but now, due to a lack of appropriate planning, a lot of problems have emerged as a result, with new conflicts. This situation is growing. Therefore, according to most stakeholders' opinion, the negative impact of tourism outweighs the positive. Employment is the most significant positive outcome of tourism in GTNP according to tour operators and tourist camps (n-60). The Park Administration (n-6), on the other hand, believes that better livelihood and the new prestige of the NP are the most significant positive impacts. (Figure 8.4).

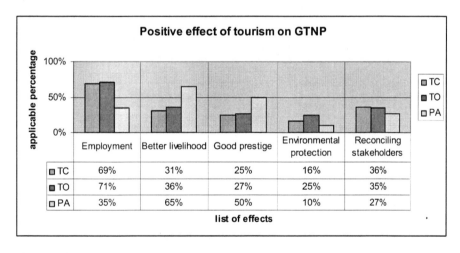

Figure 8.4   Positive Effects of Tourism

For negative impacts, almost all stakeholders agreed that the problem of overgrazing on the pasture was the most essential issue for everybody. Almost all local people interviewed were not happy that the pastoral land was used by everyone, such as tourist camps, tour operators and newly arrived herders who moved into their grazing area. Most tourist camps (85%) have their own animals (sheep, goats, cows and horses) to use in animal husbandry; they also use them to produce meat, milk and other dairy products. As noted above, tourist camps have been mushrooming in GTNP. Tour operators and their various vehicles (buses, jeeps, and minivans) with many tourists drive all over the pastures. The consequences are a lot of new pumps, littering, overgrazed lands and lack of water resources of wells and rivers. Additionally, new herders who move in temporarily expect to get benefits from tourism, such as temporary employment, additional income from domestic and foreign tourists by renting their ger, or cooking nomad food, selling souvenirs and so on. Overgrazing is a basic and fundamental issue to each stakeholder and also between them. As discussed in the first section, the key elements of the nomad community are land, animals and people. The land in GTNP is becoming overgrazed and degraded by the transition of society and the "attack" of the new tourism sector.

Overcrowding of the tourist area and environmental pollution accelerate the overgrazing problem. Tourist camps pay considerable attention to overcrowding and environmental pollution, because these create significant practical problems for them. It is quite difficult to operate a tourist camp with traditional Mongolian yurts in such a way as to provide western facilities and equipment in the wilderness and environmental issues are pressing problems for them. Tour operators are unhappy with overcrowding; thus, they like to open new itineraries far from current intensive use zones. On the one hand, nomads are also not very happy, because new itineraries increase the overgrazing problem. Yet again, tour operators consider the lifestyle of the local people important as it enhances the quality of the visitor experience. The Park Administration is mostly worried about the overcrowding and resultant environmental pollution, their most important responsibility. Tourist camps and tour operators perceive that tourism brings new problems and that these problems cause conflicts among stakeholders, but the Park Administration is not really concerned about stakeholder conflict. This is shown by Figure 8.5 (n-59).

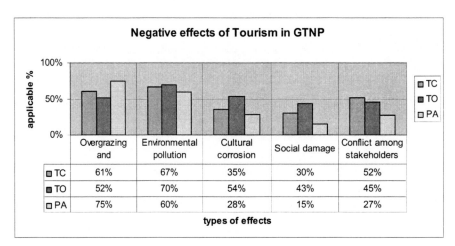

Figure 8.5   Negative Effects of Tourism

There is no clear data about how many visitors have been in the National Park, according to the official statistics,14,700 foreign tourists and 26,000 domestic tourists in 2004 (report of GTNPA, 2004). These numbers might be based on entrance fee income, but local people and staffs who work at the entrance gate believe this number is under-estimated and should be much more than this. The questionnaire revealed that tour operators prefer to decrease or keep the current number of visitors (68%) instead of increasing them. Tour operators argued that foreign tourists were decreasing in the last few years, although the price of a package offered by tourist camps was still relatively high by Mongolian standards (US$ 27-30 per person per day including 3 meals and ger accommodation). Tourist camps managers, however, wanted to maximize the number of tourists (45%). This appeared to be related to the fact that the number of tourism camps has been rapidly increasing in the last few years, and a lot of visitors prefer to stay in their own tent or in local people's satellite ger. The occupancy of the tourist camps used to be 80-100% during the tourism season; but with increased supply, it is currently around only 40-60%.

The survey asked about the current tourism programs in the GTNP. Fifty two per cent of the tour operators focused on GTNP as a destination for short programs; therefore, they saw typical tourism of

GTNP as a passive and relaxed tour where tourists stayed in a ger camp and engaged in sightseeing in close proximity around it. However, the other 48% of the tour operators who were surveyed preferred to carry out adventure and active tours with several days' programs of hiking, riding and camping.

For other National Parks, tourist camps are located near a unique cultural or natural attraction, but still far from each other; however, in GTNP, tourist camps are located close to each other in every mountain glen just like tourist hotels and amusement centres on the beach in countries with developed seaside tourism. Thus, all tourist camps form a sort of a contained resort area. This is the picture of current tourism.

Most tourist respondents to the questionnaire would prefer different types of tours than the current quality of tourism in GTNP, as the table below shows (Figure 8.6, n-78). As discussed above, most of the visitors who enter the National Park are domestic excursionists and it is quite complicated to take an entrance fee from them. In this way, the Park Administration is losing its control and power. This is probably the main reason why the Park Administration wants different types of tour programs, enabling them to channel and control tourism activities.

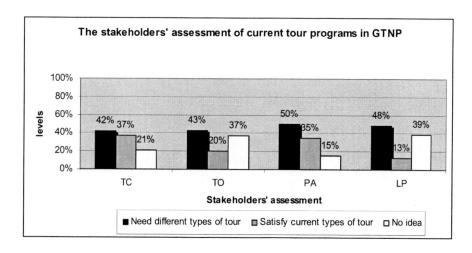

Figure 8.6   Assessment of Current Tourism Quality by Stakeholders

However, all stakeholders are ready to look at additional multi-tourism programs, which target resort and leisure tourists. It might be one mutual opportunity for establishing a common mission among the stakeholders.

Tourism has already highly impacted GKNP, which is why all stakeholders agree they can not imagine GTNP without the tourism sector. Hence, 82% of all stakeholders stressed tourism's importance for the GTNP development.

8.6   Stakeholders' Interests on Collaboration

To assess the collaboration of key stakeholders, it is significant to reveal the position of each stakeholder in GTNP. The position of stakeholders is based on their capacity and power in the tourism network, which means which stakeholder holds what stake or, in other words, which stakeholder stands on what resource in the tourism sector. In order to analyze this, the "four margins of sustainability" (Duim, 1997) were used. The functionality and accessibility of stakeholders and the assessment survey of stakeholders regarding the impact of tourism are the basis for determining the position of a stakeholder in one of the four margins.

The majority of the international tourists visit the park via tour operators, which means the operators control the marketing, distribution and product development. Therefore, most profit issues in this park depend on the capacity and the positioning of the tour operators since the main budget of GTNP, the income of local people and tourist camps come mostly from international tourists. On the other hand, tour operators are really concerned about the socio-cultural quality of local people because: i) Socio-cultural aspects are quite significant to the quality of the visitor experience. Tour operators realize that the cultural heritage and lifestyles of the nomad people is the most significant element of their current program; ii) Tour operators also want to establish more cultural and ethnic tour programs based on the nomad people's life in GTNP. Therefore, it can be stated that the tour operators' position is between profit and socio-cultural margins.

Furthermore, tourist camps are private entrepreneurs in GTNP. Their service, product and hospitality are highly significant for tourism to be profitable. Thus, tourist camps' resources and capacity is driven by profit, which in turn empowers them. On the other hand, the tourist camps' business depends on environmental quality; thus, in fact, it is very sensitive to manage tourist camps in an environmentally friendly way. Therefore, tourist camps can be placed between profit and ecological margins. The Park Administration is responsible for all legal and political aspects of the national park development and its most important function is the ecological aspect of GTNP, according to law. It is reasonable to put the PA between risk and ecological aspects.

Local people have a hold on the socio-cultural resources and capacities in the collaboration process. Indeed socio-cultural highlights and identity exist among local people; but on the other hand, local people have liability and rights, responsibility and risks to participate in local level issues. Also, the most moral and ethical powers go to the local people. In Mongolia there are quite good laws; however, enforcement is very weak. In many cases ethical, cultural and religious values drive the practical outcome of behaviour and communication in the society. This is the basis for positioning local people between socio-cultural and risk margins.

Based on the above reasons, it is possible to locate the position of the key stakeholders according to the four margins as follows (Figure 8.7):

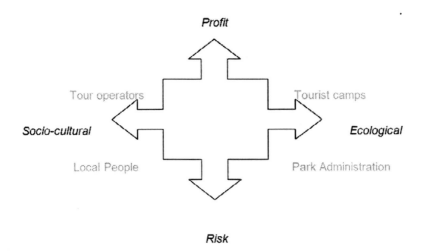

Figure 8.7   Stakeholders' Positions in the Four Margins

It is quite instructive to identify the interests and resources of the key stakeholders because, on one hand, stakeholders participate in the tourism collaboration from their position as much as possible; and, on the other hand, it is important to know where the problems are and how to solve these problems based on which resources. Therefore, it is matter of power dynamics due to which stakeholders take whatever power position is advantageous to them. Using each stakeholder's strength can be the main advantage of collaboration if they encourage and promote each other's activity to reach a common vision and to find a solution for their problems by sharing each others capacities.

8.7   Discussion

The key elements of the GTNP community are pastoral lands, animals and herder people. Thus, it is essential that the tourism sector become integrated in these key concepts of the community. In order to do that, tourism-related stakeholders (tour operators and tourist camps) have to adjust their activity to the local community needs. For example, it is important to clarify and reveal all the possibilities and capacities of local people, and to sustain these by accommodating them into an appropriate tourism development plan. The main point of this study is that the key stakeholders have to (re)establish an integrated community system between tourism and nomadic local life based on respect of key elements of traditional local community, which encompasses their identity: people, land and animals. The remarkable thing is that Mongolian nomads have several thousand years of experience on how to live together with nature in an environmentally friendly way, keeping their own unique culture, pastoral lands and social value system. This is why the main message is that the key issue of successful collaboration between stakeholders in GTNP is to (re)define and agree with the community groups about how to adapt to and take sufficient account of the local system comprised of land, people and animals.

One possible practical solution is to establish a pasture-based stakeholder collaboration system. Everybody depends on land and pasture. Tourism-related stakeholders (tour operators and/or tourist camps) and local people (primary and secondary users of pasture) can build a co-operative unity based on their common interests and efficient resource use within their land utility. For example, tourist camps located in particular pastoral lands, tour operators who send their clients through these pasture areas, and local herders (primary or secondary users) who live in the area need to combine their interests. Everybody has an interest to protect this certain place, to keep it in top quality, to manage the issues of their limited spatial environment. Therefore, local herders, tourist camp operators and tour operators have an opportunity to establish a common interest group. It could be called a pasture-based stakeholder group (see Figure 8.8).

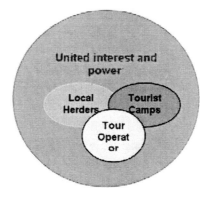

Figure 8.8   Pasture-based Stakeholder Group

There can be several pasture-based stakeholder groups at GTNP according to the particular borders of the lands. The pasture-based stakeholder groups may have direct contact with the Park Administration. Moreover, the Park Administration may establish a "local tourism policy group" which will consist of those stakeholder groups. This policy group can be a united voice of the local stakeholders towards the sustainable tourism development at community level.

Needless to say, such solutions need be negotiated through a stakeholder process and suited to the results of same. A lot of misuse of resources and costs to bring this right could have been avoided by careful planning from the beginning, some 13-14 years ago.

References:

Annual report of Park Administration (2004), GTNP, Mongolia, MNE, Mongolia (in Mongolian).

Annual report of Park Administration (2005), GTNP, Mongolia, MNE, Mongolia (in Mongolian).

Annual report of Khan Khentii Strictly Protected Area Management (2005), Mongolia, MNE: Mongolia (in Mongolian).

Annual report of GTZ projects in Mongolia (2004), Mongolia: GTZ and MNE.

Duim, V.R. van der (1997), 'The role of small entrepreneurs in the development of sustainable tourism in Costa Rica', in H. Dahles (ed.), *Tourism, Small Entrepreneurs and Sustainable Development – Cases from Developing Countries*, Tilburg: Atlas.

Fernández-Gimenenz (2001), 'Sustaining the steppes: A geographical history of pastoral land use in Mongolia', *Geographical Review*, 89(3), pp.315-342.

Germeraad, W.P. and E. Zandangiin (1996), The Mongolian landscape tradition: A key to progress Nomadic traditions and their contemporary role in landscape planning and management in Mongolia, Schiedam, The Netherlands: BGS.

Myagmarsuren, D (2000), *The Protected Areas in Mongolia*, Ulaanabaatar (in Mongolian).

Ministry of Nature and Environment (1994), *WWF action plan*. Ulaanbaatar, Mongolia.

Mongolian Tourism Board (MTB) (2005), (online), available: http://www.mongoliatourism.gov.mn (31-5-2007).

World Tourism Organization (2000), *Tourism 2020 Vision*, Madrid.

Possible Model for Culture-based Tourism Development in Japan: Implications of CVM Surveys of the World Heritage Hamlets of Gokayama, Toyama Prefecture, Japan

9.1 Overview

In the 21st century, Japanese society and the economy have matured, and the national demand for a better quality of life has increased. People are seeking their own identity and cultural and artistic activities have been integrated into local communities and are considered an important component of a high quality lifestyle. From the perspective of local development, the focus has shifted to improvement of amenities and quality of life in addition to fulfilling the minimum requirements of living standards.

Based on these trends, in 2001 the Fundamental Law for the Promotion of Culture and Arts was enacted. This law reflects a broad social consensus on the importance of culture. Also in 2004, the Act of Scenery[5] was enacted aiming to create pleasant and beautiful scenery in cities and villages. It is the first law which refers to the importance of the beauty of the cities and villages and includes provisions for tourism promotion utilizing beautiful scenery created through the interaction between nature, history and culture, and economic activities. Furthermore, in 2006 the Fundamental Law for the Promotion of a Tourism Nation (author's translation) was revised. In this new law, tourism is regarded as a symbol of international peace and an enrichment of national life, as well as a driving force in creating jobs and revitalizing the local economy.

In view of the growing importance of high value-added, service-oriented industries, the importance of tourism has gradually being recognized. In fact, the number of travelers has been increasing during recent decades (see Figure 9.1). In 2003, Japanese citizens spent approximately 190 billion US dollars for travel within Japan (including domestic travel costs for travel to overseas destinations) and 36 billion US dollars for travel overseas, while international tourists spent 12 billion US dollars in Japan. Domestic travel by Japanese and international travelers amounts to 202 billion US dollars, which is equal to 2.4% of GDP, creating 2.1 million jobs (3.2% of total employment)[6]. Cultural heritage and natural scenic beauty have been attracting these travelers; for example, in 2004 42.5% of domestic travelers who stayed

---

[5] Besides the Act of Scenery (2004), the author also cited materials from The Fundamental Law for the Promotion of a Tourism Nation (2006), The Fundamental Law for the Promotion of Culture and Arts (2001), and The Law for Protection of Cultural Properties (1950).

[6] Ministry of Land, Infrastructure and Transport Japan (2005), White Paper 2005, MLIT, Tokyo. Exchange rate as of January 2007 was one US dollar to 118 yen.

overnight visited natural scenery and 27.5% visited historical sites and heritage venues[7]. Culture is now considered a high priority among measures for realizing a country built on tourism – a "tourism nation."

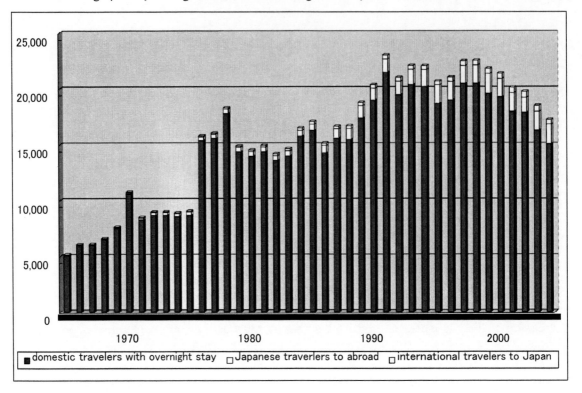

Figure 9.1   Number of Travelers (Unit:10,000)

Source: Based on data published by Japan Association of Travel Agents, http://www.jata-net.or.jp

However, culture is still treated as peripheral in general. For example, the national government has allocated only 0.1% of the total budget to culture. It is necessary to make effective investment in culture from various funding sources. Tourism is an important option to this end. At the same time, it is important for tourism promotion to maintain various cultural values, which are essential for attracting tourists. A well organized management with government-citizen collaboration is necessary to provide a positive impact on the local community by attracting tourists, and to increase total benefits and satisfaction of all the stakeholders of the society.

A possible model for community-based tourism development is examined by applying contingent valuation method (CVM) studies of the historic hamlets of Gokayama in Toyama Prefecture, Japan. These hamlets are UNESCO World Heritage sites. The focus of study will be the maintenance of cultural values. Section 2 presents an outline of the heritage sites and their problems, and Section 3 discusses the overall results and analysis, including estimates of willingness to pay (WTP) for preservation of heritage values based on the CVM surveys. Sections 4 and 5 evaluate the benefits of heritage, identify factors accounting for these benefits and the beneficiaries, and discuss the implications of possible policy measures utilizing private initiatives and public investment for heritage preservation and sustainable community development through tourism.

---

[7] Japan Tourism Association (2005), Facts and Trends of Tourism, JTA, Tokyo.

9.2 Case study: Contingent Valuation Method Studies on Cultural Landscape of Gokayama, Toyama, Japan

9.2.1 Outline of the Heritage Site

The historic hamlets are located in a mountainous area in Toyama Prefecture, in the central part of Japan (Figure 9.2). They are well known for their traditional wooden houses, one of the representative forms of Japanese architecture. Harmonizing with the surrounding harsh natural environment, the steep thatched roofs of the houses, which are made of natural materials from nearby forests, can endure the heavy snows of this region. These houses were maintained by "yui" (community cooperation), and the necessary skills were passed from generation to generation among the residents; however, due to the rapid economic growth and changes of social structure from the 1950's through the 1970's, most of these houses and historic hamlets vanished, with the exception of the Shirakawa-go hamlet in Gifu Prefecture and the two smaller hamlets of Gokayama (Ainokura and Suganuma, Figures 3–8) in Toyama Prefecture. These three hamlets are now designated as "districts of groups of important historic buildings" under Japan's Law for Protection of Cultural Properties (hereinafter referred to as "the Law"), and the UNESCO World Heritage. The two hamlets of Gokayama were also designated as "national historic sites" under the Law in the 1970's; since then changes in both the interior and exterior of houses have been strictly controlled.

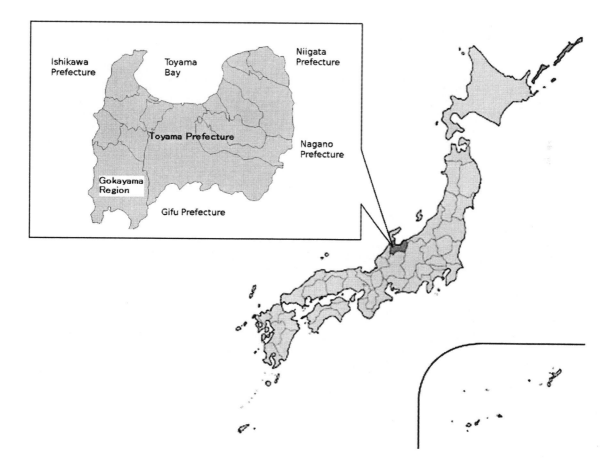

Figure 9.2   Map of Japan, Toyama Prefecture, and Gokayama Region

Figure 9.3   Ainokura Hamlet from Distance

Figure 9.4   Suganuma Village from Distance

Figure 9.5   Traditional House in Ainokura Hamlet

Figure 9.6   Traditional House in Suganuma Hamlet

Figure 9.7   Inside Traditional House
Traditional House

Figure   9.8   Repairing   Thatched   Roof   of

Both hamlets are located in villages which are "designated depopulation areas"[8] and annual expenditures of these villages were roughly 20-25 million US dollars respectively in 2000[9]. During 2000-2003, Taira village had around 1,400 residents with the financial capability indicator (fraction of the necessary expenditures which can be raised by the village itself; the remainder comes from subsidies from the national and prefectural governments) of 0.15, and Kamitaira village had less than 1,000 residents with a financial capability indicator of 0.42. The per capita income of both villages was estimated as relatively low; 25,600 US dollars per person in 2003[10], but almost no one received public livelihood aid (welfare). The house ownership was very high in these villages; for example, in Taira village 87.5% of residents owned their houses. Roughly half of the population in this region was engaged in the service sector and roughly 40% of them were engaged in the industrial sector. The Gokayama region, which includes the villages of Taira and Kamitaira, was merged into the city of Nanto in 2004.

Located in the former Taira village, Ainokura hamlet occupies 18 ha where 20 thatched-roof houses as well as temples and shrines are located and preserved. The population of Ainokura hamlet was around 90 (27 households) at the time of their inclusion in the UNESCO World Heritage List, and has continuously decreased since then. The hamlet residents are either families who are engaged in tourism-related business, or production process/construction workers who are employed by companies outside the hamlet, including a large electric company[11]. Most of the residents are also engaged part-time in agricultural production, mainly for self-consumption. Located in the former Kamitaira village, Suganuma hamlet occupies 4.4 ha, with 9 thatched roof houses. This hamlet, much smaller than Ainokura, had only 40 residents (8 households) at the time of their inclusion in UNESCO World Heritage List. Due to aging some of the residents are pensioners and others are engaged mainly in the construction industry.

These hamlets now face a serious challenge. Depopulation, rural decay due to nationwide economic development, aging and the increase in tourism-related family business have weakened various functions needed for maintenance of the hamlets: making paddy fields, managing forests and re-roofing historic houses. In order to maintain the cultural value of the heritage, the hamlets must be made sustainable and liveable. Thus, creating jobs and upgrading living conditions are essential.

9.2.2 Tourism Related Issues

As Gokayama hamlets are designated national historic sites under the Law, they are eligible for public subsidies extended by the national government for preservation and, at the same time, public access is required as much as possible to the designated historic sites. The number of travelers to Gokayama region has been growing (Figure 9.9). In 1970, when the hamlets were designated, 100,000 travelers visited Gokayama region; in 1995, at their inclusion in the UNESCO World Heritage List, the number of tourists dramatically increased to more than 900,000, but has been stabilized at the level of 700,000 today.

---

[8] Under the Law of Special Measures on Promoting Independence of Depopulated Areas (in effect since 2000) the areas which are suffering from underdevelopment of social and production infrastructure can be designated as eligible for special financial supports from the national government.
[9] The statistics sited in this paragraph were provided by the former Taira village and Kamitaira village.
[10] Japan Planning Systems (2005), Personal Income Indicator 2005, JPA, Tokyo. In this indicator estimate, the figures are based on the city, town or village tax compiled by the Ministry of Internal Affairs and Communications.
[11] The figures sited in this paragraph were provided by Gokayama Tourism Association.

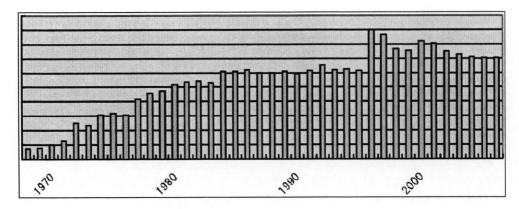

Figure 9.9   Number of Travelers to Gokayama Region (Person)

Source: Based on data provided by Gokayama Tourist Association

At the time of inclusion of these hamlets in the UNESCO World Heritage List, the Gokayama region set up a committee to plan a comprehensive development strategy, such as construction of highways connecting the historic hamlets to large cities, creation of an eco-museum and/or "World Heritage Theme Park," inviting venture business of artists' ateliers, and attracting more tourists[12]. However, the partial construction of the highway has brought about an increase of transit tourists, thus the number of tourists who stay overnight in the region has been quite low, around only 5-6% on average. On the other hand, the other items included in the strategy have not been realized and the economic and industrial structure has not changed greatly.

Heavy pressure from daytrip tourists has created difficulties for the residents; their daily life is exposed to outsiders' eyes all the time, increased waste by tourists is a concern, and congestion is notable in the high season. The hamlets have thus asked tourists to visit them only during the daytime (9:00-17:00). Still, the residents recognize the importance of tourism for maintaining the hamlets.

Ainokura established a foundation for collecting fees from tourists in 1996. The foundation also works toward maintaining the natural environment surrounding the hamlet. At present, the foundation has funds for only a few jobs, most of them part-time. The other Gokayama hamlet, Suganuma, has built a museum and accommodations at a nearby site and is trying to keep the living heritage as it was in the past. Tourists are free to enter the hamlet. Today, after ten years' inclusion in the World Heritage List, Gokayama region tries to connect these hamlets to other tourist spots nearby, the Shirakawa-go hamlet in Gifu prefecture in particular. Also, with a partnership between local government and private initiatives, they are trying to promote local production through tourism[13].

It is crucial to find a way to maximize the benefits and minimize the demerits of tourism for tourists as well as residents, rather than just increasing the number of tourists; otherwise the cultural value of the hamlets will deteriorate, which might result in a decrease of the number of tourists in the long run. Yet tourists cannot be free riders on the scenic beauty and should take responsibility in bearing some costs according to their capability to maintain the hamlets and the cultural values they enjoy. Existing public support does not fully cover the costs nor does it provide a labor force to maintain the heritage. Further support, including additional job creation and upgraded living standards, is necessary to facilitate the daily life of the hamlets and to create a new system that can replace traditional community cooperation in order to preserve the hamlets and their environment.

---

[12] Gokayama Regional Committee for Development (1996), Towards New Villages at the Inclusion of the UNESCO World Heritage List, Taira Village and Kamitaira Village, Gokayama, pp. 25-30.
[13] Gokayama Tourism Association (2006), Symposium abstract, GTA, Tokyama.

9.2.3   Method and Survey Design

The benefits of cultural heritage consist of use value and non-use value. Comparison of the results of an on-site survey of tourists and a nationwide postal survey is focused on the non-use values[14], such as option value, existence value, bequest value, educational value and aesthetic value using the contingent valuation method (CVM).

CVM is a method used to estimate economic values for a wide variety of goods and services by directly asking survey respondents how much they would be willing to pay for specific goods and services. Use of the CVM is becoming increasingly common in Japan, especially to evaluate the benefits of agricultural functions and the natural environment[15]. Several CVM surveys have been done internationally on cultural heritage and facilities[16].

The focus of heritage values has evolved from material value to more comprehensive values such as workmanship, design and setting. Accordingly, the preservation of the world heritage has evolved from preservation of historical monuments to inclusion of the surrounding environment and even intangible activities inside the heritage site as a whole. In light of this international trend, the CVM was applied to estimate willingness to pay (WTP) for preservation of the living heritage and cultural landscape. The cultural landscape includes both natural and cultural elements derived from human activities and the artefacts of human life. Preservation of the cultural landscape is thus the appropriate scenario for determining the benefits of preservation of the hamlets.

The surveys were designed to examine two issues: coexistence with tourism and upgrading community welfare, including not only preserving the physical heritage (houses) but also repairing thatched roofs, managing the surrounding forests and maintaining the technological capability needed to make repairs in the future. The surveys included personal data such as educational background and preference for cultural activities to specify the beneficiaries of heritage values.

The on-site survey of tourists was conducted as a mall-intercept, respondent-completed survey[17] over three days in September 2001; the nationwide postal survey[18] was conducted in November 2001. The questionnaire used in the nationwide survey was similar to that used in the on-site survey of tourists, and was sent to 3,000 respondents whose information was randomly extracted from a telephone database throughout Japan using a stratified two-stage sampling system.

9.3   Results and Analysis

9.3.1   Overall Results

The response rate of the surveys is shown in Table 9.1. The key statistics are shown in Table 2. Although the tourists who visited the hamlets came from throughout Japan, they came mainly from Hokuriku (location of the hamlets), Kanto (location of the capital, Tokyo), and Kinki (location of the second most

---

[14] In general, non-use value (passive use value) is considered to include option value, existence value, and bequest value. See Ohio v. Department of Interior, 880 F.2d 432 (D.C. Cir. 1989).
[15] In Japan much research was conducted on the environment, addressing such issues as preservation of the landscape of rural villages (Yoshida, et al., 1997) and the environmental value of Yakushima (Kuriyama, et al., 2001).
[16] Internationally there are several research cases, including Santagata (2000) and Rolfe (2003).
[17] The questionnaire was distributed to every third to fifth person. In Japan a respondent-completed questionnaire survey (one completed by the respondent rather than by the interviewer) is considered appropriate, as the questionnaire includes personal data such as income.
[18] In Japan, postal surveys are considered one of the most reliable survey methods.

populous prefecture, Osaka). The tourist group consisted almost evenly of male and female respondents; half of the group was either from the younger generation (27.3% were under the age of 29) or mature people (23.1% were in their 50's). Nearly half of the tourist respondents were clerical workers, professionals or housewives. The tourists had a relatively high educational background (university, 52.2%), and their income was higher than the national average.

Table 9.1   Response Rate

	Distribution-A	Usable Responses-B (B/A)	Non-response rate to WTP questions-C (C/B)	Protest NO response rate-D (D/(B-C-F))	Samples used to estimate WTP-E(E/A)	Not available-F (F/(B-C))
Nationwide survey	2,903	782 (26.9%)	40 (5.1%)	143 (20.7%)	549 (18.9%)	50 (6.7%)
Tourist survey	2,119	1,508 (71.2%)	77 (5.1%)	136 (10.8%)	1,122 (52.9%)	173 (12.1%)
Ainokura	1,353	974 (72.0%)	45 (4.6%)	89 (10.8%)	732 (54.1%)	108 (11.6%)
Suganuma	766	534 (69.7%)	32 (6.0%)	47 (10.8%)	390 (50.9%)	65 (12.9%)

Cf. Not available: Respondents who answered WTP questions but not questions about their income.

In contrast to the on-site survey of tourists, in the nationwide survey, the distribution of the residential areas of respondents was almost the same as that of the randomly extracted samples, which suggests that there is almost no regional bias in the survey. Because the telephone database was used, the respondents were relatively old and predominantly male. Their most common professions were pensioners (29.8%) and executives (15.0%). The group had a relatively high educational background (university, 36.3%) but their household income was relatively low[19]. This income represents only annual cash flow and does not consider the respondents' assets.

Respondents to both surveys were more interested in visiting temples, shrines and heritage sites, and the natural environment than is the nation on average (Table 9.2); their donation rate was lower than the national average. While the national average includes donations such as neighbourhood association fees, which are nominally difficult to refuse, the survey respondents understood donations as contributions that are truly voluntary.

Table 9.2   Activities in the Past One Year (% of Respondents) (Multiple Answers Allowed)

Activities	Nationwide survey	Tourist survey	National average
Experienced cultural activities	49.5%	60.6%	63.0%
Participated in cultural activities	7.9%	10.9%	19.5%
Visited temples, shrines, heritage sites	54.5%	49.2%	33.5%
Visited natural environment	35.3%	47.8%	30.8%
Volunteer experience	15.5%	11.5%	25.0%
Donation experience	29.2%	21.8%	68.0%

---

[19] It can be thought that the relatively low income of those who have retired and who are in their 20's resulted in the relatively low average income of this group, as the income level of those at the working age of 30's–50's of this group is higher than the national average income.

Cf. National Survey on Culture 2000 (Agency for Cultural Affairs), Leisure White Report on Social Life (Leisure Development Foundation, 1996), Survey on Time Use and Leisure Activities (Ministry of Internal Affairs and Communications, 2001), National Survey on Life Style Preferences (Cabinet Office, 2001)

The Gokayama hamlets are well known throughout Japan. As Table 4 shows, most of the respondents acknowledged the beauty of the hamlets. Of the respondents to the nationwide survey, 79.4% had at least some knowledge of the hamlets and 39.1% had visited the sites; an additional 13.7% of the nationwide survey respondents knew the names of the hamlets. Roughly half of the respondents to the tourist survey were repeat tourists (48.3%). Two-thirds of the respondents to both surveys recognized "cultural values," and roughly half recognized "bequest value" and "existence value" of the hamlets. With regard to images of the hamlets, more than half of the respondents in both surveys recognized the nostalgic Japanese landscape and traditional thatched-roof of the hamlets.

Table 9.3   Recognition and Views of the Hamlets

	Nationwide survey	Tourist survey
Aesthetic value of the hamlets		
The hamlets are very beautiful	422 (54.0%)	802 (53.2%)
The hamlets are relatively beautiful	244 (31.2%)	598 (39.7%)
Neutral	91 (11.6%)	68 (4.5%)
The hamlets are not beautiful	10 (1.3%)	36 (2.4%)
NOT AVAILABLE	15 (1.9%)	4 (0.3%
Knowledge of the hamlets		
Knew the hamlets well	84 (10.7%)	---
Learned about them at school	192 (24.6%)	---
Saw the hamlets on TV	345 (44.1%)	---
Knew the names of the hamlets	107 (13.7%)	---
Did not know	40 (5.1%)	---
N.A.	14 (1.8%)	---
Visiting experience		
Visited the hamlets many times	34 (4.3%)	215 (14.3%)
Visited the hamlets several times	272 (34.8%)	513 (34.0%)
Had seen photos of the hamlets	409 (52.3%)	---
Had neither visited nor seen the hamlets	59 (7.5%)	---
First visit to the hamlets	---	779 (51.7%)
N.A.	8 (1.0%)	1 (0.1%)
Opinions of the hamlets (multiple answers allowed)		
The hamlets have important cultural value	523 (66.9%)	1,032 (68.4%)
The hamlets should be passed on to next generations(bequest value)	393 (50.3%)	688 (45.6%)
Proud that the hamlets still exist	148 (18.9%)	192 (12.7%)
It is wonderful that the hamlets continue to exist(existence value)	372 (47.6%)	623 (41.3%)
It is fun to experience living in traditional houses	185 (23.7%)	351 (23.3%)
Want to come again(option value)	226 (28.9%)	294 (19.5%)
Images of the hamlets (multiple answers allowed)		
Mountainous hamlets	395 (50.5%)	563 (37.3%)
Nostalgic Japanese landscape	487 (62.3%)	818 (54.2%)
Traditional thatched roof	544 (69.6%)	822 (54.5%)
Living heritage	284 (36.3%)	394 (26.1%)
World Heritage	267 (34.1%)	448 (29.7%)
National Important Cultural Property	248 (31.7%)	207 (13.7%)

Regarding the unwillingness to pay, the questionnaire was intended to ask only those who refused to pay to specify their reasons; however, it was found that some respondents who agreed to pay also answered this question. Without cleaning the data, all the responses to this question are shown in Table 9.4. Most of the respondents answered that there should be another means of preserving the hamlets or that the proposed payment was too high. Thus, even quite a few of the respondents who agreed to pay still think there should be some other means of preserving the hamlets.

Table 9.5 shows the response rate regarding various possible measures for maintaining the hamlets. Respondents thought that the national and local governments should be responsible for preservation. The scenario in this survey seeks to ascertain the WTP voluntary funds for maintaining the hamlets but respondents prefer government support to voluntary support. Although respondents are willing to pay a certain amount to a voluntary fund, they also want the governments to support the hamlets at the same time.

Table 9.6 shows the willingness to do volunteer work for preservation of the historic hamlets.

From the nationwide survey, 18% of the respondents would like to work for the hamlets as volunteers, while 35.4% of tourists would like to be involved in volunteer work for the hamlets. In order to support this volunteer work, free accommodation, transport and insurance were requested. It is noted that information about the heritage villages is highly requested by tourists.

Table 9.4　Reasons for Rejection of Payment (Multiple Answers Allowed)

(Percentages in terms of total of negative responses)	Nationwide survey	Tourist survey
Total usable responses	782 (100.0%)	1508 (100.0%)
Negative responses*	338 (43.2%)	418 (27.3%)
Quasi-negative responses**	41 (5.2%)	83 (5.5%)
The bid amount is too high	85 (25.1%)	192 (45.9%)
	21 (51.2%)	39 (47.0%)
Not interested in the hamlets	22 (6.5%)	9 (2.2%)
	1 (2.4%)	1 (1.2%)
There should be other measures to preserve the hamlets	244 (72.2%)	207 (49.5%)
	25 (61.0%)	39 (47.0%)
Do not think the hamlets are valuable	11 (3.3%)	9 (2.2%)
	0 (0.0%)	1 (1.2%)
Do not understand the question	14 (4.1%)	25 (6.0%)
	2 (4.9%)	2 (2.4%)
Others	64 (18.9%)	43 (10.3%)
	3 (7.3%)	7 (8.4%)

Cf. * The responses are answers by those who refused to pay; ** The responses are answers by those who agreed to pay but answered this question.

Table 9.5　Measures to Preserve the Historic Hamlets (Multiple Answers)

	Nationwide survey	Tourist survey
Those who are concerned should preserve the hamlets	122 (15.6%)	216 (14.3%)
Residents should preserve the hamlets	43 (5.5%)	113 (7.5%)
Tourists should pay fees	201 (25.7%)	335 (22.2%)
Local governments should preserve the hamlets	411 (52.6%)	780 (51.7%)
The national government should preserve the hamlets	554 (70.8%)	987 (65.5%)
Others	22 (2.8%)	17 (1.1%)

Table 9.6   Volunteer Work

	Nationwide survey	Tourist survey
Willingness for volunteer work		
Want to do	141(18.0%)	534(35.4%)
Do not want to do	192(24.6%)	463(30.7%)
Can not do due to various reasons	397(50.8%)	404(26.8%)
N.A.	52(6.6%)	107(7.1%)
Necessary conditions for volunteer work*		
Free accommodation, transport	97(56.7%)	306(51.4%)
Insurance	58(33.9%)	181(30.4%)
Information of the hamlets	46(26.9%)	212(35.6%)
Membership system	39(22.8%)	114(19.2%)
Learning opportunities	43(25.1%)	135(22.7%)
Others	11(6.4%)	12(2.0%)

Cf. * multiple answers, percentage is the number of responses among 171samples for national survey and 595 samples for tourist survey who answered to this question.

9.3.2   Estimates of WTP and Analysis

In order to reduce bias, a double-bounded dichotomous choice CVM was applied, using a random utility model (Hanemann, et al., 1991)[20]. The scenario in the survey was to ask the respondents their amount of WTP to "a virtual fund" for preserving the hamlets, providing information about the present condition of the heritage hamlets through visual aids. The survey respondents were informed that the fund would be spent properly, that information about the fund would be open to the public and that donations to the fund would decrease the disposable income of each respondent[21].

The rate of agreement by the respondents to make the proposed payment to the fund is shown in Figure 9.10. As the proposed payment becomes higher, the acceptance rate decreases. Skew was

---

[20] Let the first bid be T, the second bid to a respondent who answers "yes" to T be Tu, and the second bid to a respondent who answers "no" to T be Td, where $Td<T<Tu$. The answers obtained by the double-bounded dichotomous choice will be yes/yes:yy, yes/no:yn, no/yes:ny, or no/no:nn. The respective probabilities (P) are shown in the equations below, where G(.) is the cumulative distribution function, X is socio-economic and attitudinal variables, and β is a parameter.

$$P_{yy}(T_i,Tu_i)=P\{T_i<Tu_i \ maxWTP_i\}=1-G(Tu_i;\beta X_i) \qquad (1)$$
$$P_{yn}(T_i,Tu_i)=P\{T_i \ maxWTP_i<Tu_i\}=G(Tu_i;\beta X_i)-G(T_i;\beta X_i) \qquad (2)$$
$$P_{ny}(T_i,Td_i)=P\{Td_i \ maxWTP_i<T_i\}=G(T_i;\beta X_i)-G(Td_i;\beta X_i) \qquad (3)$$
$$P_{nn}(T_i,Td_i)=P\{maxWTP_i<Td_i<T_i\}=G(Td_i;\beta X_i) \qquad (4)$$

If the respondent i answers yes to the bid amount T_i, $If_i=1$, and if the respondent answers no to the bid amount T_i, $If_i=0$. Also if the respondent answers yes to the second bid (Tu_i, Td_i), $Is_i=1$, and if the respondent answers no to the second bid, $Is_i=0$. The log likelihood function is shown in the following equation.

$$\ln L = \sum i\{If_iIs_i\ln P_{yy}(T_i,Tu_i)+If_i(1-Is_i)\ln P_{yn}(T_i,Tu_i)$$
$$+(1-If_i)Is_i\ln P_{ny}(T_i,Td_i)+(1-If_i)(1-Is_i)\ln P_{nn}(T_i,Td_i)\}$$
$$= \sum i[If_iIs_i\ln\{1-G(Tu_i;\beta X_i)\}$$
$$+If_i(1-Is_i)\ln\{G(Tu_i;\beta X_i)-G(T_i;\beta X_i)\}$$
$$+(1-If_i)Is_i\ln\{G(T_i;\beta X_i)-G(Td_i;\beta X_i)\}$$
$$+(1-If_i)(1-Is_i)\ln\{G(Td_i;\beta X_i)\}] \qquad (5)$$

Assuming G(.) follows a log-logistic distribution, we estimate the parameters α_0, α_1, and β using maximum likelihood estimation, where the log likelihood function is obtained below. P{"yes"} is the probability of the respondent who answers yes. By accumulating this function, the mean WTP will be obtained. In the case of P{"yes"}=0.5, the median WTP will be T.

$$P\{\text{"yes"}\}=\{1+\exp(-\alpha_0-\alpha_1 \cdot \ln T_i-\beta X_i)\}^{-1} \qquad (6)$$

[21] In the survey questionnaire, we informed respondents that the hamlets are registered as national heritage sites as well as UNESCO World Heritage sites, most of the traditional houses of the hamlets are 200–400 years old, and the roofs need to be repaired about every 10–15 years. Then we asked the questions to determine WTP to the fund only for maintaining the hamlets as they are now, by growing roofing grass, disseminating the necessary techniques for preservation of traditional houses, installing water tanks to protect against fire disasters, and other necessary measures.

relatively high, which is considered to be one of the characteristics of heritage; heritage has an extremely high value only to a certain segment of respondents.

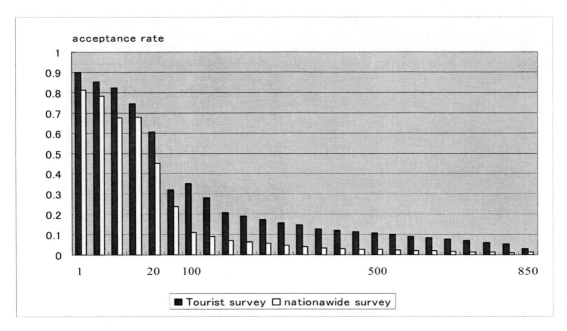

Figure 9.10   Acceptance Rate Dependence on WTP Bid Amounts (US Dollars)

Tourists were willing to pay for preservation of the historic hamlets based on aesthetic value (the hamlets are beautiful), cultural value and especially bequest value. Furthermore, the tourists' WTP has strong correlations with such variables as "volunteer experience" and "endorsement of support of the hamlets by the national government." These correlations can be interpreted as meaning that tourists are happy to be involved in preservation of the hamlets as volunteers and that they strongly wish the national government to extend support to preservation of the hamlets for future generations (Table 8).

Table 9.7   Variables and Estimated Coefficient (US$)

Variable name; quantity	Nationwide survey	Tourist survey (Ainokura)	Tourist survey (Suganuma)
Constant	3.08 (**)	8.98 (**)	5.79(**)
ln (T) bid amount	-1.19 (**)	-1.22 (**)	-1.13(**)
spontaneous visit	---	0.56 (**)	0.35
Beautiful landscape	---	0.39 (*)	0.31
Image as mountain village	---	-0.40 (*)	-0.28
Image as nostalgic village	---	0.21	-0.46(*)
Image as designated cultural property	---	0.15	0.62(*)
Recognition of cultural value	---	0.44 (*)	0.47
Recognition of bequest value	0.83 (**)	0.61 (**)	0.58(*)
Recognition of existence Value	0.63 (**)	-0.06	-0.53(*)
National gov't should supports the hamlets	---	0.39 (*)	0.85(**)
Gender(female)	---	-0.44(**)	0.58(**)
Age (years)	0.03 (**)	---	---
Income	0.59 (**)	-0.07	0.32(*)
Volunteer experience in the past one year	---	0.64 (**)	0.70(*)
N	549	732	390

Log likelihood	-649.123	-982.69	-545.13
Mean WTP (yen)	87.67	125.14	213.39
Confidence interval	56.83–179.44	90.03–208.44	114.90-661.09
Median WTP (yen)	15.98	25.75	27.54
Confidence interval	13.90–17.90	23.19-28.34	23.62-31.88

Cf.*rejected with 5% significance level, **rejected with 1% significance level. Confidence interval is set at 90%.

In general, WTP is expected to be correlated with household income, but such a correlation was not clearly observed in the tourist survey. It can be said that the tourists on average have more disposable income and the income factor does not necessarily affect their WTP. The average WTP of tourists is estimated at US$ 125 at Ainokura and US$ 213 at Suganuma, and the median WTP is estimated at US$ 26 and US$ 28 respectively for the same locations.

Based on the above results, it was concluded that tourists agreed that the village cannot be preserved solely by the efforts of its own residents, that the cultural landscape of the hamlets has significantly large social benefits and that tourists are willing to contribute not only financial support but also voluntary work to the hamlets based on their own judgment of the aesthetic, cultural and bequest values of the hamlets.

In the nationwide survey, the average WTP is estimated to be about US$ 88 and the mean WTP is estimated to be US$16. Correlation with WTP can be observed in such variables as the bequest value and existence value, age, and income factors. The correlation between WTP and income follows the general consumption rule.

Neither past visiting experience nor the intention to visit the village in the future has a significant statistical correlation with WTP. As mentioned above, the nationwide survey showed that the historic hamlets are quite well known, which may help to explain why the respondents were willing to pay for preservation of the historic hamlets regardless of whether they had visited them and/or wanted to visit them in the future.

The results of both surveys did not show any clear correlation between WTP and personal characteristics such as residential area, gender, educational background or profession. Education is not correlated with WTP in this survey, although the respondents in the survey were more educated than the average Japanese. This result can be interpreted as indicating that the benefits of cultural heritage, such as that found in the Gokayama hamlets, accrue to Japanese society as a whole rather than going only to a particular segment of society.

The survey results also suggest that heritage is an extremely strong public good and bequest value is the most important component of WTP, as was repeatedly observed in both the nationwide and tourist surveys.

A sensitivity analysis is conducted about "bequest value" and "existence value" of the nationwide survey, and "cultural value" and "aesthetic value" of the tourist survey, that showed strong correlations with the respective respondent groups' WTP. The results of this analysis are shown in Table 9.8.

Table 9.8   Sensitive Analysis (Unit: US$)

		Bequest value	Existence value	Cultural value	Aesthetic value
Mean WTP	Nationwide survey	81.2	54.9	---	---
	Tourist survey (Ainokura)	63.7	---	42.0	39.7
	Tourist survey (Suganuma)	27.2	---	81.3	218.5
Median WTP	Nationwide survey	10.9	8.6	---	---
	Tourist survey (Ainokura)	13.1	---	8.6	8.2
	Tourist survey (Suganuma)	14.3	---	10.2	7.5

9.3.3   Estimates of Total WTP (TWTP)

Table 9.9 shows estimates of the total willingness to pay (TWTP) of the national respondents and of tourists to these hamlets. TWTP is an aggregate of the groups' WTP multiplied by the population from which each sample is extracted. In this study, TWTP is estimated in the mean and the median of the respondents. The median TWTP is considered to be important for policy makers, as it is the amount which half of the population agrees to pay.

Table 9.9   Estimate of TWTP (US$)

	Nationwide survey	Tourist survey (Ainokura)	Tourist Survey (Suganuma)
Mean WTP	87.67	125.14	213.39
Median WTP	15.98	25.75	27.54
Estimated number of households (unit: thousand)	4,637.60	---	
Estimated number of tourists (unit: person)	---	56,742	38,694
Response rate (%)	26.9	72.0	70.0
Mean TWTP (1)	4,065,737,693	7,100,571	8,256,738
Mean TWTP (2)	1,093,683,440	5,112,411	5,779,716
Median TWTP (1)	740,939,330	1,461,131	1,065,551
Median TWTP (2)	199,312,680	1,052,014	745,886

Cf. (1) is a conventional model, multiplying WTP by the population; (2) is a multiplying model by the response rate of the survey, assuming that a non-respondent has zero WTP.

Considering some biases (for example, the "warm glow" which occurs when respondents agree to the payment proposed by the scenario, not because of its characteristics but because they think it is morally correct, and/or "symbolic bias" which occurs when respondents value a symbolic entity rather than actual item proposed by the scenario), two estimates are made: one is the conventional TWTP and the second is TWTP multiplied by the response rate, assuming that non-respondents have zero WTP.

As for TWTP of tourists, the number of tourists was estimated as follows: according to official data, more than 800 thousand people per year visit the Gokayama region where the hamlets are located and most of them are thought to visit the heritage hamlets. However, no detailed breakdown of the number of tourists is available and the annual number of tourists to the heritage hamlets was 95,000 in the year

2000, based on the number of cars that parked in Ainokura hamlet and the number of tourists to the museums of the two hamlets. Therefore, the concrete number of tourists was used: 95,000. Even when estimating based on this number, the mean TWTP of tourists equals at least 11 million US dollars per year.

Multiplying mean WTP in the nationwide survey (88 US dollars) and median WTP (16 US dollars) by the number of households (based on the 2000 national census) in Japan, mean TWTP amounts to 4.1 billion US dollars, with median TWTP at 0.7 billion US dollars. Multiplying by the response rate and the sample rate, they are 1.1 billion US dollars and 0.2 billion US dollars, respectively.

Although these figures are the smallest estimation, they are still enough to justify the current level of public support to these hamlets[22].

9.4   Policy Implications of CVM Studies

9.4.1   Findings of CVM Studies

Considering the above points, it can be concluded that:

- There is a strong consensus among tourists as well as the national population that the hamlets cannot be preserved solely by the efforts of their residents;

- The cultural landscape provides a large benefit to society as a whole;

- The CVM results can be said to justify more public support by both national and local governments;

- National benefits of the hamlets derive from non-use values, such as bequest value and existence value;

- The most important and fundamental value of the cultural landscape of the hamlets is bequest value;

- Cultural heritage can be said to be a public good;

- Tourists are willing to donate for preserving the hamlets and to do volunteer work based on their recognition of the aesthetic, cultural and bequest values of the hamlets;

- Tourists require governments to be more involved; and

- To facilitate the tourists' participation in the preservation of the hamlets, appropriate information should be provided in addition to provision of free accommodation and transportation, and good relationships should be established between residents and tourists.

---

[22] The public support of governments varies each year. In each year from 1998 to 2000, around 0.3 million US dollars was provided for preservation of the hamlets by the national government. The local governments added up to 0.6 million US dollars in total. An additional 1.6 million US dollars was provided for rural community development.

The above findings suggest possible options in addition to public funding by which the cultural landscape could be maintained by the tourists who are sensitive to various values of the hamlets. The residents of the hamlets, for their part, must make greater efforts to provide appropriate information and opportunities to learn about the hamlets, and to reach out to potential supporters from the large tourist pool.

9.4.2 Characteristics of Cultural Heritage

Cultural heritage has positive externality with non-use value, non-exclusivity and non-competitiveness. The characteristics can be examined in detail in order to consider possible policy measures based on the classification of public goods presented by the Organisation for Economic Co-operation and Development (OECD, Table 9.10).

Table 9.10   The Classification of Public Goods

	Non-rival	Congestible	Rival
Non-excludable	Pure public goods	Type II Open access resources	Type II Open access resources
Benefits involve only a small jurisdiction such as a municipality	Type I Local pure public goods		
Excludable only to outsiders of a community		Type III Common property resources	Type III Common property resources
Excludable	Type IV	Type V Club goods	Private goods

The cultural landscape of the historic hamlets can be classified as close to "pure public goods" due to the benefits to the nation (including non-users). On the other hand, for tourists (users), Ainokura hamlet would be classified as "club goods" because it charges fees for parking, while the Suganuma village, which is freely accessible to tourists, might be classified as "open access resources."

Open access resources are generally characterized by congestion and rivalry, which leads to over-consumption of resources. Club goods might be optimized if the number of tourists and the scale of resource consumption are balanced through good management. In this case, economic efficiency can be maximized, but it should be noted that management costs will be incurred.

Historic hamlets can be supported to a certain degree by public funding because they are classified as pure public goods. However, tourists experience benefits that the general population does not receive; these benefits derive from experiencing not only historic houses but also life inside the house and the surrounding environment, which they want to pass on to future generations. At the same time, tourists worry about over-consumption of hamlet resources and the majority think they can endure inconveniences such as lack of lodging houses and restaurants. This attitude of tourists suggests that promotion of only tourism-related business (and job creation) would satisfy neither the hamlet residents nor the tourists. Therefore, it is crucial to consider possible systems to create jobs not from ordinary tourism-related business but from the work necessary for maintaining the historic hamlets, such as growing grass for roofing, growing rice in the paddy and pruning trees in the forests.

In this sense, it is appropriate that Ainokura hamlet has established a foundation to provide services for maintaining the hamlets and to create jobs specifically for this purpose. By collecting fees from tourists, this foundation might be able to control the number of tourists, which is one of the ways to avoid over-consumption of resources. In practice, however, the foundation, with its limited number of staff, is only engaged in collecting fees from tourists. If the hamlets want to better involve tourists and improve the present tourism focusing on education, participation and awareness, they will need to provide appropriate information and create a membership system. The initial investment for this purpose should be made to develop skills and human resources. Considering the carrying capacity of the cultural landscape of the hamlets, it is also important to limit the number of tourists and avoid congestion in order to maximize the benefits for those who visit.

9.4.3   Possible Systems

Several possible systems for creating a beneficial relationship between tourists and the hamlets are compared in the following sessions:

Tax

A heritage tax might be one option. However, generally speaking, a dedicated tax is not the way to achieve optimal allocation of funds. In addition, the purpose of the tax must be narrowly defined in order to justify limiting the freedom of government budget distribution. Also, the entities to be taxed and the neutrality and fairness of such taxation would have to be clarified by governments.

Entrance fee

Since the tourists have a high TWTP to preserve the hamlets, entrance fees might be a useful option. As tourists prefer avoiding over-crowded conditions and over-consumption of resources, they are likely to agree to pay fees to cover the costs of preservation of the hamlets when they enter the sites. Taxes and entrance fees are measures to impose charges, which will not maximize the TWTP. Those who have lower WTP than the amount of introduced tax or fees might not visit the sites and thus TWTP will become smaller than estimated.

However, these systems would be effective in limiting tourists to an appropriate volume. Assume a decrease in the number of tourists to half of the present number and try to maximize TWTP. Median WTP in the tourist survey was roughly US$ 26 to 28. Sensitivity analysis focusing on values shows that the indirect use value (aesthetic value) is around 8 US dollars, while the bequest value is US$13 – 14 dollars and the cultural value is US$ 9 to 10 (Table 9.8). Therefore, the indirect use value occupies roughly 30% of the median WTP, and a fee of around 8 US dollars would likely be accepted.

The nationwide survey, on the other hand, shows that the median WTP is US$ 16, based mostly on non-use value. The difference between the median WTP of tourists (users) and national WTP (non-users) would be US$ 10 to 12, which might be considered as the WTP for use value. As a result, a fee between US$ 8 and 12 might be appropriate.

Three additional systems for creating a beneficial tourist-hamlet relationship could be considered:

Fund

Voluntary donation is one of the most powerful options to gain cooperation from those who are concerned about the preservation of the hamlets. If sufficient and appropriate information is provided, involvement of those potential supporters will be gained.

Membership

This would require an approach similar to that of seeking donated funds; in-depth information about the hamlets should be provided along with other merits for members, such as learning opportunities about the hamlets, facility use, and/or village product sales. In this case, the cultural landscape of the hamlets is classified as club goods, and the cost should be covered by members rather than by ordinary tourists.

Volunteers

Survey results show a positive correlation between volunteer experience and WTP, which implies that potential supporters might provide both financial, physical, and time resources.

In sum, several systems could be used for harmonizing heritage preservation and tourism. In order to maximize the TWTP, the voluntary donation (fund) mentioned in 1) above is most desirable.

It should be noted that the individual coverage of the cost of preservation of the hamlets should be limited so as not to impede access to the heritage. Moreover, it is crucial to have the participation of the local community for maintaining the landscape, where management plays an important role in coordinating support from all the stakeholders.

9.5 Conclusion

The results of the research show the nationwide accrual of the benefit of cultural heritage on a large scale, based mainly on non-use/non-market values such as bequest value and existence value. Even those who have not visited the hamlets are willing to pay some funds, because they want to pass on the historic houses as well as life inside the houses and the surrounding environment to future generations. These results strongly suggest that cultural heritage is a public good. Thus, more support from government for preservation of the hamlets can be justified. On the other hand, tourists benefit from experiencing the hamlets while the general population does not. Therefore it can be said that all of the beneficiaries and stakeholders – not only government, but also residents, tourists, and other concerned parties – should be involved in efforts to preserve these heritage values. In particular, tourists have the potential to play an important role in these efforts.

These heritage values, not only aesthetic values but also cultural and bequest values, are the essential core to attract tourists to the hamlets. Recognizing these values, tourists are visiting the hamlets and are willing to pay donations as well as to do volunteer work to preserve the hamlets. In order to facilitate and enhance the participation by tourists, it is recommended that local residents provide appropriate information and create a good relationship with tourists, focusing on education and awareness, which might improve the quality of culture-based tourism and lead to greater satisfaction among tourists who are sensitive to various values of the hamlets. At the same time, considering the carrying capacity of the cultural landscape of the hamlets, it might be desirable to limit the number of tourists to avoid congestion and overuse of the resources in order to maximize the benefits for those who visit and who are concerned.

This survey finds that tourists worry about over-consumption of hamlet resources and the majority believe they can endure inconveniences, such as a lack of lodging facilities and restaurants, and suggests that conventional promotion of ordinary tourism-related business might not satisfy the tourists. Therefore, it is crucial to consider sustainable systems to create jobs not from ordinary tourism-related business and events but from the works necessary for maintaining the historic hamlets, such as growing grass for roofing, growing rice in the paddy and pruning trees in the forests. Development of funds for such sustainable systems might be one option to creating such jobs as well as controlling congestion and overuse.

Without a healthy economy and community, heritage values cannot be maintained. Considering culture is an important component of tourism, tourism should be organized to contribute to local society and economy in a sustainable way rather than simply taking away something for themselves. Toward this end, the initiatives and involvement of local residents are crucial, and well-organized management is required.

References:

Hanemann, M. et al. (1991), 'Statistical efficiency of double-bounded dichotomous choicecontingent evaluation', American Journal of Agricultural Economics, 73, pp. 1255–1263.

Kakiuchi, E. (2005), Evaluating the Cultural Landscape, Suiyo-sha, Tokyo (in Japanese).

Kakiuchi, E. and Nishimura, Y. (2004), 'Quantitative evaluation of cultural capital using the CVM: The case of the world heritage villages of Gokayama, Toyama', Journal of the City Planning Institute of Japan, 39 (2), pp. 15-24. (in Japanese).

Kuriyama, K. et al. (2001), Economics of the World Heritage, Keiso Shobo, Kyoto (in Japanese).

Mitchell, R.C. and Carson, R.T. (1989), Using Surveys to Value Public Goods: The Contingent Valuation Method, Resources for the Future, Washington, D.C..

Organisation for Economic Co-operation and Development (2001), Multifunctionality towards an Analytical Framework, OECD, Paris.

Rolfe, J. and Windle, J. (2003), 'Valuing the protection of aboriginal cultural heritage sites', The Economic Record, Special Issue, 79, pp. 85–95.

Santangata, W. and Signorello, G. (2000), 'Contingent valuation of a cultural public good and policy design: The case of Napoli Musei Aperti', Journal of Cultural Economics, 24, pp. 181–204.

Yoshida, K. et al. (1997), 'Valuing economic benefits of agricultural landscape by double-bounded dichotomous choice CVM: A case study of Nose-town, Osaka Prefecture', Journal of Rural Planning Association, 16, pp. 205–215 (in Japanese).

Chapter 10 ——————————————————————

ICT Driven Business Approach for Sustainable Community-based Tourism Intervention: An Implementation Blueprint

10.1 Introduction

Of late, rural development and upliftment of backward regions is one of the prime concerns of policy makers, experts, and development specialists. The core objective is to target marginalised groups and communities in the countryside in terms of enabling economic opportunities for better living conditions. Amidst the scores of approaches adopted so far, promotion of tourism is seen as a vital measure to ensure a holistic and sustainable development of rural societies[23]. To put it explicitly, it is more of a promotion of tourism across rural culture, rural ecology and rural holistic learning and educational environment that communities should orient themselves towards.

Community-based tourism (CBT), when applied to economically marginalised populations, translates into a pro-poor tourism (PPT) intervention. Given that 70% of the world's poor live in rural areas and depend on agriculture for livelihood (Human Development Report, 2003), CBT initiatives tend to have a rural focus. In theory, CBT is initiated or managed by local communities to enhance their own interests (DFID, 1999). This "of the community, by the community, for the community" concept can therefore, it is argued, ensure retention of the revenues generated through tourism-related activities within the community, thus mitigating revenue leakages, which is a serious issue in tourism economics of developing and least developed countries (Ashley et al., 2000; Sinclair, 1998).

CBT projects/models entwined in ICT apparatus have recently appeared in developing countries and LDCs as a sustainable approach towards community development. Rural/eco-tourism is becoming one of the principal focus areas of attention. There is ample scope in India for such traditional tourism models. The Ministry of Tourism in India, for example, has launched a funding scheme for NGOs for tourism capacity-building and has adopted a cluster of villages for developing rural tourism[24]. Such initiatives implemented through NGOs with the appropriate expertise available at their disposal are showing encouraging results. A case in point is the rural heritage tourism project by the Indian National Trust for Art and Cultural Heritage (INTACH, 2007) in Raghurajpur in Orissa state.

—————————————————————————————————————

[23] Community tourism or rural or traditional tourism cannot be a sole livelihood opportunity. At best, it can complement the seasonal nature of occupational activities in the countryside.
[24] http://tourism.nic.in

From the perspective of Information and Communication Technologies for Development (ICT4D) in a tourism perspective, UNCTAD has launched an e-tourism platform which is still at a nascent stage of development[25]. UNCTAD made a presentation to this effect at the WSIS summit in Tunis in early 2006. A conference for the Asia Pacific region on this theme was organised in March 2007 in Malaysia. Something quite do-able and tangible at the grassroots level is putting together low cost technology solutions (hardware, FLOSS etc.) with a workable business plan for community-based tourism (CBT) in rural/non-urban areas. An example is the agro-sector focused e-choupal model of village internet centers established in rural

Madhya Pradesh, central India (Kumar, 2004).   Harris and Rajoura (2006b) have studied the role of ICT4D interventions   in rural poverty alleviation schemes in India and the lessons drawn would be useful in the context of ICT facilitated pro-poor tourism initiatives such as the one proposed for Dausa.

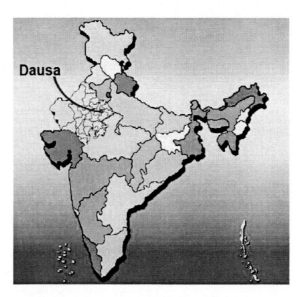

Figure 10.1   Location of the Geography of Intervention

The Dausa ICT-based CBT project is a conscious formulation of a concept for ideational and implementation purposes. The tourism model is focussed on the Dausa district community utilising its local cultural and traditional heritage assets and resources. The rich culture, tradition and history marked by age-old monuments and edifices in Dausa make it a suitable base for ICT-based CBT intervention. In this approach, the principal critical success factors are viability gap funding and sound business models to sustain operations once the funding phase is over and once the technological interventions are worked out. Another core necessity is a sound infrastructural base in Dausa including e-infrastructure[26].

Dausa is a backward district in the state of Rajasthan, 50 km from the state capital of Jaipur and 300 km from the national capital, New Delhi. The geographic location is illustrated in Figure 10.2. It is conveniently situated on the periphery of the famed Delhi-Jaipur-Agra golden triangle, arguably India's most popular tourist circuit. These pockets of urban prosperity are home to many professionals, possibly looking for rejuvenating weekend getaways, and school children (and their parents) seeking an

---

[25] http://etourism.unctad.org
[26] E-infrastructure is availability of a sound network of ICT infrastructure in terms of telephone, internet, connectivity as well as
  a computer-enabled society and institutional set ups.

educational experience of a holistic and balanced approach to life and proximity to nature. These are the principal target market segments for this CBT intervention.

Overseas visitors undertaking the golden triangle tour circuit are also an important (but not the principal) segment that will complement the market mix. There being no price differentiation between the local and foreign tourists in the CBT space, greater reliance on the more dependable and accessible domestic market segments will bode well for long term sustainability of the CBT product. This assessment is consistent with the findings of Archer's (1978) study which concludes that domestic tourism is a better local income generator in comparison to international tourism. Awasthi et al.'s (2006) observation that the recipe for success for the Indian tourism sector is a balanced mix of domestic and international markets and the domestic traveller holds the key to sustainable growth. Disintermediation (the movement of funds from one investment vehicle to another) achieved through effective deployment of ICT is expected to effectively address the problem of revenue leakages. The model also incorporates capacity-building for the stakeholders at the vocational/crafts level as well as basic business skills. Training in ICT will be an integral part of the capacity building process. This study discusses the practical modalities associated with executing this intervention. The conjectures and the proposed model are expected to serve as a blueprint for implementation of this CBT project.

10.2 Dausa Community-based Tourism

As previously stated, the focus of this study is on developing a CBT model for the Dausa community using ICT. Dausa is a poor region and is largely populated by economically disadvantaged and socially backward people. As per the 2001 India census[27], Dausa town had a population of 61,589 and the district population was around 1.3 million. The district level statistics reveal that males constitute 53% of the population and females 47%. The average literacy rate is 66%, with male literacy at 76% and female literacy at 54%. In Dausa, 16% of the population is under 6 years of age. Approximately 77% of the workforce is engaged in agro-economic activities. A case in point of its backwardness is the finding of a survey in early 2006 which revealed very low school enrolment rates among girls. Some had never gone to school and many had dropped out after two years in primary school[28]. It is also one of the largest districts in the country in terms of area. Dausa, 300 km from Delhi, would serve both foreign tourists as well the domestic tourists from the urban expanse of Gurgaon, Noida, Delhi, Jaipur and Agra. It is important for such CBT destinations to be a drivable distance from metropolitan areas so that the urbanites could be a catchment market for generating awareness of typical village life which, even though so close, may never have been experienced.

Dausa is an ancient town of archaeological importance and is the capital of the district of the same name. It is located at a distance of about 51 km from Jaipur, the capital city of Rajasthan state. The main attractions of the town are temples, the magnificently carved mansions or havelis, the mosque or dargah of Hazrat Khwaja Jamaluddin Shah Baba and Pratap Vatika, an architectural marvel. There is a fort perched atop a nearby hill, called Devgiri. In terms of its historical legacy and significance, Dausa was the first capital of the Kachwaha Rajput Empire. Though no visitor statistics are available, major tour operators include Dausa on package tour circuits of Jaipur. In addition to the heritage attractions, the Sawa and Ban Ganga rivers run through the district, thereby providing potential opportunities for eco-tourism. To the limited extent that CBT is presently practiced in Dausa, basic boarding and lodging facilities are available in some of the havelis or mansions. As such, CBT has not yet evolved into an organised product and in the absence of viable statistics it is difficult to gauge the impact of tourism on the local economy. It is expected that in addition to providing visibility and market access, the ICT

[27] http://www.censusindia.net/
[28] http://www.humana-india.org/Articel.asp?NewsID=28

intervention will mitigate this problem by facilitating easy documentation, access and interpretation of such data. Table 10.1 provides a synopsis of the benefits that will accrue to the Dausa CBT intervention from the deployment of ICT.

Role of ICT in Dausa CBT

Information and communication technology is currently not playing any significant role in the promotion of Dausa's tourism strengths. Nevertheless, there is an increasing demand for cultural, traditional and environmental tourism products. Dausa being a traditional society with a rich cultural and historical background could be a much sought-after destination in Rajasthan. Thus, if positioned appropriately it could well be poised for a significant increase in visitor arrivals. Any effort towards growth in tourism must be effectively managed in order to sustain important landscapes, protect and enhance the quality of life of the targeted community, and increase economic benefits associated with the industry. Figure 2 provides a conceptual diagram of the Dausa CBT ecosystem.

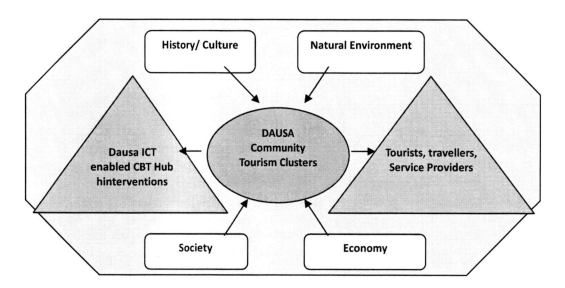

Figure 10.2   Community-based Tourism (Cbt)

Cases drawn from rural New Zealand and small island states in the South Pacific provide insights into the role that information and communication technologies (ICT) and community informatics (CI) can play in improving communication, cooperation and level of understanding between various stakeholders (tourists, residents, industry and government) in the tourism development process   (Milne, 2006). The adoption of innovative ICT tools in both business and community settings can enhance the economic performance and broader sustainability of tourism, provided this process is dovetailed with the local ethos and the essence of hospitality and tourism as a service. It is imperative that the effectiveness of an ICT intervention in tourism be gauged from the perspective of the human-technology interface, given that in this sector, "both high tech and high touch are essential success factors" (Nadkarni, 2003: 52). ICT has the potential to collect, analyse and distribute information widely across the sector, supporting a better understanding of visitors' needs, preferences and behaviours (Noddera et al. 2000). The exploitation of ICT offers the opportunity to realise significant benefits for CBT interventions, and Dausa is no exception.

Establishing the awareness of those people in local administrative capacity charged with the development of Dausa to build critical mass, nurture co-operation and facilitate specialisation using ICT as an enabler of the process is a key issue.   In this context, the effective use of ICTs offers a variety of ways to support the process of developing clusters of Small and Medium Tourism Enterprises (SMTEs) in Dausa communities. Clustering is seen as a critical success factor in the support of these businesses. Overall, the strategy to deploy ICT for Dausa community CBT would embrace the following:

- Adequate delivery of ICT infrastructure around the Dausa community and tourism clusters. Effective use of ICT as a tool to assist in relationship-building, in particular the use of cost-effective methods such as e-mail and Voice Over IP (VOIP)

- Development of improved networks facilitated by the use of ICT.

- Creation of web-based tool kits that can be accessed and updated.

- Adequate ICT training to community stakeholders.

- Developing close links between Dausa CBT requirements and ICT training providers and focusing on the labour market implications of ICT introduction into the domestic tourism enterprises.

- Pre- and post-CBT research activities to gauge the implications and impacts of ICT interventions.

- Establishment of an ICT sub-committee of the proposed Destination Management Organisation (DMO) to oversee ongoing Dausa CBT education and awareness programmes.

- Actively linking Dausa community into the broader regional and national tourism development process and contours.

- Using ICT to share resources and disseminate information.

- Improving the quality and integration of core datasets pertaining to Dausa CBT to support effective sector analysis.

Table 10.1   ICT as an Enabler of Dausa CBT Model

Strategy	Action (ICT as an enabler)
Development of a sound profile of tourism assets of Dausa District	A database to record details of tourism assets and operators in the area as well as interested individuals and parties.
Promoting participation in cluster activities through a range of product and service channels	Detailing out (mailing) related materials about clusters to operators, individuals and groups.
Facilitating an online Dausa tourism Community	Developing communications to share local, regional, national and international information about the tourism sector. This will be achieved through a new Dausa website where members having access can chat, enter discussion forums and download relevant information.
Collating and disseminating information about tourism in the local community	Electronic newsletters that summarise key statistics and research findings of Dausa, linking to other source materials and downloads
Conducting research into the needs of clusters across Dausa district	Assessing research needs of local and special interest clusters. This could be done through a variety of channels of communication – forums, email, newsletters, and online surveys.
Undertaking assessment or product development and training needs as per Dausa CBT requirements	Undertaking training needs survey (quantitative and qualitative analysis could be supported by ICT applications)
Ensuring that the district is effectively represented on the Internet in a comprehensive manner	Establishing a website to provide non-commercial information about the district and encouraging tour operators to register. *"about CBTs within the district" would seem more accurate*

10.3   Salient Features/Observations

The salient features of this proposed CBT intervention with a strong ICT component are:

- "Glocal" market mix that reduces over-reliance on a single source market;

- Strategic location by virtue of geographic proximity to the high tourist density golden triangle zone of Delhi-Jaipur-Agra;

- CBT activity as a bottom-up (not substitute) approach to complement existing agro-economic base;

- Guests experience an authentic (not "commodified") way of life in rural India, thereby contributing towards conserving a living heritage;

- Value-added role, wherein, in addition to revenues, the host community gains insight into the pros and cons of urban/foreign lifestyles from guests, broadening horizons;

- NGO-facilitated viability gap funding, capacity building and publicity;

- "For-profit" business model to ensure financial viability in the post-intervention phase;

- Dausa village community to be the sole stakeholder thereby making it the beneficiary as well as benefactor, upon attaining break-even;

- Host community's skills, time and knowledge to be deployed as "provisions" for CBT activities;

- Innovative low cost scalable ICT driven business process with dissemination and transaction capability;

- Optimal utilisation of ICT infrastructure through shared deployment in tourism and non-tourism related commercial and educational activities;

- Higher profitability through ICT-induced disintermediation in the backward/forward linkages of tourism and other commercial enterprises.

- There is presently little reference to consultation with the wider community or to the Councils of neighbouring communities. To be operating in such isolation does little to endear the Council and SMTEs to those in the community who are resistant to tourism development.

- There is also little evidence of participation by tourists or any reference made to the desires of prospective visitors to the region.

10.4   Framewok for Proposed Intervention

The Dausa CBT project is focused on community-based intervention and networking. In other words, the project would have an informal structural and functional approach. An informal approach can best suit the CBT project and serve real community needs.

10.4.1   Components of the Dausa CBT

The Dausa Community-based Tourism initiative revolves around the following community oriented components:

Historical/Heritage Tourism

From the various artefacts found and that lie scattered in the region, Dausa is believed to have been the habitation of pre-historic man. Visitors can make trips to the historical temples of Goddess Harshad Mata and the Chand bawdi (Deep Well); Mataji Ka Mandir (finely carved sculptures dating back to 12th century AD); Nilkanth Mahadev Temple on the Aravalli Hill Ranges; Century old Shrine (Mazhar) of Hazrat Kwhaja Sheikh Jamal Shah located within the Dausa city; the Buddha Stupa at Bhandarej and many other small and large monuments. Besides engaging the local community in preserving and maintaining the monuments near them, the local citizens could   be engaged in making arrangements to provide the tourists and visitors with boarding and lodging that is purely local and eco-friendly in nature.

10.4.2   Culture and Handicrafts Tourism

The Dausa CBT experience will be characterised by a strong element of local culture and tradition. Tourists shall have opportunities to become acquainted with local art, craft, dress, food, belief and festivals. Visitors can savour local culinary specialities like Choorma Dal Bati (pulse based dish); Bajre ki Rabri (flat and round eatables made of Bajra cereal), Jokhwa (item made of cereal) and the like. Among folk arts, Hela Khayal is a unique singing style of this region. Dhundhari is spoken as a local dialect. One can also come across community societies in Dausa district like the Lakhera and the Nath ethnic groups having their own community marriage practices. In terms of arts and artefacts tourists can have a real taste of these, wrought by hand in historical monuments like Abhaneri ki Bawdi. Seasonal festivals like the spring Basant Panchami Festival, Mahadev Mela, Balaji Mela, Ganagaur Mela and Paplaj Mata Mela are also part of Dausa CBT experience. The local community can have good commercial returns at the Dausa CBTRC and in cluster sites.

10.4.3   Safari Tourism

Safari trips shall be another focal attention of the Dausa CBT project. Visitors and tourists can be introduced to the natural beauty of Dausa. Potential areas for Safari are Shetal, Jhajirampura, and Ranoli. The Ghomna Bandh is a natural dam and another area of attraction, the Paproj mata Devi mandir is located in the vicinity. Jhajirampura has a spectacular water fall. Local people shall be equipped to deal with the Safari visitors. This shall serve as another revenue-generating activity for the locals while entertaining the tourists, mostly harried city dwellers, in the serene, calm Dausa surroundings.

10.4.4   Overnight Accommodation for Tourists

Boarding and lodging amenities shall be another component for the Dausa CBT. These will be basic in nature and consistent with the local ethos. Hygiene standards will be maintained through appropriate capacity initiatives and the facilities will be managed by the community partners in and around the tourism locations. This opportunity for enterprise shall earn a modest revenue stream for the locals.

Major points for developing CBT are:

- The project fits well into the concept of eco-tourism, edu-tourism, rural-tourism, holistic tourism. It is being setup in a rural belt, where the potential for use of already existing ingredients of tourism could be an added advantage.

- It would have traditional dwellings entirely made by the community from the materials which would be absolutely local.

- It would have as stakeholders all the villages around it, particularly the village which is the closest to the place of intervention.

- It would have all the fundamentals of adopting the local village/s and their practices and culture.

- It would have teaching and learning centres – one part of this will serve the villagers and the other part of it will serve the visitors.

- It will offer local cuisine prepared by the villagers using local supplies and farm fresh vegetables, and all the activities will have a local flavour without compromise.

- The visitors can share their culture to make the villagers aware and knowledgeable.

- There will be a resource centre-cum mall which will have locally produced items for sale to visitors.

- All the local historical places will be included in tour itineraries and locals will be coached in the basics of tour guiding.

- The providers and facilitators would be village community members and they would simultaneously be the direct beneficiaries.

- There will be a large scale ICT intervention at the place for the benefit of the local villagers.

- The other ICT involvement would be to sell through payment gateway-based   GLOCAL portal of the place thereby allowing the revenues from this enterprise to go directly to the village community by virtue of disintermediation.

- To reduce, if not entirely eliminate, the revenue leakages it is essential for the members of the host community to have as much direct ownership as possible of their enterprises spread across the supply-side verticals.

- On the demand side, the village-to-village and more importantly perhaps, the urban-to-village contours (weekend getaways, edu/eco tours) shall ensure the critical mass to make an entrepreneurial venture viable in a village, non-urban context.

- Micro credit, viability gap funding mechanisms could be a way out for the village, non-urban entrepreneur to become well-engaged with the Dausa CBT.

- Timely capacity-building and ICT-facilitated information access and interchange (e.g. glocal portal).

The unique feature of this intervention is that at a time when many tourism ventures are offering local content to a global audience, in this case the global audience also includes those who come from neighbouring villages. Domestic tourism in India has been witnessing a phenomenal growth and with numbers in 2006 estimated at 425 million, of which 200 million (or 47%) were rural residents (Awasthi, 2007), this grassroots segment can be an important source of custom to CBT destinations such as Dausa. On a more localised scale, these are the visiting friends and relatives (VFR), pilgrimage and business travel segments that can accentuate the tourism multiplier effect in the host community by virtue of their sheer volume. This is exactly opposite to the bottom of the pyramid concept of Prahalad (2006), where the focus is on assessing the consumption capacity and purchasing power for white goods on the part of the rural poor. In this CBT intervention, the acceptable medium and approach is that villagers at the bottom are the providers and the world at the top of Prahalad's (2006) pyramid are the consumers. Following is a synopsis of the intervention.

10.4.5 Dausa CBT Project Elements:

- A web-based community platform

- Village clusters as tourism huts/clusters

- Effective setting up and running of Community-based Tourism Resource Centre (CBTRC)

- Information and communication channels between the CBTRC and the tourism huts or clusters

- Internet working and communication between local tourism stakeholders

- An effective supply chain of local products and services for the CBTRC and tourism huts/clusters

- Marketing and Promotion

- Strong and effective information and communication networking

10.4.6 The Dausa CBT Web Portal

To be made available in English and local language (Hindi), the DAUSA CBT Web platform shall highlight the local community in different perspectives as shown in Table 10.2:

Table 10.2   Vectors of Dausa CBT Web Platform

Geography	Small scale industries & micro-enterprise	Culture and heritage assets (tangible and intangible)
Demographics	Mineral based activities	Entertainment
History	Finance	Links with newspapers and electronic media
Social profile	Self Help Group Activities	Employment, education section
Economic status	Tourism profile	Institutions profile
Agriculture and allied sectors	Pilgrimage centres	Links with other geographies and institutions

10.5   Expected Impact Analysis

The advantages and challenges from the ICT-based Dausa CBT are quite discernable. Initiating such community-oriented projects that also involve technology in an otherwise technologically resistant community has its own advantages and limitations. The traditional social and cultural features appear to give more challenges than options for easy initiation and execution of such community developmental schemes. Nevertheless, the Dausa CBT model is expected to ensure the following crucial advantages.

- Augmentation to local economy and revenue-generating activities;

- Growth and streamlining of local SMTEs in and around Dausa;

- Networking opportunities with the outside world for knowledge, information exchange and exposure to alternative lifestyles and cultures;

- Visitors and tourists coming close to a new world of local culture, tradition, way of living and natural surroundings;

- Impetus to an information and knowledge society in Dausa;

- Exchange of cultures and traditional knowledge in a bottom-up and top-down channelling processes;

- The development of small, medium and micro enterprises now has the potential to foster growth of a strong SMTEs economic base and build linkages with the rest of the economy.

- A sustainable tourism development programme;

- A fillip to existing local business and trade.

The Channel of Revenue Generation/Business Model

The stakeholders' responsibilities will be delineated in the interest of an efficient workflow process that will help sustain the proposed model. Stakeholders across the CBT value chain include the service provider (the CBT enterprise), the service consumer (the tourist) and the benign intermediaries (implementing NGOs and the local government). Revenue shall accrue from the Dausa CBTRC through the following interventions and service delivery:

- The CBTRC shall be providing a one-stop platform for tourism products and services minus e external services like sight seeing;

- Tourism clusters or huts shall have revenue generation accruing from serving visitors;

- A revenue structure shall be worked out between the CBTRC and the tourism clusters for mutual gains on the demand-supply chain;

- Community people to earn revenue from selling of products and services to the prospective buyers at CBTRC;

- Revenue shall accrue to the CBTRC thorough the provision of modest accommodation and hospitality services with a local ambience to the visitors.

10.6   Inferences/Lessons Learnt in Implementation

Community-based tourism is not always successful. It is prudent to estimate and perhaps begin to look at failures as pathways to success. Rural community tourism takes place in already marginalized areas. Created with good intentions, community-based tourism projects sometimes faqil when political pressures rise, project finances run dry, community resistance and lack of participation become pronounced, jealousies intensify or the heralded eco-tourists do not arrive[29].

There may be challenges vis-à-vis uptake of ICT by SMTE including: a lack of training and capital, limited understanding of the potential of technology, and lack of clear business strategies (Buhalis 1996; Hull and Milne 2001). The degree to which these difficulties can be mitigated depends, to some extent, on the effective implementation of government policies (Grant et al., 2001; Atkinson and Wilhelm 2002). The role of the government is to ensure that the infrastructure is available to enable full advantage to be taken of the opportunities offered by ICT. The support of the local government will therefore be crucial for the project because it is often the scale at which most direct interaction with business is felt and is often closely tied up with areas such as training and network development (Buhalis 2000). Local bodies are often best positioned to identify the policy mechanisms that suit local business and commercial needs as well as on the needs and feasibility of communication technologies that can enhance interaction amongst interested communities.

Shifting consumer demands and the need for organisations and community tourism clusters, including the Dausa CBTRC, to adjust flexibly and efficiently to a variety of external pressures, shall necessitate timely changes to their organisational strategies (Wilson, 2002). Pressure has mounted on regional and local tourist destinations to restructure, re-engineer and/or redesign hardware, software and human ware within the core and peripheral tourism businesses (Weiermair, 2001). Collaboration, community-building and communication are all areas covered by policy as are capacity-building and network enhancement (Wilson, 2002). Welcoming participation and facilitating such exchanges through the strategic use of ICT can assist Dausa's not so "stubbornly self-sufficient and competitively focused" tourism business community to engage in networks (Wilson, 2002:11).

The necessity of a sound and practical Dausa district tourism policy and strategy that is "in sync" with local environment, social, cultural and economic setups and in tune with changing technology needs for community-based development projects, including promotion of rural holistic tourism, should not be overlooked. The engagement of the local Dausa community holds critical in the success of the CBT model. There need to be regular consultations with the wider community, for the project cannot operate in isolation and instead this would boomerang on the prospective revenue-generating activities for the community clusters and the local SMTEs. The model needs to be scalable in order to ensure long-term economic viability.

10.7 Conclusion

This paper has conjectured that the Dausa intervention can embrace both ICT and tourism at a community level, however, the critical point being brought into focus is how to ensure that local involvement and participation shall be active and that the project can be sustained in a manner that leads to effective development outcomes in the medium to long run. The issues and thoughts raised in this paper highlight the fact that one of the core challenges in a backward community setting like Dausa remains as to how to effectively deploy and deliver outcomes using ICT on a large scale.

On a positive note, ICT has the capacity to affect relationships, drive effective business strategies, build and establish networks and communities (both virtual and real), and add new dimensions to the capabilities of a network of organisations to actively participate in the Dausa CBT project for mutual and multiple gains. Nevertheless, the fact does not change that in Cyberspace, just as in traditional

---

[29] http://www.planeta.com/ecotravel/tour/community.html

communities, citizens must be motivated and engaged effectively if they are to participate in a community project like the Dausa CBT. Though the Internet tends to change the capacity and quantity of information that is available, Bimber (1998:138) asserts that "it is not yet clear that it will also change motivation and interest, let alone cognitive capacity." The challenge is therefore there to see and experiment.

References:

Archer, B. (1978), 'Domestic tourism as a development factor', *Annals of Tourism Research*, 5(1), pp. 126-140.

Ashley, C., C. Boyd, and H. Goodwin (2000), 'Pro-poor tourism: putting poverty at the heart of the tourism agenda', *Natural Resource Perspectives*, 51, pp. 1-6.

Atkinson, R. and T. Wilhelm (2002), *The Best States for E-Commerce, Technology and New Economy Project*, Progressive Policy Institute, Washington D.C.

Awasthi, R., I. Dutta-Gupta and R. Singh (2006), 'Go! Trek, trip or Cruise', *The Economic Times*, Mumbai, 1 Oct., p. 6.

Awasthi, R. (2007), 'Domestic travellers too going places', *The Economic Times*, Mumbai, 15 Apr., p. 6.

Bimber, B. (1998), 'The Internet and political transformation: Populism, community and accelerated pluralism', *Polity*, 31(1), pp. 133-160.

Buhalis, D. (2000), 'Tourism and information technologies: past, present and future', *Tourism Recreation Research*, 25(1), pp. 41-58.

Buhalis, D. (1996), 'Enhancing the competitiveness of small and medium sized tourism enterprises at the destination level by using information technology', *Electronic Markets*, 6 (1), pp.1-6.

Cattarinich, X. (2001), 'Pro-poor tourism initiatives in developing countries: analysis of secondary case studies', PPT Working Paper No. 8, Department for International Development, London.

Department for International Development (1999), *Tourism and Poverty Elimination: Untapped Potential*, DFID, London.

Grant, G., C. Louis, M. Maheshwari, D. Murty and Tao Y. (2001), *Regional Initiative for Informatics Strategies: Sector ICT Strategies Planning Templates*, (Online), available: http://www.caribank.org/downloads/ICT_Policy.pdf (17-1-2007).

Harris, R., D. Vogel and L. Bestle (2006a), 'E-Community-Based Tourism for Asia's Indigenous People', in L. Dyson, M. Hendriks & S. Grant (eds.), *Information Technology and Indigenous People*, Hershey: Idea Group Inc..

Harris, R. and R. Rajora (2006b), 'Empowering the Poor: Information and Communications Technology for Governance and Poverty Reduction--A Study of Rural Development Projects in India', UNDP-APDIP Elsevier, Singapore.

Hull, J. and S. Milne (2001), 'From nets to the 'Net': marketing tourism on Quebec's lower north shore', in N. Baerenholdt & J. Aarsaether (eds.), *Coping Strategies in the North* (Vol. 2), Copenhagen: Nordic Council of Ministers.

Human Development Report (2003), Oxford University Press, New Delhi.

INTACH (2007), *Raghurajpur: A Case Study in Sustainable Rural Heritage Tourism*, INTACH, New Delhi.

Jamieson, W. (2006), 'Defining Urban Tourism Destination Management', in W. Jamieson (ed.), *Community Destination Management in Developing Economies*, Haworth Hospitality Press, New York, pp. 3-36.

Koster, R. and J. Randall (2005), 'Indicators of community economic development through mural-based tourism', *The Canadian Geographer*, 49(1), pp. 42-60.

Kumar, R. (2004), 'E-choupals: A study on the financial sustainability of village internet centers in rural Madhya Pradesh', *Information Technologies and International Development*, 2(1), pp. 45-73.

Milne, S. (2006), *ICT and Sustainable Development: cases and observations from the South Pacific*, Seminar on e-Tourism, New Zealand Tourism Research Institute, Auckland.

Murphy, P. and H. Renwick (1987), 'Tourism: A Community Approach', *Geographical Review*, 77(2), pp. 246-248.

Murphy, P. (1985), *Tourism: A Community Approach*. Methuen, New York.

Nadkarni, S. (2003), 'IT Competencies in Tourism Management Education', *Journal of Information Technology and Tourism*, 6(1), pp. 47-54.

Noddera, C., N. Cateb, K., Slaterc and S. Milne (2000), *ICT, Local Government & Tourism Development: Cases from Auckland, New Zealand*, New Zealand Tourism Research Institute, Auckland University of Technology, Auckland.

Prahalad, C. (2006), *The Fortune at the Bottom of the Pyramid: Eradicating Poverty Through Profits*, Wharton School Publishing, NJ.

Redclift, M. (1987), *Sustainable Development: Exploring the Contradictions*, Methuen, London.

Sen, A. (1981), *Poverty and famines: An essay on entitlement and deprivation*, Clarendon Press, Oxford.

Sinclair, T. (1998), 'Tourism and economic development: a survey', *The Journal of Development Studies*, 34(5), pp. 1-51.

Weiermair, K. (2001), 'The Growth of Tourism Enterprises', *Tourism Review*, 56(3/4), pp.17-25.

Wilson, H. (2002), *NZ SMEs: Annotated Bibliography, Key Findings and Recommendations for Research and Policy*, University of Auckland, Auckland.

Zurick, D. (1992), 'Adventure Travel and Sustainable Tourism in the Periphery Economy of Nepal', *Annals of the Association of American Geographers*, 82(4), pp. 608-628.

Country Experiences and Country Strategies

Chapter 11

Sustainable Development of Community-based Tourism in Iranian Rural Areas

11.1 Tourism Development in Iran

Before 1979, Iran was a relatively popular destination due to its exotic nature, rich cultural resources and impressive history of over 3000 years. Before the Revolution, many American hotel chains set up business throughout the country; and the numbers of international visitors increased. However, after the Revolution, all Western businesses were forced to pull out and Iran's tourism sector plummeted. The economy dropped further due to the eight-year war with Iraq.

Since the election of President Mohammad Khatami, Iran's image has changed significantly and tourism has become a top priority in developmental plans for the country. International visitors have increased from 70,000 in 1988 to 1.6 million in 2005 (Table 11.1) and a 20-year perspective plan targets ways in which Iran hopes to capture one and a half percent of the world's total tourist arrivals annually. This is not at all an unrealistic goal considering that the United Nations Educational, Scientific, and Cultural Organization (UNESCO) ranks Iran seventh in the world in terms of possessing historical monuments, museums and other cultural attractions. Unfortunately, however, Iran has been placed at 70th worldwide in terms of its tourism hosting capacity and 13th among Moslem countries. Iran's market share of total Middle East demand is 16.7%, but on the global scale it is a mere 0.35% (WTTC, 2005).

Table 11.1   International arrivals to Iran and international tourism receipts (1990- 2005)

Year	International Tourist Arrivals	Change (%)	International Tourism Receipts (US$ million)	% Change
1990	161954	72.4	65	38.2
1991	249103	53.8	105	61.5
1992	275672	10.7	120	14.2
1993	311243	12.9	131	9.1
1994	360658	15.9	155	18.3
1995	488908	35.6	205	32.2
1996	573449	17.3	261	27.3
1997	764092	33.2	352	34.8
1998	1007598	31.9	464	31.8
1999	1320905	31.1	586	26.2
2000	1341762	1.6	671	14.5
2001	1402160	4.5	701	4.4
2002	1585000	13.0	792	12.9
2003	1546335	-2.4	750	-5.3
2004	1649479	6.7	829	10.5
2005	1600000	-2.9	1074	29.5

Source: Iran Cultural Heritage and Tourism Organization (2005).

After the 1979 Revolution, the first official document on the development of tourism in Iran was prepared for the first Five-Year Social and Economic Development Plan implemented during the period 1989-1993 defined specific objectives, policy and framework for the development of the tourism industry after the Islamic revolution. One of the main objectives was to increase interest for visiting Iran's natural and cultural attractions both on national and international levels and developing tourist facilities, services and other infrastructure. But community-based tourism was only paid attention in the third Five-Year Social and Economic Development Plan (2000-2004), Iran's Tourism Development and Management Master Plan in 2001-2002; and again in the fourth Five-Year plan (2005-2009) with a 20-year perspective plan.

Though these national development plans have all emphasized tourism, they have mostly been concerned with increasing tourist arrivals, marketing and physical development in terms of infrastructure, access and facilities. Local involvement in tourism activities was not sufficiently emphasized. However, the introduction of sustainable development has gradually changed the role of community-based tourism in overall tourism development strategies.

Community-based tourism has been supported recently by the authorities as a tool for poverty alleviation and sustainable development in rural and remote areas. According to Iran's Tourism Development and Management Master Plan, (2001-2002) rural- and community-based tourism should be developed in the short, medium and long term. The development of community-based tourism would provide employment opportunities, particularly for women, young people and aboriginals. For many people in rural areas, especially in remote places, the opportunity to earn money doesn't come easily; for this reason, finding job opportunities in these regions has pushed immigration to urban areas. This situation, in addition to reducing agricultural and husbandry activities, has compelled officials and local governments to develop a tourism industry in high potential rural and remote areas.

At the national level, the Iran Cultural Heritage and Tourism Organization (ICHTO), Provincial Cultural Heritage and Tourism Department and tourism working groups, the Rural and Urban Municipalities

Organization, the Islamic Revolution Housing Foundation as well as the Agriculture Bank have cooperated in developing rural tourism and have set up a committee for development of community-based tourism in such areas. One of the objectives of this committee was to select and support high potential rural areas for development of the tourism industry. For this reason, pilot projects in about 360 rural sites were selected on the basis of carefully defined criteria. Technical and financial support would be given to these projects by committee members and a guidebook, containing these rural tourism attractions and related tourist facilities and services in three languages (English, Arabic and Farsi), would be published. Several meetings with national and local authorities and community members were conducted in order to attain their full support for local and national investments in their areas.

11.2   The Objectives of Sustainable Community-based Tourism in Iranian Rural Areas

Sustainable community-based tourism in Iran has a number of broadly defined objectives:

One of the most important objectives is to bring the economic benefits of income, job creation and employment in tourism. Iranian rural residents, specifically in remote villages, suffer from a high rate of poverty and unemployment, principally because the agricultural and husbandry activities are so seasonal. The tourism activity and infrastructure (hotels, restaurants, shops, etc.) should be developed and managed by local people to enable them to gain from the economic benefits of the tourism industry.

When tourism activities are developed and operated, for the most part, by local community members, and certainly with their consent and support, then the community tourism is socially sustainable. This is not to suggest that there aren't dissenting views on tourism development among the locals, but it does imply that there is a forum for discussion and participation.

Cultural heritage is one of the most important and attractive community-based tourism products. Iranian ethnic groups in rural areas have unique traditions, folklore, dance and music, cuisine, handicrafts and local products, festivals, livelihoods, etc. Preserving and respecting these cultural characteristics is necessary.

Third objective is to develop leadership and participation by local residents. Mostly, the development of community-based tourism can be linked to the initial spark and leadership of one person or a small group within the community, though fostering change and development in a community with traditional beliefs is not easy. This requires someone with vision, imagination and great energy. This important mission in Iran belongs to the private sector, NGO's and other associations.

The fourth objective is natural heritage preservation, a key factor for many community-based tourism activities. Tourism at the local level should improve the environmental quality and limit damage from negative and adverse impacts. As with heritage and culture, the influx of tourists has in many cases actually increased environmental protection and conservation. Rural areas in the north of Iran are excellent examples of cases where local communities benefit from the flow of domestic tourists attracted to the natural and environmental experience. Community-based tourism is replete with examples of community heritage and values being revitalized through the growth in tourism, thus showing that Iranian rural areas can be developed and revitalized through community-tourism.

Finally, community-based tourism should reduce immigration from rural to urban areas by providing social welfare and employment. Because of the concentration of facilities and services in urban areas, Iranian rural residents move to find better a life. Some villages have been decimated due to unemployment and the lack of social facilities and equipment. So, community-tourism aims to reduce immigration from the villages to the urban areas.

11.3   Tourism and Its Impacts on Local Communities in Iranian Rural Areas

With growing interest to community-based tourism, Iranian rural areas, because of their natural beauty, pleasant climate, and historical and architectural characteristics, have been developed as tourism destinations. These rural sites were attractive places for domestic visitors and some even for international tourists. Some of these villages in the north of Iran were considered as "holiday villages." These villages were almost all located in-route and off-route from Tehran, the capital of Iran, to the Northern provinces of Gilan, Mazandaran and Golestan. The tourism resources, facilities and services of these rural sites have already attracted a large volume of domestic tourists, mostly from within the province itself (including a very large volume of day recreation visitors), as well as visitors from other provinces. Local people in these villages were involved in providing tourist facilities and services for visitors, including: home-stay accommodations, rental villas, and sales of handicrafts, traditional foods, and other local products.

Most of these travelers were domestic, although a small group was foreign visitors. The primary purpose of the visitors is normally visiting friends and relatives, taking holiday leisure in resorts and other natural sites. Most travelers are day visitors going to historical and architectural sites such as Masoleoleh in Gilan, Javaher Deh and Kandaloos in Mazandaran, and Ziarat village in Golestan. One of the key factors in the development of tourism in these regions was active participation of locals in providing tourist facilities and services. They provided accommodation, transportation, traditional foods and beverages, local products and handicrafts, local guide services and so forth. These rural sites have suffered from the adverse impacts of tourist activities on their environments, as noted below.

11.3.1   Environmental impacts on local community

Without careful planning, development and management, tourism activity in Iran's rural areas is not sustainable. Several types of environmental problems have resulted from an uncontrolled influx of visitors. Overuse of the fragile natural environment has lead to ecological damage in some villages.

Trekkers have created problems for villagers in Iranian mountainous areas. Damavand and Tochal north of Tehran, for example, have experienced serious environmental problems from trekkers and mountaineers who left large amounts of litter and rubbish along the trails and at campsites. Tourists and their porters also cut trees for fuel, exacerbating the already serious erosion resulting from residents' removal of the forest cover. The situation in Masuleh is more critical: visitors left rubbish and litter on the mountains and all along the climbing trails, trees were cut by hikers and campers for use as fuel to make campfire, and erosion was further exacerbated by overuse of hiking and riding trails. In the high season, tourists are far beyond the carrying capacity of the area and thus the natural environment people come to see is destroyed. Congestion level is high at the peak season. By contrast, the relative lack of tourism facilities and poor condition of roads, combined with the isolation of distant areas of the west and north mountain areas, are likely to restrict an influx of visitors there

Visual, noise and water pollution in the holiday villages of Damavand, Tochal and Masuleh are other environmental problems. Because of improper sewage disposal system for restaurants, villas, second-homes, hotels and other tourist facilities, the effluence has polluted ground water and rivers, and in some cases has generated health problems from vermin and disease.

Visual pollution in holiday villages (Fasham and Maygon) has resulted from use of unsuitable building materials on external surfaces; inappropriate landscaping; poorly-designed hotels and other buildings that are not compatible with the local architectural style and scale or are not well-integrated into the natural environment; and badly planned layout of tourist facilities. Holiday villages north of Tehran, such as Fasham, Mygoon, Shamshak, Dizin, have suffered from development of second homes and city-like architectural structures.

11.3.2   Socio-cultural impacts on local community

Visitors are usually genuinely interested in local culture and traditions and one of the main attractions of Iranian rural areas is the personal interaction with local resident; this has caused both positive and negative impacts on social and cultural aspects of the local communities. The potential benefits for protecting and enhancing cultural heritage through tourism activities are significant: reinforcing village identity, creating and enhancing community pride; building or re-building cultural amenities within a region; stabilizing the community; giving purpose to community development; and broadening community horizons. However, in some rural areas, because of the uncontrolled influx of tourists or misuse of the environment by tourists and the resultant non-preservation, especially in high season, some historical buildings and attractions have been damaged and cultural patterns and traditional arts altered. Masuleh and Abyaneh are good examples. The demonstration effect of tourists from different cultural backgrounds on residents, especially on young people, has also resulted in some young people in these villages losing their cultural identity and traditional lifestyles.

11.3.3   Socio-economic impacts

The most popular positive socio-economic impact of tourism is economic benefit and an increase in social welfare for residents, especially for young people who are more likely to migrate from these areas. But in some holiday villages, tourist facilities are owned and managed by outsiders. In these villages "local elites" were created and only a few local families became involved in operating and managing tourist facilities. So, these communities received minimal benefits from tourism. Some villagers only gained economically from the occasional sale of handicrafts or when meals or accommodation were arranged in the village.

Overcrowding and loss of amenities for residents are other negative socio-economic impacts on communities. During the high season, Masuleh, Abyaneh and other villages suffered from overcrowding of amenity, shopping and community facilities and congestion of transportation systems such that the residents themselves could not conveniently use them and become irritated and resentful of the tourists.

11.4   Community's Participation in Tourism Activities

11.4.1   Different Modes of Participation

Community participation is a key strategy for ensuring that an effective structure is in place to control and manage any adverse impact that may arise from tourism development in their area. This is particularly important in the case of cultural heritage sites throughout the country, most of which are operated by a national government organization with, in the past, relatively little if any local participation. This is one of the main reasons for the poor state of most of Iran's cultural heritage – especially its potentially valuable pre-Islamic heritage.

The ability of local people to participate actively in tourism development can vary considerably depending on economic, social and political relationships as well as ecological and physiographic factors found in any particular area. But where local communities fully participate in tourism development with provincial and national government agencies, the resulting multiplication of resources enables a number of effective strategies to be adapted to control and manage the adverse impacts of tourism on a sustainable basis.

As sustainable community-based tourism has been the concern of both officials and local communities in recent years, local residents in some high potential villages are very interested in becoming involved in tourism and they have made efforts to do so. Indeed, many did not wait for government support and initiated actions of their own. Masuleh village in north of Iran is again a good example. In this village, the local people established hotels, restaurants, markets, home-stay accommodations and souvenir shops, selling their local handicrafts and products to tourists. Conversely, in other villages, this participation is weak and local communities were not encouraged to participate in tourism activities because of religious and cultural beliefs. Rural residents in the western, central and eastern part of Iran have only engaged in passive participation in tourism activities. Paving the way to encourage these communities to participate in tourism activities is necessary. There are different kinds of community participation in tourism activities to help overcome this situation, including:

Participation in planning and formulation of local area tourism plans and programs is one of the more common forms of community participation in the tourism planning process, which includes the generation of information and its analysis and subsequent use, i.e. in learning and future planning processes. The community should be consulted in order for the people to be happy with the tourism development. This form of community participation recently has been emphasized in preparation of provincial and regional tourism plans in Iran. In these local and national plans, residents were encouraged to participate in providing information, analysis of the challenges and problems or tourism leading to consideration of their requests and recommendations.

Participation in sharing economic benefits – sharing and distribution of economic benefits resulting from development of tourism on an equal opportunity basis within communities is the concern of local tourism planners. In economically depressed areas, distribution of benefits arising from tourism leads to improve living standards of local communities and helped stem migration. To sustain tourism in Iranian rural areas, benefits must accrue to residents and to those who host tourists. Establishing a committee with leadership from within the local communities in order to distribute economic benefits of tourism to local people is essential.

Participation in decision-making and management – local people play key roles in the choice, design and management of community-based tourism, including tourism enterprises, conservation activities and monitoring and evaluation. They also must take a leading role in making decisions about the level of development in their area. In Iran, Rural Councils and local NGOs, as representatives of rural residents, are generally involved in decision-making for development and management of tourism.

Participation in implementation and operations – community-based tourism requires implementation structures and arrangements to conduct activities. Participants play a key role in implementing activities, setting up institutional arrangements and in enterprise operations. This kind of participation ensures that implementation and operation of tourism activities and action plans generate the needed support of local communities in order to achieve sustainable development. With attention to this matter, local communities in Iranian rural areas were encouraged to become involved in implementing and operating their tourism activities. They were encouraged to establish tourism facilities, including local accommodations, restaurants and shopping centers, and managing resorts and recreational centers.

Participation is not a one-way process, but a mutual learning experience for all concerned: professionals, academics, facilitators, government officials, entrepreneurs and local communities. Such participation is critical.

Figure 11.1   local people are selling their agricultural products to tourists

11.4.2   Challenges and Problems

The main problems in development of community-based-tourism in Iran are:

- Lack of community interests in some rural areas. In some rural areas, because of religious and cultural beliefs there is no interest to develop tourism activities in their communities.

- Lack of integrated and comprehensive planning approaches in development of community tourism.

- Lack of active local associations and NGOs who can actively participate in planning, implementing and controlling tourism activities and distribution of benefits to local communities.

- Unsustainable tourism activities in rural areas create socio-cultural, natural and economic negative impacts on local communities.

- Passive participation of some local communities in traditional rural areas in planning, decision-making and implementing tourism activities.

- Lack of training and awareness programs for local residents plays a key role in the lack development of tourism activities.

- Limited access to the main markets because of inadequate marketing strategies, weak advertisements and no segmentation in destination markets.

- Insufficient tourist facilities and services in rural areas to serve tourist needs, such as providing B/B, good access to the region and so on.

- High immigration rate from rural to urban areas, so the rural areas become evacuated.

- One of the greatest causes of failure in development of community-based tourism and conservation work in Iran is a lack of follow-up and commitment by the community members. Continuously empowering, motivating and rewarding participants with immediate positive feedback and hope for a better future are needed.

- Insensitive planning and development leading to a lack of mutual understanding between local communities and tourists that results in resentment and, in some cases, open hostility.

- Lack of effective sustainable management approaches to the use of local tangible and intangible cultural resources resulting either in their destruction or devaluation.

- Local people feeling that they have little control over the future of tourism.

- Trivialization of local cultural values, for example by presenting ceremonies that normally only occurs once or twice a year every day.

- Pressure to conform to external forces causes rapid changes in traditional values and customs.

- Introduction of non-local staff to operate tourist facilities and services.

- Creating competition for local community land and other resources.

- Introduction of built forms and structures that detract from the unique character of the local architecture.

- Acceleration of social inequality within local communities.

11.4.3   Possible Solutions for Sustainable Development of Tourism

- Set up training and education programmes for local communities in order to show how to provide adequate tourist facilities and services, upgrading the quality of local products, learning foreign languages, etc.

- Develop the attitude and managerial skills of local people to effectively participate in tourism and provide efficient tourism services, while yet maintaining the natural friendliness of the local people toward tourists.

- For community-based tourism to be sustainable communities must develop the capacity and the infrastructure required to promote tourism while preserving natural and cultural resources.

- Since sustainable tourism must benefit the local people, they should participate fully in formulating the tourism policy; thus in tourism development plans, the integrity of the local community should be preserved.

- Promoting conservation of traditional cultures and their artistic expressions and places of specific historic and cultural importance that present the history of villages and minimizes any negative impact from tourism through carefully controlled developments.

- Preserving and maintaining the architectural and traditional texture of villages, i.e. revitalization of historic buildings and unique architectural texture.

- Improve the general income level and economic and social welfare of people in rural areas and encourage the distribution of economic benefits as widely as possible, including the development of activities related to tourism, such as handicrafts production, agriculture and local industry.

- Marketing community-based tourism products more effectively and establishing good access to the main markets.

- Establishing local associations/NGOs in order to distribute benefits to residents not to the tour operators or travel agencies.

- Low-interest loans must be provided so that local communities are not totally dependent on supplementary income from tourism.

- Low-interest loans are to be made to residents in order to establish required tourist facilities and services.

- Encouraging private and public sectors to support community-tourism at national, regional and local levels.

- Developing an innovative idea for the improvement of rural development in an environmentally friendly way.

- Environmental protection through integrated land management in which local people play a key role

- Visitors from Asian and Western countries are predominantly attracted to Iran; therefore training must be consistent with international standards in order to be successful. Local residents can be trained as home stay hosts or local tour guides, contributing to the distribution of benefits.

- Utilizing local materials and products in tourist facilities, such as converting local houses to tourist accommodation or by providing standard tourist facilities and services such as private bath, kitchen and sanitary conditions.

- Establishing good access to the remote areas and using animals as transportation vehicles such as horses, donkeys and coaches.

- Initiate special marketing programmes by local governments and tourism offices, in which tourism products and local tourism programmes will be advertised in the media.

- Preserving a community's natural heritage and maintaining environmental quality.

- Encourage local banks and other lending institutions to set up regional investment funding programmes, including micro-credit programmes.

- Special brochures and booklets should be printed to introduce community tourism attractions, invite foreign reporters to view closely the country's attractions and tourist facilities and reflect them worldwide, and organize related fairs and conferences in cooperation with the international organizations

- Conducting FAM trips to rural areas from the selected markets in order to introduce these products to these markets more effectively.

- Provide funds for applied research through pilot projects to determine optimal mechanisms for community development over a wide range of different circumstances.

- In order to achieve sustainable goals, a clear understanding of the nature of both the product and the visitor, realistic expectations of tourism revenues and appropriate interpretive strategies and guide training are factors that must be considered prior to the implementation of any tourism program. If the tourism product is to be traditional community life, then the community must address the challenge of maintaining its traditional, authentic character while still meeting tourists' needs.

11.5   Case studies

Tourism has been used as a development policy tool in rural Iran and for poverty alleviation. Some villages were selected to obtain supports to develop tourism in national and regional plans. These case studies included two traditional and historical villages in the north and west of Iran.

11.5.1   Masuleh (Msooleh)

This village is situated to the southwest of Fooman Township, 63 km. from Rasht, the centre of Gilan province in the north of Iran. It enjoys a moderate climate, local architecture, springs, waterfalls, the Rood Khan River and dense forests that combine to make it an attractive tourism spot. Msooleh as a national relic is an archetype historic habitat and has been registered as No.1090 on the national relics list of Iran since 1975.

Masuleh's integrated architecture and its houses are of two stories, comprised of an entrance corridor, cellars and unique architectural features, all linked to each other by a staircase. The terrace of each house is the courtyard of the house above.

The five shrines and ancient mosques are pilgrimage sites and hold cultural importance.

11.5.1.1   Trade Center (BAZAAR)

The Bazaar is the heart of Masuleh; it is one of the most attractive places for tourists and those who cherish historical sites and buildings. The Bazaar is built on four separate levels. The shops on the lower two levels are one-story buildings while those on the upper two levels are two-storied. It is located in the center of the town and is surrounded by four major districts. Shoemakers and knife makers occupy the lowest level, while the wholesalers occupy the second floor; the upper two levels are allocated to large merchants and traders. The shops' wooden shields, the two-story wooden decks and the large columns create an ancient and beautiful view of a traditional Middle Eastern Bazaar. The existence of so many springs and caravanserais and mosques tell us of the prosperous times of the past. Of the 160 shops, only a few are still in business today; the rest are abandoned or have become warehouses or are completely destroyed.

Traditionally, the Bazaar served as the central location for trading goods for merchants and traders, but today it is a tourist attraction and serves mostly tourists and visitors. Therefore, the manufacturers, distributors and traders of various products who were once the heartbeat of the Bazaar have been replaced by coffee shops and gift shops, which are only open for business during the travel seasons. Nearby, there are also some bakers, butchers, and general stores that serve the Msooeh residents and are open year around.

11.5.1.2   Tourism in Masuleh

Masuleh, as an historic village, receives travelers from near and far every year. Most travelers arrive during summer. The purpose of their visit is usually leisure and taking in the village's architectural-historical texture. But many visitors from surrounding areas come for the pleasant weather and natural beauty.   Most foreigners travel to Masuleh for visiting its historic, architectural and rural attractions. Small and large groups interested in natural wonders usually travel there from nearby towns; some groups visit solely for mountain climbing. The natural, architectural and historical attractions of Masuleh absorb every kind of visitor, no matter his or her interest. Even the winter snows attract tourists.

11.5.1.3   The Impacts of Tourism on Masuleh

Some tourism activities, such as trekking, picnicking and camping have caused environmental pollution from unhygienic disposal of human waste, discharge of sewage effluent into water sources, and littering. Without strict regulations on appropriate land use, high-rise buildings such as tourist hotels to cater to the increasing number of tourists, have resulted in congestion and degradation of the local scenery.   A large number of weekend travelers who visit in spring and summer have negative impacts on environment because of congestion in excess of the village's carrying capacity. The numbers of visitors in the high season has caused environmental problems, especially via access to the village which is limited because of the lack of parking spaces. Thus, travelers have damaged trees and created a disturbance for the local people.

11.5.1.4   Community Participation in Masuleh, UNESCO Eco-tourism Site

The purpose of this inter-disciplinary project was to promote community-based cultural, rural and eco-tourism in Masuleh village, with a specific focus on poverty eradication, reduction of rural-urban migration and the preservation of the cultural and natural heritage of the area. The village of Masuleh is the site of the UNESCO/Iran Cultural Heritage and Tourism Organization (ICHTO) project. Notable for its traditional wooden buildings clustered on the northern slopes of the valley, Masuleh is registered as a Cultural and Natural Heritage site in Iran, as the village is rich in tangible and intangible heritage. The surrounding mountains provide many opportunities for trekking, climbing and other eco-tourism activities. Local houses were prepared as tourist accommodations and a rural museum was established.

Figure 11.2   Masuleh Traditional Houses

A main emphasis of the project included encouraging the full participation of the local community in developing public-private sector partnerships. Promoting local community participation required training being given in the development of a local handicraft industry, as well as in the management of home-stays and in the skills needed for local people to become cultural and nature guides. A visitor centre is being developed in the village and a system of walking trails in the surrounding mountains has been drawn up.

The project sought to set up links and to establish co-operation between local communities and national NGOs on the one hand and international NGOs, tour operators and travel agencies on the other, with a view to involving the local population in income-generation activities related to tourism and marketing their products. Such activities included the training of tour guides, production and sale of high-quality craft items, promotion of home-stays and of bed and breakfast type accommodations, as well as development of traditional dance and music. As the project advances, recommendations, tour guidebooks and web sites will also be produced. However the selected marketing method has been used as a strategy for preventing mass tourism.

11.5.1.5   Role of the government in the development of Masuleh

This village has received strong support from the government of the Islamic Republic of Iran at both national and local levels. At the national level, ICHTO has actively participated in preservation and repairing historical buildings and monuments. For this reason, ICHTO started the Msooleh Great Project in 2001. The main purpose of the Great Project is to prevent the wear and destruction of the village, to protect it for the next generations and to develop tourism. Involvement of the people and the continuation of traditional life in the village distinguish Masuleh from other projects. This causes a complexity of interventions and it makes a vital and important necessity of deliberate and fundamental programming with due attention to the attendance and activity of the people and other governmental and private organs.

Because of special texture and fine architecture and natural views, Masuleh is an important center in the tourism field nationally and internationally. This is the only source of livelihood for the few people who haven't migrated. They prevent the changing of Masuleh to a museum with their involvement which necessarily increases the need for a special look at Masuleh. The most significant activities which have been carried out are as follows:

- Establishing a temporary office of the Great Project with repair to one of the Cultural Inheritance inns in order to provide accommodation for the associates of the project and needed infrastructure;

- Continuous activities for providing, collecting and computerizing documents of Masuleh, consisting of: old photos, aerial photos, design of texture, single buildings, etc;

- Collecting compiled books, university projects, studies related to Msooleh and its culture and history in order to exploit this information;

- The conservation and renovation of built cultural heritage, natural resources and the environment;

- Repairing some of residential and public buildings to make them safe;

- Repairing the old bath building as a research base of historic Masuleh;

- Studying and providing details of architectural substances to create more solidity and strength;

- Establishing a Masuleh web site;

- Providing necessary evidence in order to register Masuleh with UNESCO;

- Conducting workshops, establishing tourist facilities and services, including accommodation, and facilitating access to the region by using environmentally friendly modes of transport in order to reduce tourism-related traffic; adopting, observing, implementing and promoting codes of conduct; developing information and education programs in co-operation with local stakeholders, providing information to tourists on appropriate behavior; implementing effective control mechanisms to regulate tourist access to ecologically fragile or stressed natural areas in order to protect the sensitive natural and cultural resources in the area; and providing support for local products and handicrafts. The Great Project established sustainable tourism policies and regulations, ensuring natural and cultural heritage and resource conservation and protection in the region. Increased funding for local NGOs enable villagers to engage in tourism activities and helped local people to diversify their products, and design and implement educational and awareness programs to sensitize people to the issues of sustainable tourism development.

11.5.2   Hewraman Takht Village

The Hewraman region contains several traditional Kurdish villages which are distinguished by their own cultural and natural characteristics. These villages played a key role in formulating the history of the Hewraman region and show great potential for the development of tourism. The diversity of culture and nature in this region, especially the presence of traditional Kurdish lifestyles and architecture, with its dialects, folklore, ancient customs; and its river, springs and waterfalls, along with its pleasant climate are of great importance from the tourism point of view. These unique characteristics were perceived by local authorities, stakeholders and the private sector as being important in developing tourism in this area. Hewraman is one of the most attractive rural areas of Kurdistan, offering panoramic view with valuable tourism capabilities because of the annual performance of the ancient and wonderful ceremony of Pir-e-Shahriar in February and May of each year.

The most important village in this region is Hewraman Takht, located in an east-west orientation on the steep slope of highly scenic valley with snow-capped mountains overlooks the northern foot of the Takht Mountains 63 km. south of Marivan. The climate of this region in spring and summer is very pleasant, though it is very cold in winter. People in this region are living in traditional houses generally made of stone with beamed ceilings and constructed in a stair-like fashion so that the roof of one house is the courtyard of the other,

The inhabitants of this territory and their language are known as Hewrami. This dialect is one of the famous branches of the Kurdish language and is very similar to Avestan, the language of the ancient region of Zorasteria. The area is recognized as the center of Zoroastrian custom in pre-Islamic times and many words spoken by the local people relate to the Sassanid era (226-651 AD). Ancient fire temples, remnants of this region, indicate that the inhabitants were Zoroastrians before converting to Islam.

The Sirvan River flows from the deep valleys of this region and has created suitable conditions for agriculture; however, due to structured natural conditions such as rocky and stony fields, agriculture was not developed. But the condition for orchards is suitable.   Here the land is covered with walnut, pomegranate, fig and mulberry trees.

This village is an excellent example of the Kurdish traditional lifestyle of the mountainous people. The presentation of folk culture and heritage, such as the wedding ceremony of Pir-e-Shaliar at Hewraman Village, attracts hundreds of visitors every year. Visitors are drawn to the village almost entirely through packaged day tours by travel agents and independent travelers. Hewraman may be just one stopover on the tour, but it usually holds tourists' attention for a period of several hours. The key attractions are the heritage buildings, architectural texture, folklore, customs and traditional clothing worn by residents, carvings and other crafts, and its natural beauty allows for a chance to see living history. The people of the village dress in traditional Kurdish costume and engage in traditional economic activities, such as sheep and goat herding, and fruit and vegetable production on terraces constructed on the side of the valley and at its base. Traditionally, the agricultural activities required the physical efforts of women and children; however, a recent and modest level of mechanization has now freed the women and children from this and, within the Hewraman Village, these two groups now focus on the expanding tourist trade.

A notable and easily-seen local product is Marass, the uniquely traditional clothing for men, and Kelash, a kind of footwear. These are worn by the villagers and are readily purchasable by the tourists as a reminder of Hewraman. The combination of a highly scenic mountain area, a traditional cultural and architecture, and local legends gives this area a unique and interesting character.

The tomb of Pir-e-Shahriar Hewrami is one of the most reputable pilgrimage sites of the people. He was a Zoroastrian celestial before the advent of Islam. The inhabitants of the Hewraman Takht are Sunni Moslems from the Shafei sect. Mention should be made of the Abdollahi mosque, the tomb of "Koseh Hajij" and Soltan Eshagh, highly respected by the people of this region and other people of Kurdistan.

Figure 11.3   Traditional Wedding Ceremony of Pir-e-Shaliar

The main issues associated with the site from a tourism development point of view are:

- The currently poor and unreliable access to the site limits the number of tourists that could be taken to it;

- The current road works involving large cut-and-fill operations is impacting adversely on the scenic character of the valley as well as on the valley's streams and drainage system;

- The existing tourist facilities, including health care and communications, are rudimentary; the hygiene is doubtful and not suited to tourism at this point in time;

- Limited production and provision of local handicrafts;

- Basic sanitation facilities are lacking with garbage being simply dumped down the slope of the road and raw sewerage running along the side of the road from the main village posing a health hazard to villagers and tourists alike, coupled with pollution of the valley stream from garbage and raw sewerage from the village;

- Lack of suitable parking facilities off the main road at the village limits visitor access;

- Lack of clearly marked and directed access trails leading to the natural areas of the valley;

- Lack of any directional signs or explanation of the village features;

- Lack of appropriate tourist facilities and services including accommodations, restaurants, camping areas, handicraft shops, tour and travel agencies, and banking system.

These factors currently impede the opportunity to use tourism as a factor in strengthening the socio-economic base of these villages. The outstanding natural and cultural tourism resources of this area have the potential to attract a range of sightseeing and eco-tourism market segments in the domestic and international market. Since the natural and cultural environment of this site is fragile, the strategy should develop low volume but high value tourism, rather than mass market-based tourism. To fully exploit the potential of the tourism resources of the area, it is recommended that:

- Development of an appropriate road access structure, including control of adverse impacts upon the scenic and ecological values of the area;

- Providing hygienic solid and liquid waste treatment facilities at the villages, collecting all garbage and litter currently distributed along the road and in the valley floor as part of a campaign among the villages emphasizing the importance of controlling waste due to its effect on their environment;

- Developing visitor centers in the village offering tourist information, transportation, local guides, accommodation, hygienic restaurants and sanitation facilities, and a tourist village bazaar;

- Connecting the other villages by a walking trail that traverses the high mountains and valleys of the area allowing visitors to undertake graduated one hour, half day, one day, two day, three day, and four day outings;

- Developing mountaineering and other outdoor mountain sports areas in the range opposite one of the main villages;

- Revisiting emergency medical services and a helicopter pad for emergency evacuation at the main village;

- Encouraging the development of a local handicraft industry for sale in the villages and for export to other parts of the Province;

- Training local villagers in the operation of small tourist-based businesses, including handicraft production sites, food and beverage services, small accommodation facilities and guiding services;

- Developing cultural tourism in the village on the basis of the traditional Kurdish culture in order to preserve the cultural and natural heritage for sustainable development of tourism;

- Encouraging local community participating in tourism activities;

- Training local guides and other stakeholders in tourism activities.

The local residents in Hewraman are strongly committed to a tourism development plan based on community development objectives. These include:

- Developing and implementing tourism plans for which "community life" will be central;

- Developing income-generating activities for community members through handicrafts, food preparation and community tours as a substantial source of employment and increased income;

- Visual representations of strategic community sites as a guide for the physical development of the village and to encourage community participation;

- Designing marketing and promotional materials, including brochures and postcards, where local officials are responsible for supplying data such as for key points of interest in the village and appropriate wording for the print materials.

As a tourism destination, Hewraman is still very much at the formative stage. However, as tourism development progresses, efforts are being made to help the community to identify and achieve tourism objectives by emphasizing principles that support community participation, environmental sustainability and cultural integrity.

11.6 Conclusion

In conclusion, national and local authorities in Iran have developed interests to develop tourism in rural and remote areas in order to bring them economic benefits of increased employment and income, while preserving and maintaining the cultural and environmental heritage and integrity of these small and fragile communities. The cases also show that community-based tourism can be helpful for the development of Iranian rural areas and also for poverty alleviation.

While community-based tourism is now growing in rural areas and has substantial potential for economic growth, it potentially carries with it significant negative social and environmental impacts. The art of the tourism development and management process should be to balance the opportunities and costs for the community, the environment and the tourists. Before applying this approach, tourism activities in some popular rural areas in Iran should be limited in order to not create adverse impacts on natural, socio-cultural and socio-economic environments. Community participatory planning process should enable the community to perceive and understand the potential negative impacts from the tourism and proactive actions are taken. Nevertheless, government support for community tourism is crucial for its success.

References:

Boyd, C. (ed.) (2002), *Tourism, the Poor and Other Stakeholders: Experience in Asia*, Nottingha: Russell Press Ltd.

Commission on Sustainable Development (1999), Seven Sessions, 19-30 April 1999, New York.

Conference Proceedings (2003), Development of Cultural and Ecotourism in the Mountainous Regions of Central and South Asia, August 26-30, 2003.

Ghaderi, Z. (2006), *Development of Agro-tourism in Iran,* Paper Presented at the Multi-Country Study Mission on Agro-tourism for Enhancing Business Opportunities in Rural Areas, 20-27 June 2006, China Taipei.

Ghaderi, Z. (2005), *Sustainable Tourism Development Planning Principle in Rural Areas*, first edition, Munucipility Publication, Tehran, Iran (Farsi version).

Iran Cultural Heritage and Tourism Organization (2002), *Iran's Tourism Development and Management Master Plan (2001-2002)*, Regional Strategies.

Iran Government Five-Year Social and Economic Development Plans, 1st (1989-1993), 3rd (2000-2004), and 4th (2005-2009).

Mountain Institute (2000), *The Community-based Tourism for Conservation and Development: A Resource Kit.*

Richards, G. and D. Hall (2002), *Tourism and Sustainable Community Development*, London: Rutledge.

WTTC (2005), *Blueprint for New Tourism*, World Tourism Council, New York, (online), available at: www.wttc.org/frameset5.htm (31-5-2007).

Chapter 12

Tourism and Community Development in Sri Lanka

12.1 Introduction: Early Development

Sri Lanka's tourism in a formal sense got into the act almost 40 years ago, in the mid-1960s. Recommendations were made by the consulting group invited by the Sri Lankan government, Panel, Kerr & Foster of Hawaii, to help Sri Lanka build beach-based tourism. The Tourism Master Plan, (1978), emphasized the need for integrated resort development. The products of the resultant work were the resorts at Bentota, Pasikuda and Koggala. The five-star business hotels of Ceylon Inter-Continental, Lanka Oberoi, Taj Samudra, Le Galadari Meridian, Ramada Renaissance and Colombo Hilton were products of this early direction. In 1982, for the first and only time in Sri Lanka, a demand analysis for the destination was carried out covering all the generating markets of Europe, through an extensive consumer -based market survey, engaging market research companies. The global demand was then found to be seeking the three "S" (Sun, Sea and Sand) type tourism (Ceylon Tourist Board, 1983).

Community tourism was recognized as a special tourism segment. Community tourism is a subset of sustainable development and focuses on the ecology, heritage, culture and way of life of the rural community. Eco-tourism, Heritage tourism, Cultural Tourism and Adventure Tourism are a few examples of community tourism. Sri Lanka is a good example of traditionally oriented community-based tourism that existed before 1980, but due to speedy urbanization communities automatically modernized due to the drastic economical and political changes and thus revealed that unplanned construction is destructive of the environment with the result that some rural areas have acquired an urban atmosphere (Premaratne, 2004).

The main objective of the 1982 study was to identify and raise awareness of the socio-economic, cultural and ecological impacts of community-based tourism, and to contribute to sustainable community-based tourism development models that would generate sustainable income for Sri Lanka's poorest and least advantaged communities, while at the same time helping to maintain culture and biodiversity in rural areas.

12.2 A Different Challenge

Sri Lanka in the meantime grappled with a "sick" tourism industry and was affected by over 20 years of civil war with the many terrorist attacks dotting the canvas of a dark period. During this period (1983 –

2000), it was a scenario of "too many operators chasing too few tourists." Price undercutting to gain business shares was not only prevalent, but was the order of the day. Risk averting fixed price forward contracts for all inclusive hotel stays and tours, meals served buffet style; cordial-based fruit juice drinks and mostly untrained seasonally recruited staff were the sad products of the survival game. Successful survival at the operational level with hard fought battles by many industry operators was achieved during this period. A strategic focus and a professional development thrust for the industry was found wanting.

A little after the dawn of the new millennium, several bold initiatives were taken jointly by the public and private sectors of the travel and tourism industry, forming into an alliance called "Sri Lanka Tourism." The alliance's work resulted in a re-positioning of the then predominant beach-based focus of Sri Lanka on a "Beyond Beaches: Nature, Culture and Adventure" platform. A new logo depicting a natural and cultural symbolism and a tag line of "Sri Lanka: A Land Like No Other" was launched by this new alliance, which also reached beyond tourism to incorporate the airlines, sports, investments and exports sectors of the economy as partners in the endeavour. A medium term marketing programme was prepared through a participatory process involving both public and private sectors.

Efforts were undertaken utilizing major international media and the approach resulted in a relative lift in bringing a positive recall for Sri Lanka Tourism among target audiences.

In 2002, a major breakthrough was achieved as a relative calm on the political front emerged, with the signing of an accord between the government and separatists to end hostilities. This opportunity offered a solid launching pad for Sri Lanka Tourism to take off with investments in products and marketing efforts such as the New Oriental Hotel being turned to Amanwella by the Aman Group and the Deer Park Resort to Banyan Tree.

12.2.1   The Role of Government in Tourism Planning

In many developing countries, including Sri Lanka, the government has discovered tourism as a source of modernization. Tourism is supposed to contribute significantly to economic development in terms of measuring growth. Sri Lanka has now adopted an environmental- and community-friendly tourism approach somewhat similar to that prevalent in countries such as New Zealand, and Hawaii.

The Sri Lanka government had previously put much effort into large scale tourism development, the national strategic plans emphasizing the construction of integrated resorts as a strategy for tourism development. In order to cope with the changing strategies, the Sri Lanka Tourist Board (SLTB) initiated several community-based projects to develop this segment. With the technical advice offered by SLTB, private sector investors were encouraged to develop community-based tourism projects to demonstrate their social responsibilities and respect for the environment (Gurusinghe, 2006).

The SLTB highlighted its objectives for the benefit of the sustainability of community tourism as follows.

- Community/eco-tourism should be used as a tool to alleviate poverty in the tourism-generating areas of Sri Lanka

- The institutional capacity of communities should be strengthened and, in the process, motivated to be involved in the complete tourism development process from the planning stage to implementation and management through avenues of consultation and partnership.

In this endeavor, Sri Lanka focuses mainly on Rural Tourism. Rural Tourism has been defined as a process which leads to a rise in the capacity of rural people to control their environment, increase their share of benefits through tourism activities and therefore ensure sustainability.

12.2.2 Segments of Community Tourism

The rural tourism development initiatives included three tourism segments: natural tourism, cultural tourism and community-based tourism. Nature Tourism is mainly concerned with recreational aspects having little or no ecological impact. Cultural Tourism covers tourism based on the culture, history and archeology of the local people. Community-based Tourism (CBT) includes Village-Based Tourism, Eco-tourism, Agro-tourism, Adventure tourism, Sports tourism (if it is local community oriented only).

In Sri Lanka, there is an indigenous community still in existence called "Veddahs" who practice communal living, survive through hunting and gathering, maintain traditional dances, and retain a unique language It is now possible for tourists to visit this community without disturbing their way of life. In visiting the people of Dambana, indigenous tourism is presented as an encounter with the primitive that embraces two dominant myths--primitivism and nostalgia (De Alwis, 2006a).

12.3 The Impact of Tourism in Community

The development of rural tourism has been found to have created substantial negative impacts.

12.3.1 Negative Economic Impact of Rural Tourism

The rate of economic return to rural communities has been rather low (Samaranayake, 1998) due to the following:

- Facilities such as hotels, resorts and tour companies belong mainly to investors from cities who take most of the profits back to the cities.

- Food, beverages and other daily necessities used by tourists are largely imported from outside, not produced locally.

- Revenues in the form of taxes and fees do not go to the rural community directly, but are returned to the central government.

- Local labour is only employed at operative and unskilled levels. Employment opportunities for local people are thus limited.

- Over the past 10 years, rural people have not benefited much from the "multiplier effect" with reference to the development of local handicrafts or agriculture. This undesirable situation is caused by poor linkages between tourism operators and local producers.

12.3.2   Socio-cultural Impact

Since the income from tourism is much higher than what rural people can earn from agriculture, according to Samaranayake (1998), tourism has been accepted willingly in many rural areas in spite of its negative effects, resulting in:

- Disruption to rural culture

- Decline in participation in rural traditional and cultural practices

- Traditional architecture replaced by modern buildings

- Local culture eroded

- Agriculture, which was the basis of traditional life, replaced by and become secondary to tourism

12.3.3   Environmental Impact

In 2005, almost 600,000 tourists visited Sri Lanka and the average length of stay was eight days. Such numbers of visitors can overexploit natural resources and have a heavy impact on the environment. In addition, tourism may require infrastructure, transportation and other facilities which can cause environmental disturbance through :

- Trekking and camping

- Unhygienic ways of disposing of human waste

- Discharging of sewage effluent into fresh water sources

- Inappropriate land use without complying with regulations

- Over-construction of buildings resulting in congestion and destruction of local scenery (SLTB, 2005b)

12.4   Community Tourism Planning

While community participation in tourism development is desirable, there seem to be formidable operational, structural and cultural limitations to this approach to tourism development in many countries, including Sri Lanka. Some of these barriers are caused by centralized decision-making and administration for the tourism industry; lack of cooperation and coordination between agencies and sectors; inadequate financial and human resources; and the domination of community ventures by the elite members of the said communities. These challenges are not insurmountable (Cohen, 1984). Instead, the success of community tourism ventures is dependent on four primary features, namely:

Empowerment

Members of the community should be included in the decision–making process and also have a share in the rewards of the business. While it is equally important that the concept and management of tourism projects be generated within the community, it is also important that the locals are provided with the required technical and financial assistance from government and other organizations. Empowerment should be taken as an action rather than a process facilitated by participation or genuine partnership, knowledge, access to resources, training and education, and social services.

Protection of Stakeholder Interests

Stakeholders should be clearly identified and their interests protected by legal and policy statements. Stakeholders would normally include community members and/or "outside" private or government investors.

Accountability

Mechanisms should be in place to ensure that decisions taken in the interest of the business do not create problems for the wider community. Also, that the interests of the tourists are taken into consideration and that those responsible for taking decisions which run counter to the benefits of the community are identified and are dealt with appropriately.

Monitoring/Evaluation

There should be a continuous assessment of the product, constantly remedying negative impacts in the community and the product.

12.5 Government Programs on Community Tourism

On the part of the government of Sri Lanka, several projects and programmes were initiated through the Sri Lanka Tourist Board in developing communities through tourism (De Alwis, 2006b). A policy decision was made to the effect that any new tourism development project/programme should incorporate a community development component in addition to providing employment opportunities for the community, purchasing goods and obtaining services from them, etc. The following programmes were conducted under this scheme.

12.5.1 Community Awareness Programmes

Community awareness progammes were conducted by the Sri Lanka Tourist Board, which falls under the purview of the Director/Community Relations. The programmes were carried out to convince the local community, the residents within the tourist areas, on the economic benefits that tourism brings. SLTB allocates Rs. 500,000 annually to promote and conduct awareness programmes. The Director/Community Relations conduct an awareness programme every year for local communities in every district (Pathirana, 2006).

12.5.2   Training Programmes (Table 12.1)

The Director/Community Relations carry out training programmes in interpretation for tourism which last for two weeks. After giving a basic training on area guiding, the youths are issued a valid license to operate as an Area Tourist Guide albeit only within the specified area. SLTB allocates a budget annually to train the area youths as area guides (SLTB, 2005a).

In view of training the youth in rural areas that function as informal interpreters to tourists, a Tourist Facilitators Training Programme was introduced. Under this programme, training programmes have been held in several areas and action has been taken to issue Tourist Facilitators Licenses to them.

12.5.3   Promotion of Youth Travel

Every year the Director/Community Relations visits leading schools in Sri Lanka to promote Youth Travel Clubs by which students are encouraged to travel within the country. After the one-day training programmes, Travel Clubs are formed in schools with the help of the teachers. There is no special budget offered by SLTB but the expenses for traveling and specific funds for the tours are collected by students themselves.

The club is anxious to encourage the youth to appreciate the value of the country's cultural and natural heritage. It also fosters friendship among school children in different parts of the country. The Board is also keen on imparting knowledge of tourism and related benefits and developing necessary attitudes in prospective aspirants for careers in tourism.

In furtherance of these objectives, the Board has set up a number of School Travel Clubs in different parts of the country where schools have responded positively. The Board, with the co-operation of government and private sector agencies, provides concessionary accommodation and transport for the members of these school travel clubs. Some of the activities planned through the school travel clubs include educational tours to places of interest, identifying new places of tourist interest in the region, becoming involved with the beautification programmes of cities and other places.

The aim of the School Travel Club programme is to motivate students to travel on the theme, "Travel to Learn, Learn to Travel."

- The programme provides opportunities not only to travel but also to acquire a wide knowledge of tourism and its activities.

- It will be useful for students to foster friendship and understanding among students of different regions in the country and other countries.

- It will help them develop and appreciate the culture and natural heritage of Sri Lanka and other countries.

- It will foster friendship and understanding among the students of different regions and countries by playing host to visiting guests of schools or youth organizations from different regions of Sri Lanka and other countries.

- It will provide knowledge of tourism, its benefits and potential adverse effects.

- It will organize educational visits to places of cultural and natural interests and explore new places of tourist interest around the areas where the school travel clubs are formed.

- It will assist in making the cities more interesting and beautiful for tourists.

Table 12.1   Example training programs

Name of the training programme	Duration	No. of Students	Budget
National Tourist Guide Training Programme	Three (03) months	65	Run from fees collected from students
Chauffeur Tourist Guide Training Programme	Two and a half (2½) months	65	Run from fees collected from students
Area Guides	One week	30	Funded by Provincial Councils

Source: SLTB (2005a).

12.5.4   The Activities Envisaged are as Follows

- To conduct community awareness programmes by means of workshops, discussions and lectures in the main tourism development areas

- To conduct school programmes for senior students and teachers in the provinces where large-scale tourism development has taken place

- To formulate tourism communities at local levels to monitor the adverse effects of tourism development on the culture and society and undertake programmes to minimize their impact.

- To conduct exhibitions of arts and crafts of the local community with the sponsorship of the Travel and Hotel Industry.

- To provide information to tourists at the point of entry to enable them to understand the local cultural value system and to educate them on the need to respect local traditions and cultural values

12.6   Community Tourism and Heritage Protection

A major step in achieving community tourism and heritage protection is the establishment of the "Responsible Tourism Partnership (RPT) Sri Lanka." The RPT was created by the Travel Foundation in the UK identifying Sri Lanka as a favorite destination among British tourists.

RPT is incorporated as a non-profit making public company and it actively promotes sustainable tourism solutions for the country. The aims of RPT include developing and implementing practical sustainable tourism solutions to help protect and enhance Sri Lanka as a tourist destination, promoting the country as a highly valued 'responsible tourism' destination for visitors, and coordinating and managing delivery of tourism related projects with the objective of contributing towards the economic, environmental and social well-being of the people.

RPT prioritizes issues affecting the future sustainability of Sri Lanka's tourism and implements a programme of activities to address the issues. It engages in projects to help communities enhance their livelihoods and generates resources for environmental conservation, it supports activities directed towards long-term sustainable tourism priorities and it disseminates information on tools and best practice guidelines for the tourism industry and for visitors on responsible tourism.

RPT has called upon the tourism industry and others directly and indirectly involved in tourism and visitors to Sri Lanka to actively participate in responsible tourism so that Sri Lanka will be a special destination for all.

The case of the Sarvodaya Community Tourism Initiative is a positive outcome of the above initiatives, spearheaded by the private sector.

12.7   Case Studies

12.7.1   Sarvodaya Community Tourism Initiative

Sarvodaya is a Sri Lankan voluntary organization, funded by volunteers from Sri Lanka and other countries, engaged in community and human development in various fields.

The Community Tourism Initiative (CTI) was established to develop sustainable livelihoods and build capacity in village communities by sharing natural resources, village culture and Sarvodaya's vision with visitors who seek meaningful and enlightening experiences. Each project is run by the villagers with assistance in training and marketing from CTI. Any surplus income from CTI projects goes directly to support the capacity-building activities of the village itself. CTI was conceived and developed by British travel and tourism professional Catherine Leech and is now managed by a Sri Lankan hotel professional.

Polhena and Mirissa

These two sites are situated in the southern coastal belt of Sri Lanka. They are 100 miles away from the capital of Colombo. The climate in these areas is fairly warm and the temperature between 27 - 37 C year round. The main occupation of the community is fishing. The miles-long golden sandy beaches are a prime product for tourism. The total population living in these areas is around 300,000. But the youth population is around 200,000; 70% of them are unemployed. The living standard of the community is still very low compared to Matara, the main city of Southern Province. Total income level per person is less than US$ 75.00. per month (Southern Provincial Council, 2005).

Figure 12.1   Rural Traditional Transportation System

Saliyapura

Saliyapura is located in the North Central Province of Sri Lanka about 140 miles from Colombo. The climate is fairly dry and is in the dry zone of Sri Lanka. The main occupation of the local community is paddy cultivation. The local community utilizes tank water for farming and agricultural purposes. The total population is around 250,000. Males and females both involve themselves in agriculture. This is an ideal place for tourists to visit a traditional farming village where dry zone fruits are grown (Central Provincial Community Tourism, 2006).

Balapitiya: Cultural Performances by Children

A natural amphitheatre on the grounds of a new community centre was the inspiration for a children's programme of teaching cultural performances in traditional low country dance. Opened in December 2006, performances are from 4.00 p.m. to 5.00 p.m. on Saturdays. The café is open daily.

Polhena: Sri Lankan Cooking

This community offers tourist the opportunity to learn about traditional Sri Lankan cooking over a "daralipa" (wood-fired stone hearth) and enjoy a traditional meal prepared by the villagers. Established in November 2006, the community restaurant is open daily with cooking demonstrations every Saturday morning.

Mirissa: Women's Handicrafts Market

The Women's handicrafts market in Mirissa provides a cultural shopping experience for tourists, which also has them supporting the local community by purchasing authentic Sri Lankan handicrafts. Local children perform traditional local dances on Saturdays from October to April.

Saliyapura: Educational Farm Visit

At Saliyapura tourists can enjoy a village-prepared lunch and a tour of Sarvodaya's show-farm; see traditional vegetables and fruits grown using traditional non-chemical fertilizer and pest control methods.

"Voluntourist" Village Stays

Another activity promoted and supported by Sarvodaya is home-stays in a purpose-built village house where tourists can help the villagers with a range of capacity-building activities, such as teaching English and Sports activities, farming, clearing land, etc.

Living and Learning Tours

Sarvodaya is also working on 'Living and Learning' tours based in village communities where groups of 6-20 people can enjoy a unique experience for a week or more, with a theme tailored according to their interests and centered on Sarvodaya's work, e.g. post-disaster management, micro-lending, peace and conflict resolution, community health, early childhood development, etc.

Difficulties in Maintaining the Projects

Although the global movement for sustainability has been favorable to the new era of Sri Lanka tourism development, Community tourism development has encountered many problems:

Inadequate Authority and Disharmony in Development

The authority of existing legislative organizations is still restricted as far as tourism development is concerned. The legislation which gives governing bodies their authority does not clearly state their power to manage and develop rural regions. Other government organizations are thus unwilling to cooperate unless a direct order or financial aid is given from the top administrators of the nation. Furthermore, organizations often encounter bureaucratic red tape and their decisions are influenced by political interference. Another major constraint is conflict between government organizations, each of which tries to protect its own bureaucratic territory and authority.

Legislation Problems

To limit the impact of tourism on rural communities, it is recommended that tour operators limit the number of tourists in each group or in each visit period, and supply well-trained staff to accompany the group. However, this adds to the cost and operators may be unwilling to meet strict requirements unless there are official regulations which are strictly enforced. Some irresponsible business operators who want to minimize their costs and undercut the prices of their competitors bring in very large groups of tourists, who may spoil the ecology and culture of the villages.

Lack of Manpower

Though there are various training courses organized by universities, the number of personnel with specific skills such as interpretation of nature, local culture, history and archeology, is still limited. In particular, local authorities do not have staff experienced in tourism management and development. To some extent, the manpower problem is caused by the present economic crisis, as well as unrealistic government policies for the development of human resources.

Insufficient Financial Support

Although a large amount of funding is needed to develop rural tourism, only a limited budget is given because funding is determined by the size of the local population. As a result, essential developments such as human resource management, enforcement of regulations, building of physical structures and land use management are not being implemented efficiently.

Lack of Local Involvement

Though the concept of local participation is strongly emphasized in rural tourism, in practice local people are seldom involved in decision-making, planning and implementing policies. Many rural communities have no knowledge of tourism and are misled by outside investors who hope to take most of the economic benefits from rural areas. Consequently, local people become confused or divided about what kind of tourism they want to establish in their area.

12.7.2   Case of Jetwing Youth Development Project

Like most other rural villages in Sri Lanka, the hamlet of Rangirigama and the surrounding villages of Rotawewa and Kimbissa also are burdened with youth unemployment. From a society predominantly involved in cultivation, either due to a surplus of manpower or unwillingness to take up agriculture as a livelihood, youths end their school careers and, unable to pursue higher education and being under-skilled, wait with little hopeof fitting into the available employment opportunities the country offers. The wait can be long and frustrating and may end with youths taking up whatever may come their way, simply for existence. The prime of their youth can be marred with an inability to obtain work, a meagre income and an abundance of financial and social problems.

Jetwing is a large Sri Lanka hotel management company with properties throughout the island. Jetwing Youth Development Project is an initiative designed to help rural youth find suitable employment within Jetwing Hotels or create the opportunity to find employment with other hotels in the country or overseas. The strengths, especially positive attitudes, natural talents, keenness to learn and good discipline, are often overshadowed by the poor knowledge of English of these youths. This is the biggest hindrance to finding themselves jobs that might be available in the country, especially with the private sector.

A programme of training to fill the "skills gap" was commenced by Jetwings with an English training programme that continued for six months. The youths were invited to the programme with the assistance of the incumbent monks of the two village Buddhist temples where classes also were held in the "Dharmasalawas." In the second month of the programme, from a process of selection, the youth were categorized into areas as per their personality traits, and entry-level industry training was conducted at the nearest hotel site in Front Office service, Housekeeping, Restaurant & Bar Service and Cookery.   Parallel courses in English, Nature and wild life, customer care, the Japanese 5S system, personality development, life skills and many other helpful topics were added to the programme for the benefit of the youth. Hotel visits were arranged for exposure and to build confidence.

On successful completion, 60 youths passed at a ceremony held at Vil Uyana (latest boutique hotel managed by Jetwing) under the patronage of the Secretary to the Ministry of Tourism and other dignitaries. The trainees are now employed at Vil Uyana furthering their skills to become the professionals of tomorrow.

12.8   Conclusion

Community-based tourism faces considerable challenges.   Not least is the challenge to keep foremost a supply-oriented management perspective. The tourism industry has traditionally catered to market demand, attempting to foster, maintain and expand the market, rather than focusing on maintaining the product or experience. The addition of facilities and improving infrastructural facilities for other attractions often occurs in order to keep the tourists coming, resulting in a tourist experience more and more divorced from the original attractions.

The challenge of community-based tourism is to avoid this process and focus on maintaining the original product/experience. Growth can only go so far but not nearly as far as with other forms of tourism, given the dominance of ecological considerations. A supply-oriented management perspective has its primary considerations based on the nature and resilience of the resources, such as cultural or local community preferences, in order to support conservation programmes. By positioning such programmes, additional costs to undertake community-based tourism may require rigorous standards as operators will have to comply with the distinctive industry segment or, alternatively, will be required to disassociate with the term community-based tourism, possibly reverting to nature tourism or other more generalist categories such as eco-tourism.

The sustainability of the tourism sector depends on finding and developing constructive business relationships with key segments of society. In creating community-based special interest tourism, research-based judgment is essential to plan future development. Clearly identified goals must be assigned to educated, trained, experienced and motivated tourism experts, ideally within the local communities, in order to carry out tasks and complete missions. In the real world of tourism, there is no perfect ending, no plain sailing and no solution of the past can be successful for the future.

References:

Central Provincial Community Tourism (2006), *Community Tourism Products Development--Regional Tourism Master Plan*, Kandy: Central Provincial Council, pp.114-118.

Ceylon Tourist Board, Research Division (1983), 'Tourism Trends in Sri Lanka', *Colombo: Annual Statistical Report*, 32, pp.16-18.

Cohen, E. (1984), 'The Sociology of Tourism--Approaches, Issues and Finders', *Annual Review of Sociology*, 10, pp.373- 392.

De Alwis, R. (2006a), 'International Trends and Challenges in Tourism and Hospitality Business, Sri Lanka Tourism, Continued Challenges',HCIMA Sri Lanka Chapter Annual Publication, pp 49-50.

De Alwis, R. (2006b), Challenges Faced by Tourism Industry for Future Development, 'Sri Lanka Tourism, Continued Challenges', HCIMA Sri Lanka Chapter Annual Publication, pp 44-47.

Dissanayake, J.B. (2007), 'Ethical Values in a Changing Village', *Sri Lanka Traditions and Customs*, University of Colombo, Colombo, pp.26-30.

Gurusinghe, P.F. de Silva (2006), *Ecotourism in Sri Lanka*, Presidential address, Sri Lanka Ecotourism Foundation, Colombo, 22 Oct.

Southern Provincial Council Master Plan for Tourism Development, (2005), Development of Community Tourism, in Coastal Areas, Ministry Tourism, Southern Tourism Bureau, Galle, pp. 23-32.

Pathirana, S. (2006), 'Lesser Known attractions in Sri Lanka', Namal Uyana Crystel Rock, Sri Lanka, p.12.

Premaratne, S.K. (2004), 'Challenges and Barriers to Develop Eco-tourism in Sri Lanka', Research Paper completed for the PhD, University of Washington, Seattle, USA, pp.203 – 248.

Samaranayake, H.M. (1998), 'Impact of Tourism Development', A Paper submitted to the Conference by World Tourism Organization, Madrid, Spain, pp.45-46.

Sri Lanka Tourist Board (2005a), *Annual Budget for Tourism Development*, Publication on Tourism Planning and Development, Colombo, 18, pp.48-51

Sri Lanka Tourist Board (2005b), Environmental Impact Assessment, 'Development of Madhu River Community based tourism Project', Development Division, Colombo, pp14-15.

Southern Provincial Council (2005), *Annual Report*, Sri Lanka.

Chapter 13

Tourism and Community Development Cases in Nepal:
A Sustainable Development Deception or the Sustainable Alternative Approach?

13.1 An Overview of Tourism Development in Nepal

In many developing countries, tourism has been taken as one of the alternative outward- and growth-oriented economic development strategies (Zurick, 1992; Brohman, 1996; Tosun and Jenkins, 1996), or one of the sustainable development strategies (Carter, 1993; Gill and Williams, 1994; Orams, 1995), and it is one of the fastest growing industries. Nepal is one of those developing countries and it has taken tourism with high hopes in its overall economic development (Zurick, 1992; Shackley, 1994; Nepal, 2000; Tiwari, 2006). In recent years, despite a negative growth in tourist arrivals, tourism is contributing about 10% of the foreign currency earnings, which is second to remittances, with a 3% gross domestic product and an employment opportunity for about 2.5% of the total labour force, directly or indirectly (National Planning Commission, 2002).

Nepal has gained its name synonymous with tourism and Nepal's tourism is synonymous with adventure tourism, that is mountaineering, followed by nature-based tourism, which is basically visiting parks and protected areas as well as trekking and white water rafting.

Two of the most admired tourist destinations in the world are located in Nepal, namely Sagarmatha (Mount Everest), including the Himalayas which is an attractor to all sorts of tourists, and Lumbini, the birthplace of Lord Buddha, which is a representation of ancient culture and world peace. Furthermore, four heritage sites in Nepal have been listed in the UNESCO World Heritage, namely, the Kathmandu valley; Lumbini; the Sagarmatha National Park; and Chitwan National Park, constituting the first two cultural and the last two natural heritages, respectively. Similarly national parks, wildlife reserves and conservation areas; river systems; religious sites; unique arts & crafts; cultural artefacts; exotic food; indigenous music; unique cultural, social and economic practices; historical and emerging places; existing sight seeing and the settlements of various ethnic groups are common attractions in Nepal. The prominent tourism attractions are as follows (see Figure 13.1):

- So far 326 mountain peaks have been opened up for expedition. These are the major peaks which can easily accommodate 3,000 expedition teams per year without any congestion.

- The Government has designated 25 exciting world class trekking sites, which generally overlap with the conservation areas.

- The total conservation reserves cover an area of 26,971 sq km, i.e. 18.3% of the total area of the country.

- There are a total of 23 world-class rivers for rafting, 16 of them with about 1,244 km available for rafting, mostly ranging between three and five in the total grade of one to six in terms of difficulty.

- There are 14 highly revered religious sites for pilgrimage, some of which are the most important sites of Hindu and Buddhist religions, including Pashupatinath, Changu Narayan and Janakpurdham (for Hindus) and Lumbini (for both Buddhists and Hindus).

- Some world class unique architecture and crafts.

- More than twelve historical sites of international significance.

- A rich cultural diversity and a lasting traditional way of life of the people.

- By now, the government has designated over 50 villages as rural tourism sites.

- Kathmandu is also a paradise for competitive-price shoppers and book lovers.

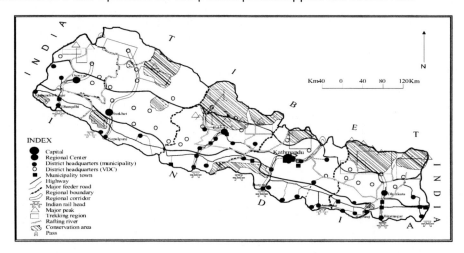

Figure 13.1   Location of the Study Areas and the Major Tourism Development Attributes in Nepal

Nepal initiated its first planned development in 1956, with the implementation of the first National Five Year Development Plan (1956-61). So far, nine periodic plans have been completed, and the tenth plan (2002-07) is currently ongoing. The major policies and programmes incorporated in these plans are summarized in table 13.1 and outlined in the following few paragraphs.

Table 13.1   Highlights of the Tourism Policies in National Plans

Plan period \ Objectives	Tourism policies and plans
First plan (1956-61)	• No specific policy or plan
Second plan (1962-65)	• Institutional development: Establishment of the Tourism Development Board (1957) and the Department of Tourism (1959)
Third plan (1965-70)	• Development of infrastructure, like hotels and airports • Conservation of historic and cultural places • Publicity.
Fourth plan (1970-75)	• Nepal Tourism Master Plan 1972, a comprehensive 10 year plan developed.
Fifth plan (1975-80)	• Policy of extending tourism outside the Kathmandu valley. • Establishment of the Ministry of Tourism (1977).
Sixth plan (1980-85)	• Improvement in previously set policies and programs. • Review of the Tourism Master Plan.
Seventh plan (1985-90)	• Continuation of earlier policies and programs in line of the structural adjustment and macroeconomic policy emphasis.
Eighth plan (1992-97)	• Revitalization of earlier policies. • New open policy in aviation. • Increased budget allocation. • Developed tourism policy (1995), with the establishment of Tourism Council and Tourism Development Board.
Ninth plan (1997-2002)	• Bringing tourism development to village and local level with vigorous publicity, using information and communication technology
Tenth plan (2002-2007)	• Even more emphasis on previous policies and their strengthening. • Establishing regional tourism hub centres. • Creating pollution free environment. • Development of ecotourism sites. • Tourism for rural poverty alleviation with concerted efforts of the Government, donor agencies and local community.

Source: Author's compilation from 10 plan documents.

Actually the first plan did not have any policy and plan related to tourism. The second plan introduced necessary institutional arrangements, including the establishment of the Tourism Development Board and the Department of Tourism under the Ministry of Commerce and Industry. Developing tourism aimed for developing infrastructure, particularly hotels and airports; conservation of historical and cultural places; and publicity for tourism were spelled out in the third plan (1965-70) (National Planning Commission 1965). Thus, from this point onward, tourism policies, strategies, plans and programs have been incorporated in all subsequent plans, including the ongoing tenth plan (2002-07) (see Table 13.1 for summary). In the 10th plan, Nepal aimed to increase foreign currency earning and increase opportunities for employment by recognizing the importance of tourism to national economic growth and development as well as poverty alleviation. During this course of planning, a Tourism Master Plan was prepared in 1972 and revised in 1984; the Ministry of Tourism was established in 1977 and Tourism Policy developed in 1995. During the last 40 years, many aspects of tourism development have been accomplished.   These include extending and diffusing tourism destinations, services and length of stay of the tourists; basic tourism infrastructure development; private sector involvement in decision making; cultural and pilgrimage tourism; eco-tourism and environmental conservation; community participation in tourism; and creating tourism regional hubs.   Diffusing tourism to local and village levels has been undertaken with a view to alleviating rural poverty through establishing and strengthening forward and backward linkages in all areas of tourism with a targeted programme, with four basic principles of pro-poor, pro-women, pro-environment and pro-rural communities.

13.2   An Overview of the Problem at the National Level

Despite all of the tourist attractions and governmental efforts, tourist arrivals in Nepal peaked at 496,000 in 1998, and began a declining trend in subsequent years. A second aspect of the development of tourism is the length of stay of the tourists, which has been steadily growing over the same period and currently has reached more than 12 days on average. And the third indicator, which shows the role of tourism in the national economy, is the earnings and income from tourists. Over this period, income from tourism matched the same pace as tourist arrivals, i.e. the income per tourist per day grew at a low pace, and it just reached US$ 45 per day per tourist as against an expected income of US$ 60 in 2000 (National Planning Commission, 2002). This indicates that tourism in Nepal is low-budget tourism. Similarly, as tourism has contributed, as mentioned earlier, about 3% of gross domestic product and employment opportunity for about 2.5% of the total labour force, its contribution to the national economy is substantially low.

When disaggregating the tourist distribution by purpose, the scenario seems more fragile. On average, only 121 teams per year, comprising eight members in each team on average, have been participating in mountain climbing expeditions since 1992. This shows that only about 1,000 people come for expeditions; however, they are the longest staying tourists and make the overall stay of tourists that much higher. The other popular activity is trekking, which totalled 66,832 tourists in 2004. Similarly, the total number of nature tourism and park visitors was 74,014 in 2004 (Ministry of Culture, Tourism and Civil Aviation, 2005). The largest number of tourists participating in rafting reached 7,799 in 1998.

Particularly, tourist visits for the much promoted types of tourism, eco-tourism, rural tourism, village tourism and home-stay tourism, are unexpectedly small and negligible, i.e. just a few thousand in total.

Tourism development in Nepal has been planned within the broad framework of national planning and regional policies. There are also plans for diversifying tourism industries out of the capital, Kathmandu, to regions by establishing regional and sub-regional tourism hubs with benefits down to local and village levels. At present, tourism development reinforces regional disparity rather than equal regional development (Tiwari, 2006).

Furthermore, despite the various initiatives taken by the government, tourism in Nepal has often developed spontaneously and has basically remained as private sector-driven. It has not been contributing much to the development of larger communities in rural and peripheral regions, neither are communities largely involved in the process. Particularly, many of the trekking tourists, who trek in groups, spend little money along the trekking routes and their contribution in the area is minimal as many stay in open camps, use tents and prepare their meals carried along with them by porters. They contribute to pollution by littering empty cans, plastics, water bottles and so on. Thus, its sustainability in the community context is also highly questionable (Tiwari, 2006).

Though Nepal wants high quality tourists, there is no provision for defining quality of tourists and tourists are welcomed regardless of their quality. Therefore, the high Himalayan fragile environment is at risk. The natural environment is basically threatened by hotel and resort developers, garbage disposed by tour operators and tourists; forests are utilised for fuel by camp setters and local hoteliers; wildlife and their habitats are disturbed. Sanitation is a big problem.

Some social problems include drugs, alcoholism and prostitution. There is a widespread unfriendly attitude and frequent rude behaviour of various service provider groups toward tourists, in particular against certain specific groups of tourists. Such behaviour can be observed at the airport and bus stations by transport service providers, around markets and tourist sites by general market vendors and souvenir vendors, in hotels and motels by their staff, and in routes and sites by the general public.

13.3 The Context of Justification for Searching an Alternative Approach to Tourism and Community Development Nexus

Community tourism provides a solution to the problems identified above. Such community development is governed by self-reliance-community culture-assets management – livelihood (SCAL) system. It encompasses the principles of: (i) self-reliance, that deals with the dynamics of the community towards self-realization, self-help, self-amelioration and self-empowerment; (ii) cultivation of community culture by virtue of organizing and participating in community affairs and development activities, the decision-making process, contributing to community life and accruing benefits from the development activities; (iii) sustainable community assets management, which is taking charge of and having control over a community's own environment, by enhancing the community's capabilities for efficiently managing (i.e. developing, generating, conserving and utilizing) natural, physical, social, human and financial assets; and (iv) ensuring sustainable livelihood, i.e. meeting (individual) household needs.

The paper is based on secondary data, derived from published sources, and relevant information and references have been used to discuss particular issues with a view to the four principles of community development outlined above. The study has thus analyzed and explained the structure, process and stage of community tourism development in Nepal with a view to a sustainable approach to tourism development. The paper has presented various forms of community approaches to tourism development and three prominent best practice cases: Ghandruk, Sirubari and Briddim community-centred tourism initiatives with their basic profiles and processes. The lessons learnt from these initiatives and cases have been presented with a view to improvement in the process and their replication for a sustainable community tourism development framework as an alternative to the present-day spontaneous process to tourism development.

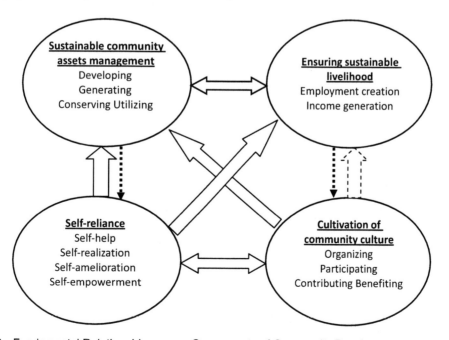

Figure 13.2   Fundamental Relationship among Components of Community Development

13.4   An Overview of Tourism and Community Development in Nepal and the Background of the Cases

There are various forms of tourism and community development in Nepal. However, given the nature of tourism and community development relationship, the following four forms of tourism and community development can be identified.

- Non-government organization initiative

- National parks and wildlife conservation initiative

- Tourism for rural poverty alleviation initiative

- Spontaneous village tourism initiative

13.4.1   Non-government Organization Initiative

This form of tourism and community development was first initiated in Nepal by the Annapurna Conservation Area Project (ACAP) in 1986. This area is the largest protected area in Nepal (7,629 sq km) and the most popular trekking area, with over 60,000 tourists visiting per year.   The major objective of the project was not tourism development but the protection of the environment with sustainable community development managed by the local people with minimal external intervention from the Government and/or other actors. The initiative was launched under ACAP as a non-governmental organization (National Trust for Nature Conservation, 2007) and has been supported by various trusts and the fees collected from tourists. The underlying objective of sustainability is based upon the financing of the project through the collection of fees from tourists. The project has been recognized as a model for conservation all over the world from its inception and it has won international prizes and awards for outstanding conservation (DRU International Environmental Award in 1989) and for promoting a tourism site (Tourism of Tomorrow in 1992).

The project implementation was divided into three pivotal modalities, one of which was tourism management. Under the ACAP functional modality, each village development committee is responsible for the conservation and protection of all natural resources, and their management and utilization. The King Mahendra Trust for Nature Conservation (2005) outlined the following community activities:

- *Conservation of resources:* Under this broad activity group, community works constitute forest management; soil and water conservation; wildlife management; training for local nursery workers, forest guards and leaders; promotion of alternative energy and fuel-efficient technologies; restoration of sites of historical, cultural and archaeological importance; research and survey on subjects such as biodiversity and wildlife census; and formation of local institutions, such as conservation area management committees and conservation sub-area management committees.

- *Community development:* The activities under this category constitute repair, maintenance, improvement and construction of rural infrastructure provisions such as schools, trails and bridges; general health and sanitation facilities, such as   health and family planning clinics, toilets and rubbish pits; extension of agro-forestry and agriculture through training, demonstrations and seed distribution; adult literacy; and programmes targeted specially for empowerment and income-generation of women, youth and economically and socially deprived groups.

- *Tourism management:* Formation of local lodge management committees; preparation of brochure and publicity materials; establishment of information posts and visitor centres; operation of hotel and lodge management training for lodge operators; training for trekking guides; eco-camp site development; and search-and-rescue arrangements for emergency helicopter-evacuation for visitors constitute this activity group.

- *Conservation education and extension:* The activities under this category constitute operating conservation education classes in schools; conducting conservation awareness camps; development of education materials; village clean-up campaigns; mobile audio-visual extension; establishing natural history museum and visitor information services; operating environmental resource libraries; arranging study tours and training for villagers; and establishment and operation of outdoor conservation education centres.

13.4.2 National Parks and Wildlife Conservation Initiative

A second type of tourism and community development initiative is the protected area and buffer zone area management initiative. This was initiated by the Department of National Parks and Wildlife Conservation with a fundamental objective of biodiversity conservation. As protected areas are among the major tourist destinations, it stands as a form of tourism and community development. The first project in this direction was started with the Makalu-Barun National Park and Buffer zone area (previously conservation area), established in 1992. This park, administered and managed by Department of National Parks and Wildlife Conservation, with financial and technical support from The Mountain Institute (TMI), is an innovative conservation model that integrates protected area management and community development. The generic objective of this initiative is to conserve natural resources and promote sustainable development in the area by strengthening the capacity of local communities and improving their socio-economic conditions (Department of National Parks and Wildlife Conservation, 2006).

This approach actively involves local people in protecting their local natural resources, including forests upon which their lives depend, and conserving their rich cultural heritage. The functional modality is the formation of user groups and user committees, thereby initiating income-generating activities, creating a plan for tourism development, working on literacy and capacity building and mitigating human-wildlife conflict. Importance is given to strengthening the traditional resource management systems, such as community-controlled grazing and forest guardianship, as well as to modernizing traditional and indigenous technologies, if appropriate. Thus, the fundamental of this initiative is the cooperation of Government agencies (with technical and financial support of donor agencies and international non-governmental organizations) with community-based organizations (CBOs), already established or newly established for the purpose in the area for the participatory management of natural resources, and also to improve local people's living conditions through integrated conservation and development (Department of National Parks and Wildlife Conservation, 2006).

At the activity level, the Department of National Parks and Wildlife Conservation has been working with UNDP, WWF and The Mountain Institute for the past decade on a couple of projects such as the 'Parks and People Programme', followed by a follow-up participatory conservation programme. This form of community development allows 30 to 50% of the revenue earned in the conservation area to be spent in the same area, with a plan basically developed by the CBOs (Department of National Parks and Wildlife Conservation, 2006). ¨

13.4.3　Tourism for Rural Poverty Alleviation Initiative

A third model of tourism and community development is the tourism for rural poverty alleviation programme (TRPAP) initiative, which is based on the principles of pro-poor, pro-woman, pro-rural and pro-environment, and was initiated in 2001 having undergone its full-fledged implementation since the current tenth five year plan (2002-2007) by recognizing tourism as a priority sector as well as considering it as a major contributor to the overall development of Nepal and rural tourism as a viable area of intervention. The objective of the programme is to create and raise the community's awareness on conservation and utilization of local natural and human resources for sustainable tourism development through social mobilization and community development (Tourism for Rural Poverty Alleviation Project, 2007).

The Ministry of Culture, Tourism and Civil Aviation is the executing ministry at the central level, whereas TRPAP works with District Development Committees under the Ministry of Local Development and with existing or newly formed community organizations, user groups, user committees and functional groups at the grassroots level. The Government, under this initiative, has supported establishing tourism sections within the district development committees (DDCs) and tourism development committees at the level of village development committees (VDCs). This empowers local authorities to manage local resources efficiently and effectively, including tourism development, and to promote forward and backward linkages of rural tourism in prospective villages. In this regard, these local bodies have been empowered by the Local Self-Government Act 1998, which included a number of legislative measures designed to decentralize administration and government service to the district and village levels. The Act has a mandatory provision for formulating plans and their implementation at the local level (DDC and VDC) through community-based organizations like user groups, user committees and local non-governmental organizations. For the management of the community development, the Act provided for a definitive share of the respective revenue to be spent locally in addition to authority for the local government to collect revenue from local natural resources and cultural establishments.

In the first phase, this initiative was implemented in 48 VDCs in six districts across four development regions, representing the mountain and plain ecological zones, as a joint programme of the Government, UNDP, DFID and SNV-Nepal. The programme attempted to serve a total population of slightly more than 160,000 for more than 28,000 households during its pilot phase (UNDP, 2007). The objective of the programme was to support the Government's policy in poverty alleviation by establishing and strengthening forward and backward linkages at the local level. Furthermore, to attain resource sustainability, the programme established a Sustainable Tourism Development Fund and a Sustainable Tourism Village Fund at each programme DDC and VDC, respectively. These funds were provided to the participating local community organizations for the development of tourism infrastructure, soft loans for undertaking micro-enterprises by the target groups, i.e. poor, women and people from disadvantaged groups and communities and other capacity building and enhancing activities (Tourism for Rural Poverty Alleviation Project, 2007).

The village-level functional groups were formed on the basis of occupation, such as lodge management, poultry and vegetable farming, cottage industries, and so on. However, in order to efficiently take responsibility, the community organizations were formed either of females or mixed groups at the settlement level. In programme areas, about 80% of people were organised into groups, with women as a majority of members. Where protected areas fell under this initiative, buffer zone user committees acted as respective Village Tourism Development Committees, and buffer zone user groups, buffer zone user committees and functional groups were recognized as community organizations.

The community organizations could undertake virtually any activity that supported income-generation of the local people through the utilization of local resources, but was also expected to undertake activities, like lodge management training, trekking guide training, improvement of sanitation and hygiene, water supply improvement, trail repair and management and promotion of clean energy. By completing these activities, the initiative expected to be a best practice model for the rest of the country where rural tourism was a prospective activity for rural poverty alleviation, and provide an institutional mechanism for sustainable rural tourism.

13.4.4 Spontaneous Village Tourism Initiative

A new wave of national development in Nepal came along with the change of 1990. Regarding the extent and coverage by such an initiative in the area of tourism, there is no clear data. It was largely initiated along with the establishment of community-based organizations and non-governmental organizations. With this development, like-minded people gathered together and initiated community resource-based development initiatives or particular development activities with the assistance of local government, local/national non-governmental organizations and donor agencies or international non-governmental organizations. Such an initiative included community forestry, school building and management, drinking water, microfinance, cooperatives, promotion of micro-hydro power, tourism development, etc. In this spontaneous initiation, activities were undertaken in urban areas as well as in rural areas – particularly numerous, though of small magnitude, in the latter case.

In this category of tourism and community development, community participation in various forms and financing of local activities largely varied. They ranged from full financing from external sources as donations or grants to full management by the community through charity and donations, members fees, revenue collection from local natural resources and cultural heritage, and utilization of local resources. In many cases, however, a combination of various financing was applied, using a pragmatic approach to financing community development activities. With this approach, full responsibility rests upon the participating organization(s) and members of the community.

As far as the formation of community organizations is concerned, various formats can be observed, ranging from narrowly focused exclusive occupational groups, gender-based groups like Mothers' Groups, or widely focused settlement specific groups. Their responsibilities are defined by the provisions of the user group as set out in the decentralization and local development legislation or by provision of the status of the organization, which is basically a non-governmental organization or cooperative.

13.5 Three Cases of Tourism and Community Development in Nepal

On the whole, Nepal is considered as one of the better sources of best practices in various community development initiatives, which are largely backed up by an exemplary practice in people's participation and decentralization. Three cases are presented in this section. Each case is discussed as to its location, extent and coverage, and activities performed and accomplishments.

13.5.1   Case 1: Non-government Organization-initiated Tourism and Community Development in Ghandruk (Kaski, Nepal)

Ghandruk was the first pilot project on tourism development based on community development principles initiated by non-government organization in Nepal. Ghandruk village is located at an altitude of about 2000 metres, at the foot of Mt. Annapurna, 43 km by road from Pokhara, (the famous tourist destination and headquarters of the western development region of Nepal), followed by   a 4-6 hour up-hill trek. It is located on the main trekking route to the Annapurna base-camp and one of the two entry points to the Mustang trekking route and/or the start or the end stop for the Annapurna trekking circuit. Ghandruk village consists of about 235 households with about 1,400 population mostly consisting of Gurung community, one of the famous Gurkha ethnic groups (see Figure 13.3). The traditional economic sector is agriculture and animal husbandry, but the major income source of the village is remittances, as 90% of the Gurung households receive remittances from the British or Indian army active services or pension.

Figure 13.3   Location Views of Ghandruk Village

Source: Ghandruk Village Photo Gallery
(http://www.nepalphotogallery.com/village/ghandrung/index.htm)

Under the ACAP functional priority, Ghandruk was given priority for tourism management. In a broader framework, there is the main Conservation and Development Committee, which covers the whole Ghandruk VDC, and is responsible for the management of conservation and overall development of the village. Local institution-building includes a separate independent committee, the Mothers Group (colloquially known as Aama Toli) is which undertakes capacity-building of the women, income-generation, social and health and hygiene improvement, performance of cultural programmes and conservation of cultural heritage, construction of a latrine in every house and village clean up, health post, literacy classes for women, and micro-enterprises. There are other sub-committees, namely the Lodge Management Committee, the Forest Management Sub-committee, the Electricity Management Sub-committee and the Campsite Management Sub-committee,

ACAP community development activities are comprehensive and include:

- Conservation activities, such as reforestation and forest management, soil and water conservation, wildlife management.

- Organization of training for local nursery workers, forest guards and forest leaders.

- Conservation of cultural heritage.

- Promotion of alternative energy and fuel-efficient technologies.

- Construction, rehabilitation and maintenance of trails.

- Construction, rehabilitation and maintenance of social infrastructure, such as schools, toilets and rubbish pits.

- General health and sanitation improvement, including health clinics, family planning and village cleanliness.

- Programmes targeted for women, youth groups and economically and socially deprived groups.

- Literacy for women and adult education.

- Income generation for women.

- Agro-forestry and agriculture extension through training, demonstrations and seed and seedling distribution.

- Conservation awareness camps and conservation education classes.

- Gurung museum management.

In addition to community development, Ghandruk undertakes tourism promotion and management. This is basically carried out by the Lodge Management Committee, the, dominant committee in relation to tourism management and development. It consists of all those who run lodges in the area. Normally, general meetings of the Committee are held twice a year with the first taking place before the trekking season. The Committee mediates competition among the lodge owners and sets the standards and prices of lodging and food and also collects hotel and lodge taxes. A flat rate is imposed on the lodges; however, taxes are collected on the basis of established businesses, for new establishments (which attracts a lesser rate) and renewal for which rates differ. This tax money is used to finance loans given to lodge owners for small-scale projects, like electric rice cookers and other utensil purchases, improvement of kitchens and lodges, etc. In addition, the following tourism management activities are undertaken in the area by this Committee and other various committees and sub-committees.

- Hotel/lodge management training for lodge operators.

- Trekking guide training.

- Eco-tourism campsite development.

- Publication of brochures and publicity materials.

- Establishment of information posts and visitor centres.

- Security arrangement of tourists including search and rescue.

Actually, most community development activities supplement tourism promotion as well. So far as performance is concerned, the community, particularly under the Mother's Group initiation, has raised funds, collecting money from tourists and locals performing cultural events during festivals and frequently during peak tourist visits. Thus, in Ghandruk proper, the community has successfully managed to run a well-maintained drinking water supply system, a community health post, a model high school, a Gurung museum, a women's cooperative shop and a micro-hydroelectric power plant. The community has managed garbage collection and keeps the village clean. The Mother's Group has liberated its fellow women members from illiteracy, helping them to attain self-empowerment, increase their share and say in asset management, increase opportunities for contributing to livelihood and fostering pride towards a community culture.

The community activities in Ghandruk have successfully generated social assets through all of these activities. They have been able to revitalize some of the functional traditions like forest guardianship, cultural performance, and so on.

13.5.2   Case 2: Spontaneously Initiated Tourism and Community Development in Sirubari (Syangja, Nepal)

Sirubari, a well known name in sustainable village tourism, is located in Syangja district at a distance of 25 km by road from Pokhara and four hours' walk from Nagdanda, or alternatively by a rough road journey of 28 km from Syangja, which is 35 km far from Pokhara. Both Nagdanda and Syangja lie along the Siddhartha Highway (AH42), the road that connects the famous tourism corridor in Western Nepal, i.e. Pokhara with Lumbini.   The village lies at an altitude of 1,700m and some of the most spectacular views of the central Himalayas, including Machhapure, Dhaulagiri and Annapurna peaks, can be seen from this village (Figure 13.4).

Figure 13.4   A View of Sirubari Village

Source:
http://www.nepaltourismdirectory.com/nepal_travel_destination.php?id=25&did=41&title=Nepal+Village+Touris
m.

Like Ghandruk, with 80 households the population of Sirubari village is about 480 and is a mainly Ghurka community.   Given the traditional occupational affiliation, most males have joined the British, Indian and Nepali armies, which is the main source of livelihood at the village by remittances from active services or pensions.

Sirubari tourism is a first in village tourism practice in Nepal, based on the farm-stay concept of Australia or Israel. It is a private sector-community partnership initiative. Unlike Ghandruk community tourism, which is basically organized group trekking tourism of long standing, Sirubari village tourism was conceptualized by its members who approached the government for assistance in developing village tourism. The response of the government fror an approach to village tourism resulted, in 1997, in a partnership between the Sirubari Village Tourism Development and Management Committee (SVTDMC) and a newly established Nepal Village Resort (NVR) company based in Kathmandu as marketing and promotion partner. At present, out of the 80 households in the village, 40 households are directly engaged in tourism.

A community member who wants to participate in the programme first must develop at least two rooms of his/her house for tourist accommodation, construct a toilet and connect running water. Thus, only some internal adjustments are needed to make the homes reasonably comfortable for stay-overnight, yet the house remains a traditional Nepalese house and the regular residence of the hosts. Then he/she has to become a member of SVTDMC and agree to the rules and regulations of SVTDMC. The marketing for tourism is done by NVR and tourists are sent to the village in groups to stay for a minimum of two nights, under a package tour. Visitors are welcomed by a group of residents and then guided to the small central square next to the village temple where plans are made for each individual's stay. The SVTDMC distributes visitors on a strict roster basis across available guestrooms and each visitor is taken to the assigned house at which point he/she has no option for making a choice for home-stay. The host provides accommodation and three meals a day. The SVTDMC gets a certain amount of tariff, agreed upon between SVTDMC and NVR, for a minimum stay for two nights and an additional amount depending upon any extension of stay. The SVTDMC arranges for porters to carry the luggage of the tourists. Upon arrival there is a welcome ceremony and upon departure a farewell ceremony. Portering and arrival and farewell ceremonies are performed by members of a traditional occupational group. Another typical service is an afternoon tea which is provided by another resident who is not a guestroom owner. Then the tariff is shared between SVTDMC and guestroom owner, which at the present rate, is a proportion of approximately 40/60%, respectively. From the share of SVTDMC, money is given as per the decision of the Committee to the porters, welcome and farewell performers and afternoon tea providers.

This tourism provides an opportunity for visitors to be exposed to community and rural life through the rich Ghurkha culture and traditional practices. Visitors are served typical Nepali food prepared in the traditional way and they normally take their meals with their hosts. Visitors travel around the village to see the living, working, socializing and spiritualizing environment, behaviour and culture and practices of the villagers. They are guided to sight-seeing, always including to the hilltop of the village for views north to the Himalayan peaks. In the evening, cultural programmes are arranged.

Visited by about 9,000 tourists since its opening in 1997, i.e. nine years of tourism service, the Sirubari village tourism's innovative initiative won the Pacific Asia Travel Association Gold Award in the heritage category in 2001. Unlike in Ghandruk, where community self-development while strong has received very significant outside assistance, community development in Sirubari is more indigenous and villagers have clearly demonstrated the community principles of self-reliance, cultivation of community culture, sustainable community assets management and generation of sustainable livelihood. The local community has been able to conserve the cultural heritage of the area, manage natural and physical assets, and develop social, human and financial assets.

13.5.3   Case 3: Rural Poverty Alleviation Programme Initiated Tourism and Community Development in Briddim (Rasuwa, Nepal)

The Briddim village, at an altitude of 2,290 m, is located in Rasuwa. The village can be reached after a walk of three hours from Syabru-Bhesi, which is located at a distance of about 170 km from Kathmandu. The village lies at the last stop of the newly designated Tamang Heritage trail running from Syabru-Bhesi through Briddim to Langtang National Park. The majority of the villagers are ethnic Tamang, a community of Tibetan origin with a strong Tibetan culture. There are a total of 43 households in the village, with a population of about 260. Since 2002, through the Tourism for Rural Poverty Alleviation Programme, the Rasuwa District Development Committee and Langtang National Park obtained financial support from the Canadian International Development Agency, and Briddim has emerged as a model rural tourism village.

"Home-stay" is one of the TRPAP modalities of rural tourism, which was selected by the Briddim TRPAP programme. Out of the total of   43 households in Briddim, 23 have developed home-stay for tourists with adequate physical facilities of room, toilet, shower, kitchen and so on to provide   reasonable and comfortable services and facilities. The programme offers support of 5,000 rupees ($\approx$ US\$ 75) to each household that decides to partake in the home-stay programme.

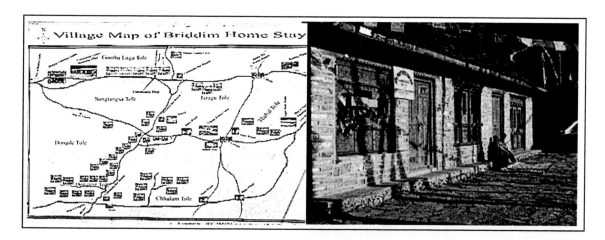

Figure 13.5   Briddim Village Map Showing Home-stay and Village Centre

Source: http://www.lamonda3.ch/TRPAP.htm.

The village is located in the fold of Langtang Himalaya and maintains a rich Tibetan culture. The people have organized in groups, formed a home-stay management sub-committee, undertaken lodge management training, visited Pokhara, Ghandruk, Sirubari and Sauraha (Chitwan) for observation of innovative tourism facilities and services with community approaches, and participated in conservation management training. They are thus highly aware of their local physical and natural assets via conservation, utilization and sanitation, and the preservation of their cultural heritage.

The home-stay management sub-committee, which is joined by all home-stay participating households, manages everything related to tourist home-stay, including reception and hospitality of tourists, supply of facilities, managerial workers, tariff determination and service standardization. Like Sirubari, the tariff for home-stay is the same throughout the village. A separate community development fee, at present 100 rupees ($\approx$ US$ 1.50), is collected from each tourist. Various community development works, including conservation of natural assets and cultural heritage, are financed from this fee.

Unlike Sirubari, there is no marketing partner in Briddim's home-stay initiative, only an open market channel. When the hosts hear about the arrival of tourists, all the villagers dress in Tibetan costumes and gather together to welcome the tourists as if in a festival. They greet the tourists as guests, offer garlands, i.e. offer Khada (silk scarves), and entertain them with different types of music and dances. All then proceed in a procession towards the Ghomba (Buddhist monastery), situated at the centre of the village, where the official welcome ceremony takes place. The chairperson of the sub-committee formally welcomes the tourists; the Buddhist priest wishes peace to all by reciting verses from the holy scriptures; and the ladies offer welcome refreshment, which typically includes Tibetan yak butter tea, Briddim white wine, apple wine, Tibetan bread and local yak cheese, among local delicacies.

The home-stay tourism initiative has not only directly benefited the participating households, it has also provided opportunities to rural unemployed youths to become tourist guides and porters, as well as for women to open small businesses, including home-stay, small hotels and lodges, tea houses and small retail shops. At least one member of each household operating a home-stay has already taken training in cooking, English language, tourist guiding, handicraft production or vegetable cultivation. Signs of revitalizing handicrafts have been seen. Similarly, encouraged by local demand, production of vegetables, poultry, and livestock has been intensified.

Community activities in Nepal date far back in history, but conventional community activities were limited to natural resource preservation and management of cultural matters in religious or traditional terms, and they were fundamentally different than the community activities performed by local people today. The local community today is more aware of the strength-of-community approach to economic matters and the revitalization of their centuries old community cooperation works, yet with a more scientific and reasonable justification. The human assets have been strengthened by receiving training on guiding trekkers, tourism management, food and services, cooking and portering, sustainable rural tourism, financial management, English language training, and biodiversity and conservation. Some also have taken loans from the venture capital fund of TRPAP to improve accommodation facilities, install solar water heaters and purchase sufficient utensils as required for kitchen and furniture, fittings and utensils for bedrooms.   The success of this venture has seen many of the households repay their micro loans.

Local infrastructure, i.e. community physical assets, have been developed and improved, particularly through stone-paved trails, potable drinking water, waste management, community lodges, campsite development, public toilets and bathrooms, monastery maintenance and visitor information centres and signage through the tourism development infrastructure fund provided by TRPAP.

People have become aware of conservation of the local environment, particularly the declining forest stock due to household energy requirements. There was no shortage of drinking water in the village, but a good management of water taps which has controlled some water wastage was started only with this development. Similarly, measures have been applied to reduce the use of firewood for household energy by using energy efficient and clean energy technology like improved cooking stoves, solar home heating systems at all home-stay houses, and bio-gas generated from human and animal excreta. Similarly, copper fin solar water heaters have been installed in five community-owned bathrooms. People have learnt how to keep their homestead sanitary by constructing toilets and keeping them clean. The village roads and surroundings have been kept clean by installing dustbins around the village and collecting rubbish regularly. Residents learn about conservation of natural and cultural assets including local costumes, food, music and festivals, leading to revitalization of their traditional practices.

Though this was not exclusively a community initiative but involved significant external intervention, it has shown strong signs of an effective impact on both the individual economic progress of the households and the community's physical, natural, human, social and financial assets. It has empowered the local community, particularly the women, opened up avenues of employment creation and income-generation by enhancing a way towards a sustainable livelihood, and thus exhibited a strong culture of community cooperation.

13.6   The Lessons Learnt

Unexpectedly, despite a big name in tourism, an outstanding performance towards contribution to gross domestic product and employment opportunities, Nepalese tourism has not performed at the level of the world average. Tourism has been declining since 2000 due to the Maoist insurgency[30] and rural areas were especially hard hit. Yet, the number of tourists is not the key issue for sustainable development but the process and the likely maintenance of cultural and environmental status quo ante combined with a positive economic impact on the host communities are very important. Similarly, from

---

[30] Though the threat was not one of life-taking, tourists do not want to face any state of uncertainty in their travels, nor encounter any intimidation or extortion when the purpose of the visit is leisure and pleasure. The situation of insurgency has improved since this paper was first drafted, and life in Nepal has been returning to normal when the Maoists gave up their policy of violence after the Peace Accord signed by the Government and the Maoists in November 2006 and joined in a Government of National Unity in March 2007.

the point of view of host communities, tourism should not only be taken as an opportunity to take short-term economic benefit, but also as a mode of sustainable livelihood in situ where socioeconomic, cultural and environmental entities should be sustainably conserved, rationally utilized and accrue a reasonable benefit to the community as a whole.

Despite a planned development, much Nepalese tourism has been developed spontaneously by business- and demand-driven phenomena. What the community approach to tourism development needs is a supply-driven approach to meet tourism demand. The community approach is designed to increase benefits to communities and encourage them to take charge on matters of local socioeconomic, cultural and environmental concerns, and to support conservation in tandem with tourism.

All cases demonstrate similarities in implementation modalities, though their origins have taken place under different circumstances. The Ghandruk and Briddim initiatives were based on the demand side of tourism, encouraged by the respective popular trekking routes. Sirubari village tourism, on the other hand was a supply-driven phenomenon, but it has successfully demonstrated that new tourism development can be created provided some primary and conducive conditions are met in order to call it a real sustainable initiative.

The Ghandruk initiative was of a more regulatory nature in matters of tourism management per se and, as the village is large, its scope of community development is wider, whereas the Sirubari and Briddim initiatives had a higher participation of the community in overall tourism service matters. In all three cases, participation in various community matters is mandatory, once a household decides to become a member of a particular activity. The arrival of tourists in Sirubari is highly regulated due to its exclusive contract with a tour operator in Kathmandu, and the distribution of tourists among households is controlled on a strict roster basis. In the other two destinations however, tourist arrivals are derived from existing demand and their distribution across households for home-stays is left to the choice of the tourists.

Some other underlying differences between Sirubari and Ghandruk and Briddim are: firstly, the prices in Sirubari are several times higher than that of tourism prices in popular trekking destinations like Ghandruk and Briddim, where bargaining provides the opportunity to adjust the price according to the contemporary situation of tourism. Secondly, Sirubari is a supply-driven phenomenon and rigorous marketing and promotion is required to receive the critical mass of tourists and to run businesses with reliable income-generation. Thirdly, whatever eye-catching observations were made, including winning an award, the arrival of tourists in Sirubari is not great enough to be termed critical in meeting the minimum requirement to run a business profitably like an enterprise at this stage, particularly in terms of sustainable earnings (Banskota et al., 2005); rather it remains a goal yet to be fully realised.

However, it remains to be seen if the communities in the respective sites can maintain the cultural and environmental status quo ante, particularly in Ghandruk and Briddim, where there is a long-established trekking attraction, after the anticipated influx of tourism now that the security situation has been normalized. This concern is raised here because, even with a smaller number of tourist arrivals, the economic impact was higher in Ghandruk and the environmental impact was negative compared with a fully community-operated tourism venture in the same area where the environmental impact was positive and the economic impact not as significant (Nyaupane and Thapa, 2004). In both cases, tourism was not as desired; Ghandruk risks environmental unsustainability, and the other venture is economically unsustainable at present.

Positives that can be taken from these three case studies include the state of empowerment of the communities themselves, and awareness about cultural and environmental niches to which they can assimilate and create opportunities for sustainable livelihood. In this respect, the communities have accepted and fully participated in the innovative approaches prescribed by the respective initiating organizations. Furthermore, the communities have taken steps towards activities that would enhance their capabilities in a range of different areas, increase the stock of various assets, and they are working by showing vigorous community solidarity.

Moreover, when the community approach is intact, there is no logical ground to be overly concerned about the destruction of the environment, since they recognise that their sustainable livelihood is attained from within. If the activity is not sustainable due to low tourist arrivals, there is no threat to the environment directly from tourism unless local people underestimate their efforts and keep a blind eye to their achievements and start a search for an unsustainable livelihood from the stock of local assets.

The community approach to tourism from these pioneer villages demonstrates alternative approaches to empowering the local people by building local institutions; and to generating and managing natural, physical, social, human and financial resources, which are the basis of the avenues for employment creation and income generation, thereby ensuring sustainable livelihood. The collective profits generated from tourism, are presently being used to develop various components of the local economy. These activities have been accomplished by raising the level of the people to a community culture, not only in matters of community issues, but also over the issues of economic life. Nevertheless, there is need for caution, particularly in the environment with a supply-driven tourism, though it can logically be concluded that, as it is working in this crisis situation, it would work when the security situation improves. What is certain is that in popular tourism destinations, the community approach can be replicated more confidently than in areas introduced as new tourism destinations, like Sirubari, with a view to focusing on management of local resources and a sustainable environment in the interest of the community. In those places where tourism attractions are to be created, this can be taken as a secondary economic activity, yet a sustainable socioeconomic, cultural and environmental approach, to tourism development.

References:

Banskota, K. et al. (2005), 'Economics of sustainable village tourism: experience and lessons from Sirubari, Nepal', *ICIMOD Newsletter*, 48, pp. 29-31.

Brohman, J. (1996), 'New Directions in tourism for third world development', *Annals of Tourism Research*, 23(1), pp. 48-70.

Carter, E. (1993), 'Ecotourism in the Third World: Problems for Sustainable Tourism Development', *Tourism Management*, 14(2), pp. 85-90.

Department of National Parks and Wildlife Conservation (2006), (online), available: http://www.dnpwc.go.np, (4-3-2007).

Gill, A. and P. Williams (1994), 'Managing growth in mountain tourism communities', *Tourism Management*, 15(3), pp. 212-220.

King Mahendra Trust for Nature Conservation (2005), *Annual Report 2005*, Kathmandu.

Ministry of Culture, Tourism & Civil Aviation (2005), *Nepal Tourism Statistics 2004*, Kathmandu.

National Planning Commission (1965), *Third Plan (1965-1970)*, Kathmandu.

National Planning Commission (1975), *Fifth Plan (1975-1980)*, Kathmandu.

National Planning Commission (1980), *The Sixth Plan (1980-1985)*, Kathmandu.

National Planning Commission (1992), *The Eighth Plan (1992-1997)*, Kathmandu.

National Planning Commission (1997), The Ninth Plan (1997-2002), Kathmandu.

National Planning Commission (2002), *The Tenth Plan (2002–2007)*, Kathmandu.

Nepal Trust for Nature Conservation (2007), Annapurna Conservation Area Project Introduction, (online), available: http://www.ntnc.org.np/ (31-5-2007).

Nepal, S. K. (2000), 'Tourism in protected areas: The Nepalese Himalayas', *Annals of Tourism Research*, 27(3), pp. 661-681.

Nyaupane, G.P. and B. Thapa (2004), 'Evaluation of ecotourism in Nepal: a comparative assessment in the Annapurna Conservation Area Project, Nepal', *Journal of Ecotourism*, 3(1), pp. 20-45.

Orams, M. B. (1995), 'Towards a more desirable form of ecotourism', *Tourism Management*, 16(1), pp. 3-8.

Shackley, M. (1994), 'The land of Lō, Nepal/Tibet', *Tourism Management*, 15(1), pp. 17-26.

Tiwari, I. P. 2006), 'Regional and poverty orientation of the tourism development in Nepal', Proceedings of the International conference on Tourism and New Asia: Implication for Research, Policy and Practice, Beijing, China, 9-12 Aug. 2006, pp. 571-583.

Tosun, C. and Jenkins, C. L. (1996), 'The need for regional planning approaches to tourism development: The case of Turkey', *Tourism Management*, 17(7), pp. 519-531.

Tourism for Rural Poverty Alleviation Programme (2007), *Tourism for rural Poverty Alleviation Programme*, (online), available: http://www.welcomenepal.com/trpap/ (31-5-2007).

UNDP (2007), *Tourism for Rural Poverty Alleviation Programme*, (online), available: http://www.undp.org.np/energy/projects/trpap/index.php?ProgramID=20 (5-3-2007).

Zurick, D. N. (1992), 'Adventure travel and sustainable tourism in the peripheral economy of Nepal', *Annals of the Association of American Geographers*, 82(4), pp. 608-628.

Chapter 14

Tourism and Community Development: UNWTO Projects in Asia

Rural Tourism Development Master Plan for Malaysia

2000-2001

Rural tourism development has been a priority area of development in Malaysia, not least due to the country's unique natural environment and the prime opportunity it has presented to diversify the country's tourism product. Moreover, rural tourism has the potential to generate annual revenues of up to RM 1 billion and create 6,000 new jobs. With the aim of delivering an increased level of socio-economic benefits to rural-based communities, a project was implemented by UNWTO with UNDP funding, in cooperation with the Government of Malaysia, to provide policy formulation guidance on a broad range of issues for its integrated development. The project undertook a number of key activities which were focussed on primarily determining the market potential of rural tourism within the country, together with providing institutional strengthening assistance to the main stakeholders for the management of the tourism industry. A comprehensive audit and inventory were made across the 13 federal states to assess the existing rural tourism products from the tourist perspective; Research was also undertaken with a survey of foreign and domestic visitors, international tour operators and travel trade organizations from main source markets; training workshops were held with the participation of state officials and representatives of the local tourism workforce, to provide training on managing the local tourism sector and developing effective tourism services in rural areas.

The Rural Tourism Development Plan developed for the Government outlined a long-term vision for rural tourism development in Malaysia together with a strategy to create a new brand of tourism experience for visitors to Malaysia from new market segments. The vision would aim to showcase the highly attractive scenic and tropical attractions in the country through focussing on developing environmentally friendly activities and attractions of high visitor interest including scenic touring, wildlife, flora and arts and crafts. The central purpose of this vision was to sustain and reflect the culture and surroundings of local communities and enhance the authenticity of a tourist's visit. In addition, the plan recommended to spread the concentration of tourism activities to a greater number of rural areas in the country; offering a higher quality of local accommodation including guesthouses and homestay houses. The Plan proposed a series of implementation mechanisms for adoption at the National, State and District levels, including the appointment of locally engaged Rural Tourism officials and the establishment of a national Rural Tourism Action Committee, to monitor the development progress within each State.

Community-based Tourism Development Plan for Indonesia

2003

UNWTO conducted a community-based tourism project in Indonesia, in cooperation with the Government of Indonesia and the United Nations Development Programme (UNDP). The primary aim of the project was to support the tourism sector in the context of the Government's decentralization reforms which would granting of greater regional autonomy to provinces, districts and communities, to enable regional authorities undertake more effective management and operation of the tourism sector. The central component of the project was therefore to develop a broad strategic framework to take into account the new changes to regional authorities which would facilitate effective coordination between central government and local authorities for the local tourism sector and deliver enhanced socio-economic benefits to the local areas. Two communities in Banten Lama (West Java) and Candireko (Central Java) were selected as locations to conduct case studies to assess the prevailing constraints and opportunities for community-based tourism. The case studies played a key role in underlining the strong range of natural and cultural tourism resources in Indonesia, and served to highlight the importance of inter-community participation and shared responsibility for developing community-based tourism; the need for a broad based partnership between public and private sectors and community groups; and the central role of education and environmental awareness programmes to broaden the understanding of local stakeholders on the long-term sustainable and tourism-related benefits. Overall, the project formulated a strategy that would seek to improve the tourism management functions carried out by provincial authorities through community empowerment and place poverty alleviation at the heart of community-based tourism projects.

UNWTO formulated a Plan which proposed the establishment of two key mechanisms: A Community-based Tourism Task Force (CTTF) and a Community Tourism Unit (CTU), which would support community projects both centrally and in local areas respectively through the active participation of local citizens in the planning and implementation process. These agencies would bear the responsibility for the mobilization of resources; defining the roles and responsibilities of regional stakeholders and community members; setting the policy direction for community-based tourism; and promoting training and skills programmes. The proposals were designed with a view to strengthening accountability, tourism awareness and impact at the local level, to enable community residents play a major decision-making role in how tourism affects and benefits their lives and environment; to ensure the costs and benefits from tourism are distributed on an equitable basis; and that natural resources are used in a ecologically sustainable manner.

Development of Community-based Tourism Guidelines for Mongolia

2006

In collaboration with the UN Development Programme (UNDP), UNWTO conducted a two month project in Mongolia to prepare a broad range of guidelines for the development community-based tourism (CBT) in the country's rural areas. The project was undertaken within the framework of the countrywide UNDP project Enterprise Mongolia, which focuses on diversifying and improving livelihoods and developing entrepreneurial skills in rural communities through supporting small and medium enterprises.

In view of the increasing activity and importance of CBT in Mongolia's tourism sector, there is a prime opportunity for communities to benefit significantly from socio-economic development through greater enterprise at the local level. Currently, community tourism in Mongolia is focused on tours to the nomadic herder communities and the project aimed to assess the potential for developing additional tourism-related activities at the local level. The guidelines would therefore assist the Government to broaden the scope of community-based tourism activities in the countries to include all community tourism initiatives in Soum Centres. A key component of the project was to establish a set of criteria for the selection of future CBT projects. These are based primarily on their market potential; range and diversity of tourism attractions; quality of local services and infrastructure; and levels of community cohesion and active interest in tourism. The project also devised pro-poor criteria for the selection of CBT sites as a key aim of the guidelines would be for community groups to receive optimum socio-economic benefits through increased tourism revenues and the creation of additional employment. To this end, the proposed guidelines proposed recommendations for the development and further strengthening in quality of existing tourism goods, services and infrastructure, as well as market pricing. These included homestay accommodation, handicrafts, guide services, trekking, agricultural products and cultural performances, which would collectively foster a more integrated CBT product for Mongolia.

Another important aspect of the formulation of the guidelines was to enable central and local government officials, community groups and the private sector to gain an enhanced understanding of CBT in Mongolia and have outlined a phased approach for establishing the activity on a wider scale within communities and improving the operational and structural management of the sector by its stakeholders. In this regard, the guidelines provided recommendations for the improvement of provisions of basic services including on health, safety and accessibility for visitors. Other recommendations made also highlighting the need to link CBT more closely with tourists, through improving English language skills and IT access, and identify appropriate partners to undertake promotional and marketing activities at the local level.

Institutional Strengthening and Capacity Building Project for Timor-Leste

2006

As one of the youngest countries in the world, it is evident that tourism in Timor-Leste is at a nascent stage. The Sustainable Tourism Sector Development and Institutional Strengthening Project, which was implemented by UNWTO with UNDP funding, has assisted the National Directorate of Tourism (NDT) in formulating a comprehensive policy document to establish a common approach for the management and development of the country's tourism sector. One of the key conclusions made by the project was that supporting entrepreneurship would be a highly effective means for reducing poverty in Timor-Leste. In addition, and owing to the country's unique natural and cultural heritage which is focused primarily on marine and coastal resources, tourism represents a significant opportunity to make a significant contribution to local economic development and job creation, as well as environmental conservation and greater equity at the local level.

As an important step towards tapping the tourism potential of the country, 15 diverse areas were identified in the country for their protection and management during the project. The criteria which were applied in the selection process included the quality and range of tourism attractions; physical and market accessibility; partnerships with the private sector; level of amenities; and community attitude towards tourism. The criteria were designed to ensure that only those villages and communities suitable for tourism would be selected, and that areas endowed with precious local resources are used for the most effective purposes for the benefit of the local communities. To assist in this process, the town of Com (Lautem), a large coastal fishing area and beach resort, and Ilimano (Metinaro), a small coastal village known as a diving resort, were selected as pilot sites to help gauge the quality and potential of prospective areas. Both sites are highly representative of the country's wider tourism product, and also reflected the size and level of awareness of tourism in communities, which has been assessed to contrast widely. In order to raise standards and under the project's proposals, local communities have been encouraged to participate more closely in the development process at an early stage to provide basic tourism infrastructure and services, such as lodging and guide services. Additionally, local communities would play an important role in conserving these areas to reduce the degradation of natural resources and further promote community-based tourism based on the sustainable use of resources.

Appendix A ————————————————

Advisory Committee and Editorial Committee

Advisory Committee

Mr. Francesco Frangialli, Secretary-General of the World Tourism Organization (UNWTO),
Mr. XU Jing, Regional Representative for Asia and the Pacific, UNWTO,
Mr. Eugenio Yunis, Director of Programme and Coordination, UNWTO,
Mr. Gabor Vereczi, Chief of Environment and Quality Section, Sustainable Development of Tourism Department, UNWTO,
Dr. Walter Jamieson, Dean, School of Travel Industry Management, University of Hawaii,
Dr. Sasithara Pichchaichannarong, Deputy Permanent Sec, Ministry of Tourism, Thailand,
Mr. Douglas Hainsworth, Senior Advisor, Sustainable Pro-poor Tourism, SNV
Ms. YANG Shengming, Director General, Guizhou Provincial Tourism Administration, China.

Editorial Committee

Chief Editor

Dr. BAO Jigang, Professor and Dean of the School of Tourism Management and the School of Geography and Planning, Sun Yat-sen University, China and a member of UNWTO's Tourism Panel of Experts.

The Editors

Dr. Xu Honggang, Professor and Vice Dean of the School of Tourism Management,
Sun Yat-sen University,
Dr. Trevor Sofield, Professor of Tourism at the University of Tasmania and Guest Professor at the the School of Tourism Management, Sun Yat-sen University,
Dr. Sun Jiuxia, Associate Professor of the School of Tourism Management,
Sun Yat-sen University,
Ms. Ma Ling, Teacher of of the School of Tourism Management, Sun Yat-sen University.

Appendix B

About the Authors

Dr. BAO Jigang is professor and dean of the School of Tourism Management and the Dean of the School of Geography and Planning at Sun Yat-sen University, China. His research interests include tourism geography, theme park, tourism planning, urban tourism, tourism impacts and community tourism. He is a member of International Academy for the study of Tourism, a member of WTO's Tourism Panel of Experts, the Chairman of the China Tourism Academy (2001-2003), a member of the National Technical Committee for Tourism Standardization of China, deputy president of the Geographical Society of China, and Chair of Tourism Geography of the Geographical Society of China. He is the regional editor of China Tourism Research. Dr. BAO Jigang has published and presented more than 100 publications, papers and presentations. He has also been the team leader for many tourism master plans in China, such as Huangshan Tourism Master Plan, Guilin Tourism Master Plan, Hubei province Tourism Master Plan, Kanas Tourism Master Plan, Shangri-La Tourism Master Plan and Hunan Province Tourism Master Plan.

Mr. Jan Burrows has been involved in tourism and conservation for over 25 years working in a variety of positions. Though Mr. Jan Burrows's academic background is in Biology he has always found this useful in his tourism work particularly in the training and coaching of naturalist guides. His early career was as director of an environmental education centre for residential school groups in New York State. Later moving to the private sector to manage Ecology and train rainforest guides in Costa Rica. His NGO work began as an ecotourism advisor to voluntary service overseas (VSO) based in Sulawesi Indonesia for 3 years before taking an assignment with SNV in Laos. Recently he completed his assignment for Netherlands development organization (SNV) as a pro poor sustainable tourism advisor based in the province of Khammouane in Laos.

Mr. Zahed Ghaderi worked for Iran Cultural Heritage Handicrafts and Tourism Organization for more then 8 years in a wide range of areas. He was tourism development planner and monitoring expert for Iran's tourism development and management master plan under supervision of the World Tourism Organization and United Nation Development Program (2000-2001) and then worked for this organization as tourism management and development expert in planning, statistics and information. His key areas of expertise are: rural and eco-tourism planning, tourism development, destination management and tourism research. Zahed has been technical advisor in preparation of provincial tourism development plans and other pilot projects in Iran. He has also handled many tourism development projects for private sectors, and has been involved in development of community-based tourism in Iran's rural areas.

Mr. Douglas Hainsworth holds a MA (Community and Regional Planning) and a BA (Geography-Natural Resource Management) from the University of British Columbia, and diplomas in Tourism Management and Tourism Marketing from the British Columbia Institute of Technology. His 20-year experience in the tourism sector reflects work in Southeast Asia, Central and North America. In pursuing his interests in tourism as a tool for local development he has worked with bilateral and multilateral development agencies, INGOs, the business sector and as a volunteer. Currently a Senior Advisor and Practice Leader on Pro-poor Sustainable Tourism with SNV (The Netherlands Development Organization) he is assisting the Government of Vietnam in developing sustainable tourism that addresses poverty reduction. He has contributed articles in leading tourism journals and other publications and is a frequent contributor at conferences and workshops in the Asia region.

Mr. Kamal S. Hapuwatte is the Principal of the Sri Lanka Institute of Tourism and Hotel Management, the only such state-run educational institute in Sri Lanka. He has experience in international hospitality management and human resource management spanning 35 years. He has held numerous senior positions in industry including as Chairman of the Sri Lanka International Group of the Hotel & Catering International Management Association [UK] in 2005; Chairman of the International Affairs Committee of the Institute of Personnel Management of Sri Lanka, and a Member of its Executive Council for several years; and Chairman of the Advisory Committee on Hotel & Catering Trades of the National Apprenticeship and Industrial Training Authority of Sri Lanka for five years. Kamal also served as National Consultant for an ILO/ UNDP Project which was responsible for the restructuring of curricula of courses currently conducted by the SLITHM and capacity building of its faculty members in pedagogical aspects.

Dr. Walter Jamieson is dean of the University of Hawai'i School of Travel Industry Management and Professor Emeritus of the University of Calgary. He currently chairs the Pacific Asia Travel Association (PATA) Human Resource Advisory Committee, and serves as a UNESCO Heritage Resource Management and Tourism consultant. Walter has been involved in a significant number of academic and consultancy activities over the last 30 years. His activities include working with the World Tourism Organization, ESCAP and UNESCO on more than 70 international research and consultancy projects at the local, national and international level. He has been director of research and outreach centers at the University of Calgary and team leader on a number of projects in Asia. He has also been active in training and facilitation on a worldwide basis and has published and presented widely with more than 135 publications, papers, presentations and outreach lectures. In 2003 he was awarded the Queen's Jubilee Medal.

Dr. Emiko Kakiuchi obtained her doctoral degree in Urban Planning, University of Tokyo, Japan. She is Professor and Director of the Cultural Policy Program of the National Graduate Institute for Policy Studies; a member of the National Land Council of Japan; and was a member of the Senior Staff of the Japanese Government for more than twenty years. Her experience extends to various positions in the Japanese government and international organizations, such as the Ministry of Education, the Agency for Cultural Affairs, the staff of the House of Representatives of the Japanese Parliament, the Institute of Advanced Studies at the United Nations University and teaching positions at universities in Japan and overseas. She has conducted consultancy activities for the central and local governments of Japan and international institutions including the World Bank. In most of her publications have been in the field of cultural policy. She received the City Planning Institute of Japan Award in 2002.

Dr. Timothy Lee was awarded his B.A. (Forest Environmental Science) at the Seoul National University. This was followed by a Masters in International Hotel Management and a PhD in Tourism & Hospitality Development from the University of Surrey. His industry experience includes working as a director of the Tourism Sciences Society of Korea, as a consultant in tourism marketing and educational tourism development in the Korea Culture & Tourism Policy Institute, and a variety of tourism and hospitality industries in Manhattan, New York for 6 years. Dr Lee joined the School of Tourism at the University of Queensland, Australia in 2005, shortly after he completed his doctoral degree. His research interests cover cultural heritage tourism, cultural hospitality, community issues in tourism and destination image development, and are still expanding.

Mr. Osama Manzar is a physics graduate with post graduate qualifications in journalism. He was awarded a joint Chevening/Young Indian IT Professional Programme 2002 Scholarship by the UK Foreign and Commonwealth Office to study Advanced IT Management Programme at Manchester Business School, University of Manchester from 2001-2002. A multi-skilled new media specialist, he is deeply involved in bridging the information barrier between India's rural and social sector, and the so-called developed society, through the Digital Empowerment Foundation. He has launched India's first ever award, the 'Manthan Award' for choosing the best e-content practices in India. Osama and his organization, the DEF are part of the Rural Entrepreneurship Program developed by the Indian Institute of Management (Ahmedabad). Among other things, he is Vice Chairman and cofounder and of the Hong Kong based Global Alliance for Bridging Digital Divide, and. a founder of the New Delhi based ICT solutions company '4Cplus'.

Dr. Sanjay Nadkarni has a Ph.D. from the University of Hull, UK, an MSc in Physics and Mathematics from the M.V. Lomonosov Moscow State University and a Master's degree in Operations Research and Technology Management from the Inter University Institute of Macau-Portuguese Catholic University. He is an Assistant Professor at the Faculty of Management and Administration, Macao University of Science & Technology, a Research Fellow of the International Institute of Macau and concurrently Research Affiliate with the School of Travel Industry Management, University of Hawaii. He has been an Asian Development Bank Consultant in ICT and is also a UNESCAP-APETIT Resource Person in Information Technology for Tourism. He has undertaken advisory and consultancy missions, principally to developing and least developed countries in the Asia-Pacific region. His research interests include ICT in tourism, pro-poor tourism and tourism education and capacity building and he has numerous publications in these areas.

Dr. Trevor Sofield is foundation professor of Tourism at the University of Tasmania, Australia, and holds a fractional conjoint appointment as Professor of Tourism at Sun Yat-sen University, China. Since 2005 he has also been Team Leader of the Mekong Tourism Development Project based in Cambodia that is funded by the Asian Development Bank. This project is active in the six Mekong countries of Cambodia, PRC (represented by the Provinces of Yunnan and Guangxi), Lao PDR, Myanmar, Thailand and Viet Nam. Dr Sofield has presented numerous papers on the issues of tourism development in the Mekong and is a leading academic on poverty alleviation through tourism. He holds degrees in social anthropology and environmental science, has more than 200 publications to his name, and his expertise has been applied to issues of tourism development in many countries in the Asia Pacific region.

Dr. SUN Jiuxia is an associate professor at the School of Tourism Management, Sun Yat-sen University, China. She obtained her doctoral degree in Tourism Management in Sun Yat-sen University. Her research interests are anthropology of tourism, community tourism, consumer behaviour in tourism and tourism and ethnic Groups. Dr. Sun Jiuxia has been involved in a number of research projects as well as tourism master plans in China. She is now the member of Institute of China ethnology and member of Institute of Guangdong Sociology.

Ms. Pawinee Sunalai graduated from Chulalongkorn University, and then obtained her MSc in Urban Environmental Management from the Asian Institute of Technology (AIT). After finishing her Masters degree, she served as Project Coordinator for the Canadian Universities Consortium Urban Environmental Management Project of Thailand at AIT. Currently she works for the University of Hawai'i School of Travel Industry Management based in Bangkok, Thailand. She also serves as a Manager for the Asian Center for Tourism Planning and Poverty Reduction (ACTPPR), a collaborative effort between the School and the Faculty of Social Administration, Thammasat University, Thailand. She has been involved in a number of research and demonstration projects throughout Southeast Asia, and in consultancy activities in several areas of tourism e.g. strategic tourism planning, community-based tourism, interpretation, visitor management, destination management and impact assessment.

Dr. Indra P. Tiwari holds multidisciplinary academic degrees in Geography, Law, and Human Settlements Development, including a Ph.D. in Regional Development Planning from the School of Environment, Resources and Development, Asian Institute of Technology, Bangkok, Thailand. Currently he is a Faculty Expert in the Graduate School of Management and Innovation, King Mongkut's University of Technology, Thonburi, Bangkok, Thailand. Dr. Tiwari previously worked for 10 years as Executive Director of the Rural Self-reliance Development Centre in Kathmandu; as an Expert in the Transport, Communications, Tourism and Infrastructure Development Division of the United Nations ESCAP, Bangkok. Dr. Tiwari has research and professional interest in human settlements development, dealing with the fundamentals of development and planning, spatial organization and reorganization, including both national and international regional issues; urbanization and development; population and migration; tourism; movement and transport system; community development and people-centred development studies.

Mr. Jan Wigsten is the head of the Sustainable Tourism Development Centre, Mongolia. He graduated from the University of Oriental and Mongolian Studies with an MA in Mongolian Nomad Philosophy and Culture. In 1995 he started his career with tourism as a lecturer in the Institute of Tourism Management in Ulaanbaatar and was then head of Tourism Management Department for another two years. Professional training has included courses for Tourism Marketing Management in the Free University of Brussels in Belgium, Tourism Planning and Policy in the University of Balearic Islands in Mallorca, Spain and Sustainable Tourism Management from Wageningen University, Netherlands. His main concern is to develop tourism as a tool for reinforcing Mongolian identity and cultural immunity by promoting mobility-based nomad-friendly tourism and travel technology. Mr.Jan Wigsten is also a board member of The International Ecotourism Society, and has been a co-partner in Nomadic Journeys Ltd. (Mongolia) since 1993.

Dr. XU Honggang is professor and vice dean of the School of Tourism Management, Sun Yat-sen University, China. She was awarded her B.A. at Beijing University. This was followed by MA and Ph.D from the School of Environment, Resources and Development, Asian Institute of Technology, Bangkok, Thailand. Dr. XU Honggang has been one of the key members in several important tourism master plans in China. Her research interests are sustainable tourism development, resource management, regional tourism planning and system dynamics modeling.